ANALECTS OF CONFUCIUS

Translations by Arthur Waley

THE NINE SONGS

THE REAL TRIPITAKA

THE POETRY AND CAREER OF LI PO

THE LIFE AND TIMES OF PO CHÜ-I

CHINESE POEMS

MONKEY

THREE WAYS OF THOUGHT IN ANCIENT CHINA

THE BOOK OF SONGS

THE WAY AND ITS POWER

THE TALE OF GENJI
by Lady Murasaki

THE NO PLAYS OF JAPAN

THE TEMPLE

MORE TRANSLATIONS FROM THE CHINESE

THE PILLOW-BOOK OF SEL-SHONAGON

BALLADS AND STORIES FROM TUN-HUANG

THE OPIUM WAR THROUGH CHINESE EYES

THE SECRET HISTORY OF THE MONGOLS

YUEN MEI

The Analects of Confucius

Translated and annotated

by

ARTHUR WALEY

London
GEORGE ALLEN & UNWIN LTD

FIRST PUBLISHED IN 1938
SECOND IMPRESSION 1945
THIRD IMPRESSION 1949
FOURTH IMPRESSION 1956
FIFTH IMPRESSION 1964
SIXTH IMPRESSION 1971

ISBN 0 04 181002 3

PRINTED IN GREAT BRITAIN BY
JOHN DICKENS AND CO LTD, NORTHAMPTON

TO

C. G. SELIGMAN

*True philosophy lies in being Humpty Dumpty
without a great fall.*
MAY CHESSHIRE

CONTENTS

	PAGE
Preface	11
INTRODUCTION	13
The Ancients	17
The Disciples	19
The *Analects*	21
Terms	27
Written Tradition	51
Ritual	54
Appendix 1, The Interpretations	71
Appendix 2, Biographical Dates	78
TRANSLATION	83
Additional Notes	235
Textual Notes	253
Index	263

PREFACE

★

THIS BOOK, begun years ago, has been several times rewritten and laid aside. My difficulties were due to the fact that the *Analects* really consist of two parts: Books III to IX, which form a perfectly consistent whole and apparently belong together; and Books I and II and X to XX, which are extremely miscellaneous in content and character. I thought at one time of dividing the translation into two parts, and writing a separate introduction to each. But this would have involved altering the order of the chapters, and such a re-arrangement, with its obvious inconveniences, is only worth while in cases (like that of the *Book of Songs*) where a text is impossible to study satisfactorily in its existing order. The introduction as it stands refers to both sections of the work; but it will be seen that the account of early Confucian ideas is based chiefly on Books III to IX.

The present book is somewhat dry and technical in character. But I would not have it supposed that I have definitely abandoned literature for learning, or forgotten the claims of the ordinary reader. My next book, *Three Ways of Thought in Ancient China*, will be wholly devoid of technicalities and indeed in most ways a contrast to this work on the *Analects*.

I wish to thank in particular Dr. Walter Simon, of the School of Oriental Studies, who supplied many valuable suggestions and corrections. Some Chinese characters have more than one reading, and where such characters occur in proper names there is often a doubt as to which reading should be followed. In several instances (e.g. Ch'ü Po Yü, P'i Ch'ên, Prince Ch'ao of Sung), Dr. Simon indicated to me which reading was followed by the seventeenth century Manchu translation, and I have thought it best to follow the Manchu readings, which are authoritative in such a case. I wish also to thank Professor Pelliot for lending me a reproduction of the Tun-huang MS., Professor Haloun for many valuable hints when the book was in its earlier stages, and Mr. R. C. Trevelyan for the great trouble he took in detecting misprints.

A.W.

INTRODUCTION

I

THOUGHT grows out of environment. Ideally speaking the translator of such a book as the *Analects* ought to furnish a complete analysis of early Chinese society, of the processes which were at work within it and of the outside forces to which it reacted. Unfortunately our knowledge of the period is far too incomplete for any such synthesis to be possible. The literary documents are scanty and of uncertain date; scientific archaeology in China has suffered constant setbacks and is still in its infancy. All that I have attempted in the following pages is to arrange such information as is accessible under a series of disconnected headings, in a convenient order, but without pretence of unity or logical sequence.

CONFUCIUS

The Confucius of whom I shall speak here is the Confucius of the *Analects*.[1] One could construct half a dozen other Confuciuses by tapping the legend at different stages of its evolution. We should see the Master becoming no longer a moral teacher but a 'wise man' according to the popular conception of wisdom that existed in non-Confucian circles in China and in our own Middle Ages, an answerer of grotesque

---

[1] I omit the obviously legendary material in Book XVIII, and the ritual portrait in Book X, for reasons explained below, p. 55. Also a few passages akin to Book XVIII (such as XIV, 34, 41, 42, and XVII, 1) in that they clearly emanate from circles hostile to Confucius.

conundrums, a prophet, a magician even. We should see the disappointed itinerant tutor of the *Analects* turning into a successful statesman and diplomatist, employed not only in his own country but in neighbouring States as well.[1]

But I shall act here on the principle recently advocated by that great scholar Ku Chieh-kang, the principle of 'one Confucius at a time.' Not that we can regard the Confucius of the *Analects* as wholly historical; still less, that we must dismiss as fiction all data about the Master that do not happen to occur in this book. But in the first place the biographical facts deducible from the *Analects* are those which are most relevant to an understanding of the book itself; and secondly, the picture of Confucius given in the *Analects*, besides being the earliest that we possess, differs from that of all other books in that it contains no elements that bear patently and obviously the stamp of folk-lore or hagiography. What then was Confucius? It appears from the *Analects* that he was a private person who trained the sons of gentlemen in the virtues proper to a member of the ruling classes. It is clear, however, that he was not content with this position and longed for a more public one, either in his own State or in some other, which would give him the opportunity to put into practice the Way which he regarded as that of the Former Kings, the Way of Goodness, long ago discarded by the rulers of the world in favour of a Way of violence and aggression. There is not the slightest indication that he ever obtained such a position. Twice, however, he speaks of himself as 'following after' the Great Officers of Court. Those who ranked

[1] The legend of Confucius's worldly success, transferred to the West, has continued its growth on European soil. Meyer's *Konversationslexicon* (1896) goes so far as to say that he was 'received with the highest honours at every Court' in China.

next to the Great Officers (*Ta Fu*) were the Knights (*shih*), and if Confucius ranked immediately after the Great Officers (as he seems to suggest) he must at the time have been *Shih-shih*,[1] Leader of the Knights, which was not politically speaking a position of any importance. Discontented with the slow progress of his doctrines in the land of Lu, Confucius travelled from State to State,[2] seeking for a ruler who would give the Way its chance. The only disciples actually mentioned as accompanying him are Jan Ch'iu, Tzu-lu, and his favourite disciple Yen Hui. The States and towns which they visited (Ch'i, Wei, Ch'ên, Ts'ai and K'uang) all lay within the modern provinces of Shantung and Honan. The strangers evidently met with a hostile reception, and had occasionally to endure severe privation. Several of the disciples were in the service of Chi K'ang-tzu, the dictator of Lu; and it may have been owing to their good offices that Confucius was at last encouraged to return to his native State.

Concerning his private life, we learn from the *Analects* that he had been brought up in humble circumstances.[3] Of his marriage nothing is said; but two children are mentioned, a daughter[4] and a son

[1] The original function of the *shih-shih* was to 'keep the Knights in order'; Cf. *Mencius* I, 2, VI, 2. In practice he acted under the orders of the Minister of Justice and functioned as a sort of police-magistrate. In the second stage of its development the Confucian legend represents the Master as achieving the position of Minister of Justice, an idea which may well have grown out of his having in fact been Leader of the Knights.

[2] This mobility was typical of Chinese society. Not only moralists, but warriors, craftsmen and even peasants moved from State to State, if they thought that by doing so they could improve their chances of success.

[3] IX, 6. But the saying from which we learn this was a disputed one, and an alternative version of it is given immediately afterwards, 'But Lao says the Master said . . .' etc. This alternative version refers to lack of official employment, but not to poverty.   [4] V, 1.

whom the Master outlived.[1] An older brother is mentioned, but Confucius seems to have acted as head of the family, and this is explained by later tradition as due to the fact that the elder brother was a cripple.

Confucius speaks of himself in one place (II, 4) as being over seventy. As to the exact dates of his birth and death the *Analects* tell us nothing. It can be inferred, however, from references to contemporary persons and events, that the time of his main activity was the end of the sixth and the first twenty years or so of the fifth century.[2]

After his apotheosis in the Han dynasty Confucius was credited with the omniscience and moral infallibility of the Divine Sage. This view of him appears, indeed, to have been current even during his lifetime; for we find him at pains to disclaim any such attributes.[3] Nor would he allow himself to be regarded as Good,[4] a disclaimer that is natural enough, seeing that he accords this title only to a few legendary heroes of the remote past. Even in the social virtues which formed the basis of his teaching he claimed no pre-eminence. There was not, he said, a hamlet of ten houses but could produce men as loyal and dependable as himself. He denied (though one disciple at least seems to have had the opposite impression) that he possessed any unusual stock of knowledge;[5] still less would he admit that such knowledge as he possessed was innate or inspired.[6] What he regarded as exceptional in himself was his love of 'learning,' that is to say, of self-improvement, and his unflagging patience in insisting upon the moral principles that had (in his

---

[1] XI, 7.

[2] I will not here enter into the difficult question of how the dates (551–479 B.C.) later accepted as official were first arrived at. Cf. Maspero, *La Chine Antique*, p. 455, and below, p. 78.

[3] VII, 33.   [4] *Ibid.*   [5] XV, 2.   [6] VII, 19.

view) guided the godlike rulers of the remote past. His task, then, like that of the English trainer of *chün-tzu* (gentlemen's sons) in the great Public Schools, was not so much to impart knowledge as to inculcate moral principles, form character, hand down unaltered and intact a great tradition of the past.[1] He speaks of himself as a veritable P'êng Tsu (i.e. Nestor) in his devoted reliance upon 'antiquity'; and if we want further to define what he meant by this reliance on the past, we find it, I think, in Mencius's saying: Follow the rules of the Former Kings, and it is impossible that you should go wrong.[2]

What then was this antiquity, who were the great figures of the past whom Confucius regarded as the sole source of wisdom?

THE ANCIENTS

Were we to take them in the order of their importance to him, I think we should have to begin with the founders and expanders of the Chou dynasty; for in his eyes the cultures of the two preceding dynasties found their climax and fulfilment in that of the early Chou sovereigns.[3] Above all, we should have to deal first with Tan, Duke of Chou, who had not only a particular importance in the Lu State, but also a peculiar significance for Confucius himself.[4] But it is more convenient to take them in their 'chronological' order, that is to say, in the order in which the mythology of Confucius's day arranged them. We must begin then with the *Shêng*, the Divine Sages.[5] These were mythological figures, historicized as rulers of human 'dynas-

---

[1] VII, 1.   [2] *Mencius*, IV, 1. I.   [3] III, 14.   [4] VII, 5.
[5] See *The Way and Its Power*, p. 91. Mencius and later writers use the term *shêng* in a much wider sense, applying it even to a comparatively recent person such as Liu-hsia Hui.

ties'; but still endowed with divine characteristics and powers. The *Analects* mention three of them, Yao, Shun and Yü the Great; but they occupy a very restricted place in the book.[1] Yao and Shun are twice[2] mentioned in the stock phrase (if a man were to do this), then 'even Yao and Shun could not criticize him'; meaning that such a man would himself be to all intents and purposes a *shêng*. Yao appears otherwise only in the eulogy of VIII, 19, where he is exalted as the equal of God.[3] The eulogy of Shun which follows tells us that with only five servants to help him he kept order 'everywhere under Heaven.' Elsewhere[4] he is said to have ruled by *wu-wei* (non-activity), through the mere fact of sitting in a majestic attitude 'with his face turned to the South.' We have here the conception, familiar to us in Africa and elsewhere, of the divine king whose magic power regulates everything in the land. It is one which is common to all early Chinese thought, particularly in the various branches of Quietism that developed in the fourth century B.C. The *shêng*, however, only 'rules by non-activity' in the sense that his divine essence (*ling*) assures the fecundity of his people and the fertility of the soil. We find Shun assisted in his task by 'five servants,'[5] who are clearly conceived of as performing the active functions of government.

Yao and Shun are not mentioned in the *Book of Songs*, and there is reason to suppose that their cult did not form part of the Chou tradition. The third

[1] I except Book XX, which has not necessarily anything to do with the beliefs of Confucius. Yü is legendary; but the Hsia dynasty is probably not wholly mythological.

[2] VI, 28; XIV, 45.

[3] *T'ien*; literally, 'Heaven'. [4] XV, 4.

[5] VIII, 20. One of them was presumably Kao Yao, mentioned in XII, 22.

Divine Sage, Yü the Great, generally[1] associated in Chinese legend with a Deluge Myth akin to that of the Near East, figures in the *Analects* not as the subduer of the Flood but as patron of agriculture. He drains and ditches the land[2] and tills the fields,[3] his name being coupled with that of the harvest-god Hou Chi. Yü the Great is 'historicized' as founder of the Hsia dynasty, whose 'times' (i.e. calendar of agricultural operations) Confucius recommends, in answer to a question about the ideal State.[4]

T'ang, the founder of the Shang-Yin dynasty which preceded the Chou, is only once mentioned. It was supposed in Confucius's day that the remnants of the Shang-Yin people had settled in Sung and that the Sung State perpetuated the traditions of the fallen dynasty. But Confucius himself doubted whether Yin culture could really be reconstructed by evidence supplied from Sung.[5]

THE DISCIPLES

Later tradition credits Confucius with seventy-two[6] disciples; but the compilers are hard put to it to bring the number up to anything like so imposing a total. In the *Analects* some twenty people figure, who might possibly be regarded as disciples, in so far as they are represented as addressing questions to Confucius. But far fewer appear as definite 'frequenters of his gate.' The most important of them, in the history of Confucianism, is

---

[1] But not in the *Songs*, where he generally appears as a Creator connected indeed with irrigation, only once as a flood-subduer.

[2] VIII, 21. [3] XIV, 6. [4] XV, 10.

[5] III, 9. Systematic excavation at An-yang, the site of one of the Yin capitals, has put us in possession of far more information about Yin culture than Confucius was able to obtain.

[6] Seventy-two is a sacred number, connected with the quintuple division of the year of 360 days. Cf. XI, 25.

Master Tsêng, who is credited in the *Analects* with twelve sayings of his own. The Master Tsêng of Book VIII is, however, a very different person from the Master Tsêng of Book I, the latter resembling far more closely the Tsêng of later tradition, and of the *Tsêng Tzu* fragments.[1] Humanly the most distinctive of the disciples are Yen Hui and Tzu-lu, who are perfect examples of the contrasted types of character that psychologists call introvert and extravert. Both of them died before Confucius, and were thus unable to influence the subsequent development of the school. Tzu-lu played a considerable part in contemporary history and is mentioned in the chronicles from 498 down to the time of his death in 480. Two other disciples are well known to history, Jan Ch'iu appears as a lieutenant of the usurping Chi Family from 484 till 472; and Tzu-kung figures largely in inter-State diplomacy from 495 till 468.

The name of Master Yu, who figures so prominently in Book I, only to disappear almost completely in the remaining Books, happens by chance to occur in the *Tso Chuan* Chronicle under the year 487. But he was evidently not a person of high social status; for he served as a foot-soldier.

It is clear that after the Master's death, Tzu-hsia, like Master Tsêng, founded a school of his own; for his disciples are spoken of in Book XIX. To him, too, are attributed about a dozen sayings. Two other disciples, Tzu-chang and Tzu-yu, are also obviously regarded by the compilers of the *Analects* as being of special importance; for they, too, are credited with sayings of their own.

[1] Collected by Yüan Yüan, *Huang Ch'ing Ching Chieh*, 803–806.

THE ANALECTS[1]

There is not much doubt that *Lun Yü* (*Analects*, to use the English equivalent that Legge's translation has made so familiar) means 'Selected Sayings.' *Lun*, as a term connected with the editing of documents, occurs indeed in *Analects*, XIV, 9. The contents of the book itself make it clear that the compilation took place long after the Master's death. Several of the disciples already have schools of their own, and the death of Master Tsêng, which certainly happened well into the second half of the fifth century, is recorded in Book VIII. It is clear, too, that the different Books are of very different date and proceed from very different sources. I should hazard the guess that Books III–IX represent the oldest stratum. Books X and XX (first part) certainly have no intrinsic connexion with the rest. The former is a compilation of maxims from works on ritual; the latter consists of stray sentences from works of the *Shu Ching* type. Book XIX consists entirely of sayings by disciples. The contents of XVIII and of parts of XIV and XVII are not Confucian in their origin, but have filtered into the book from the outside world, and from a world hostile to Confucius. Book XVI is generally and rightly regarded as late. It contains nothing characteristic of the milieu that produced Books III–IX, and it would not be difficult to compile a much longer book of just the same character by stringing together precepts from works such as the *Tso Chuan* and *Kuo Yü*. Only in one passage of the *Analects* do we find any reference to ideas the development of which we should be inclined to place later than the ordinarily accepted[2] date of the book,

[1] This section might well be omitted by readers without special knowledge of Chinese literature.

[2] I mean accepted by scholars as the date of the material contained in the book. The date of its compilation may well be later.

namely the middle of the fourth century. I refer to the disquisition on 'correcting names' in XIII, 3. In *Mencius* (early third century B.C.) there is not a trace of the 'language crisis,'[1] and we have no reason to suppose that the whole sequence of ideas embodied in this passage could possibly be earlier in date than the end of the fourth century. That the writer of the passage realized its incompatibility with the doctrines of Confucius—the insistence on punishments is wholly un-Confucian—is naïvely betrayed in the introductory paragraphs. Tzu-lu is made to express the greatest astonishment that Confucius should regard the reform of language as the first duty of a ruler and tells him impatiently that his remark is quite beside the point.

We may, of course, be wrong in thinking that the whole complex of ideas connected with 'reforming language in order to adjust penalties' dates from as late as the end of the fourth century. There may be special reasons why we find no echo of such ideas in *Mencius*. Or again, the compilation of the *Analects* may be much later than we suppose; but this alternative involves linguistic difficulties. It may, on the other hand, be a better solution to regard this passage as an interpolation on the part of Hsün Tzu or his school, for whom the absence of any reference in the sayings of Confucius to what they themselves taught as a fundamental doctrine must certainly have been inconvenient.

It is curious that only one pre-Han text shows definite evidence of familiarity with the *Analects*. The *Fang Chi* (part of the *Li Chi*; supposed to be an extract from the *Tzu Ssu Tzu*) quotes *Analects*, II, 11, and names the *Lun Yü* as its source. The *Fang Chi* also quotes books of the *Shu Ching* which were unknown in Han times, not being found either in the official

[1] See *The Way and Its Power*, p. 59. *Mencius*, VI, 2. VI, is unintelligible, and has in any case never been interpreted as relevant.

collection or among the books rediscovered but un-interpreted. It is therefore certainly a pre-Han work. There are, apart from this, many cases in which pre-Han authors, such as Hsün Tzu, Lü Pu-wei, Han Fei Tzu, use maxims or anecdotes that are also used in the *Analects*. But there is nothing to show that the writer is quoting the book as we know it now. Mencius, it is clear, used a quite different collection of sayings, which contained, indeed, a certain number of those which occur in the *Analects*, often differently worded and allotted to quite different contexts; but he quotes at least three times as many sayings that do not occur in the *Analects* at all.

It would be rash, however, to conclude that the *Analects* were not known or did not exist in the days of Mencius and Hsün Tzu. We possess only a very small fragment of early Confucian literature. Could we read all the works that are listed in the *Han Shu* bibliography, we should very likely discover that some particular school of Confucianism based its teaching on the *Analects*, just as Mencius based his on another collection of sayings. The *Doctrine of the Mean* and the *Great Learning*, works of very uncertain date but certainly pre-Han, both use sayings from the *Analects*, which may well be actual quotations.

The history of the text from *c.* 150 B.C.[1] till the time (second century A.D.) when at the hands of Chêng Hsüan the book received something like its present form I must leave to others to write. The task is one which involves great difficulties. The data are supplied not by scientific bibliographers but by careless repeaters of legend and anecdote. Some of the relevant texts (e.g. *Lun Hêng*, P'ien 81) are hopelessly corrupt; the real dates of supposedly early Han works which show

[1] It is quoted by name in the *Han Shih Wai Chuan*, which presumably dates from the middle of the second century.

knowledge of the *Analects* are impossible to ascertain. At every turn, in such studies, we are forced to rely, without any means of checking their statements, upon writers who clearly took no pains to control their facts.

This much, however, is certain: during the period 100 B.C. to A.D. 100 two versions were currently used, the Lu version (upon which our modern version is chiefly based) and the Ch'i version,¹ which had two extra chapters. Much later (second century A.D. ?)² a third version came into general use. This was the Ku Wên (ancient script) text collated by Chêng Hsüan when he made his famous edition, of which fragments have been recovered from Tun-huang. We know³ some twenty-seven instances in which the Ku version differed from the Lu, and in all but two of these instances the version we use to-day follows Ku not Lu. I state these facts merely that the reader may know roughly what is meant when in the course of this book I mention Ku and Lu readings. The real origin of the Ku version⁴ remains very uncertain and a discussion of the question, bound up as it is with the history of the other Ku Wên texts, would lead us too far afield.

¹ Now lost, save for a few fragments.
² Legge's suggestion that Chang Yü (died 5 B.C.) used the Ku version is not borne out by the texts.
³ Through the *Shih Wên* and the fragments from Tun-huang. The *Hsin-lun* of Huan T'an (*c.* A.D. 1) says that Ku had four hundred characters different from Lu.
⁴ Alleged to have been found, (1) during the Emperor Ching's reign (156–141 B.C.); (2) at the beginning of the Han Emperor Wu's reign (140 B.C.); (3) at the end of his reign (87 B.C.); by (1) Prince Kung of Lu (in Lu from 154–127 B.C.; (2) the Emperor Wu himself; (1) during the demolition of Confucius's house; (2) before the demolition, which was at once suspended; (1) according to some accounts without supernatural manifestations; (2) according to others, to the accompaniment of supernatural music.

The accounts also differ considerably as to what books were found and as to who hid them there.

A last question remains to be answered. How far can we regard any of the sayings in the *Analects* as actual words of Confucius? In searching for such authentic sayings we must use certain precautions. Obviously, we shall not find them in Book X,[1] nor in Book XX.[2] Books XVI–XVII clearly do not emanate from a source at all near to the earliest Confucianism. Book XVIII is, indeed, full of anti-Confucian stories, of just the same sort that we find in Taoist works, naïvely accepted by the compilers; Book XIV has a considerable element of the same description (34, 41, 42). The story of the meeting with Yang Huo (XVII, 1) is of just the same kind. We shall have to remember that in ancient Chinese literature sayings are often attributed to a variety of people; (indifferently, for example, to Master Tsêng and Confucius, or to Confucius and Yen Tzu) and bear in mind that such sayings were probably more or less proverbial. We certainly must not forget that Confucius describes himself as a transmitter, not an originator, and that the presence of rhyme or archaic formulae, or of proverbial shape in the sayings often definitely stamps them as inherited from the past. Bearing all these facts in mind I think we are justified in supposing that the book does not contain many authentic sayings, and may possibly contain none at all. As I have already pointed out, I use the term 'Confucius' throughout this book in a conventional sense, simply meaning the particular early Confucians whose ideas are embodied in the sayings.

Supposing, however, someone should succeed in proving that some particular saying was really uttered by the Master, it would still remain to be proved that

---

[1] Which is simply a collection of traditional ritual maxims.

[2] Which, apart from the few sayings appended at the end, is a collection of sentences from texts of the *Shu Ching* type.

the context in which the remark occurred in the *Analects* was really the original one; and the context of a remark profoundly affects its meaning. In later literature, particularly the *Li Chi* (Book of Rites) and *Shih Chi* (Historical Records), we find a good many of Confucius's more cryptic remarks given contexts, put into settings of an explanatory description, and it has been suggested that in such cases we have the original form and intention of the sayings, which in the *Analects* have for some reason become divorced from their proper surroundings. That this should be so is against all the canons of textual history. Always, in similar cases, we find that the contexts have been invented as glosses upon the original *logia*. In the oldest strata of the Synoptic Gospels isolated sayings occur which in the more recent strata are furnished, often very arbitrarily, with an explanatory setting. It is a process that we can see at work over and over again in Buddhist hagiography. I have therefore seldom called attention to these manipulations of the text by the later Confucian schools, and have been content to leave the isolated *logia* as I found them.

II

TERMS

JÊN[1]

This word in the earliest Chinese means freemen, men of the tribe, as opposed to *min*, 'subjects,' 'the common people.'[2] The same word, written with a slight modification, means 'good' in the most general sense of the word, that is to say, 'possessing the qualities of one's tribe.' For no more sweeping form of praise can be given by the men of a tribe than to say that someone is a 'true member' of that tribe. The same is true of modern nations; an Englishman can give no higher praise than to say that another is a true Englishman. In the *Book of Songs* the phrase 'handsome and good' (*jên*) occurs more than once as a description of a perfectly satisfactory lover. *Jên*, 'members of the tribe' show a forbearance towards one another that they do not show to aliens, and just as the Latin *gens*, 'clan,' gave rise to our own word 'gentle,' so *jên* in Chinese came to mean 'kind,' 'gentle,' 'humane.' Finally, when the old distinction between *jên* and *min*, freemen and subjects, was forgotten and *jên* became a general word for 'human being,' the adjective *jên* came to be understood in the sense 'human' as opposed to 'animal,' and to be applied to conduct worthy of a man, as distinct from the behaviour of mere beasts.

Of this last sense (human, not brutal) there is not a trace in the *Analects*. Of the sense 'kind,' 'tender-

[1] See textual notes.
[2] See the *Way and Its Power*, p. 148.

hearted' there are only two examples,[1] out of some sixty instances in which the word occurs. Confucius's use of the term, a use peculiar to this one book, stands in close relation to the primitive meaning. *Jên*, in the *Analects*, means 'good' in an extremely wide and general sense. 'In its direction'[2] lie unselfishness and an ability to measure other people's feelings by one's own. The good man is 'in private life, courteous; in public life, diligent; in relationships, loyal.'[3] Goodness (on the part of a ruler) is complete submission to ritual.[4] The Good do not grieve[5] and will necessarily be brave.[6] At the same time, it cannot be said that *jên* in the *Analects* simply means 'good' in a wide and general sense. It is, on the contrary, the name of a quality so rare and peculiar that one 'cannot but be chary in speaking of it.'[7] It is a sublime moral attitude, a transcendental perfection attained to by legendary heroes such as Po I, but not by any living or historic person. This, however, is far from being understood by the disciples, who suggest as examples of goodness not only Tzu-wên (seventh century B.C.), Ch'ên Wên-tzu (sixth century), Kuan Tzu (seventh century), but even contemporaries and associates such as Tzu-lu, Jan Ch'iu, Kung-hsi Hua, Jan Yung. All such claims the Master abruptly dismisses. Indeed so unwilling is he to accord the title *jên* that he will not even allow it to a hypothetical person who 'compassed the salvation of the whole State.'[8] Such a one would be a Divine Sage (*shêng*), a demi-god; whereas *jên* is the display of human qualities at their highest. It appears indeed that *jên* is a mystic entity not merely analogous to but in certain sayings practically identical with the Tao of the Quietists. Like Tao, it is contrasted with 'know-

---

[1] XII, 22 and XVII, 21.   [2] VI, 28.
[3] XIII, 19.   [4] XII, 1.   [5] IX, 28.
[6] XIV, 5.   [7] XII, 3.   [8] VI, 28.

ledge.' Knowledge is active and frets itself away; Goodness is passive and therefore eternal as the hills.[1] Confucius can point the way to Goodness, can tell 'the workman how to sharpen his tools,'[2] can speak even of things 'that are near to Goodness.' But it is only once, in a chapter bearing every sign of lateness,[3] that anything approaching a definition of Goodness is given.

In view of this repeated refusal to accept any but remote[4] mythological figures as examples of *jên*, to accept[5] or give a definition of Goodness, there is surely nothing surprising in the statement of Book IX (opening sentence) that 'the Master rarely discoursed upon Goodness.'[6]

It seems to me that 'good' is the only possible translation of the term *jên* as it occurs in the *Analects*. No other word is sufficiently general to cover the whole range of meaning; indeed terms such as 'humane,' 'altruistic,' 'benevolent' are in almost every instance inappropriate, often ludicrously so. But there is another word, *shan*, which though it wholly lacks the mystical and transcendental implications of *jên*, cannot conveniently be translated by any other word but 'good.' For that reason I shall henceforward translate *jên* by Good (Goodness, etc.) with a capital; and *shan* by good, with a small g.

---

[1] VI, 21. For the capital G, see below.

[2] XV, 9.   [3] XVII.

[4] Po I, Shu Ch'i, Pi Kan, Wei Tzu and Chi Tzu is the complete list. All of them belonged, according to legend, to the end of the Yin dynasty. The last three occur in Book XVIII, which emanated from non-Confucian circles.   [5] Cf. XIV, 2.

[6] A vast mass of discussion has centred round this passage. Cf. *Journal of the American Oriental Society*, December 1933 and March 1934.

TAO

Unlike *jên*, *tao* has not in the *Analects* a technical or peculiar meaning, but is used there in just the same sense as in early Chinese works in general. *Tao* means literally a road, a path, a way. Hence, the way in which anything is done, the way in which, for example, a kingdom is ruled; a method, a principle, a doctrine. It usually has a good meaning. Thus 'when *tao* (the Way) prevails under Heaven' means when a good method of government prevails in the world; or rather 'when *the* good method prevails,' for Confucius 'believed in the ancients,' that is to say, he believed that the one infallible method of rule had been practised by certain rulers of old, and that statecraft consisted in rediscovering this method. But there seem to have been other 'Ways'; for Confucius[1] speaks of 'this Way' and 'my Way.' Moreover, in one passage[2] he is asked about *shan-jên chih Tao*, 'the Way of the good people,' and replies (according to my interpretation) disapprovingly that 'those who do not tread in the tracks (of the ancients)' cannot hope to 'enter into the sanctum.' 'Good people' is a term often applied in Chinese to those who share one's views. Thus Quietists called other Quietists 'good people.' The 'good people' here intended evidently sought guidance from some source other than the example of the ancients, and they may well have been Quietists.

But we are also told that Confucius did not discourse about the Will of Heaven[3] or about 'prodigies' and 'disorders' (of Nature).[4] We have only to read other early books to see that the world at large attached

---

[1] It would be pedantic always to say 'the early Confucians' or the compilers of the *Analects*; though that is, strictly speaking, what I mean when I say 'Confucius.'

[2] XI, 19.　　　　[3] V, 12.　　　　[4] VII, 20.

extreme importance to the Will of Heaven as manifested by portents such as rainbows, comets, eclipses;
and to monstrosities such as two-headed calves and
the like. It may be that the doctrine of those who
sought guidance from such signs rather than from the
records of the Former Kings came to be known as the
'Way of the good people.' In general, however, the
word *Tao* in the *Analects* means one thing only, the
Way of the ancients as it could be reconstructed from
the stories told about the founders of the Chou dynasty
and the demi-gods who had preceded them.

The aspect of Confucius's Way upon which Western
writers have chiefly insisted is his attitude towards the
supernatural. It has been rightly emphasized that he
was concerned above all with the duties of man to man
and that he 'did not talk about spirits.'[1] From a false
interpretation of two passages (VI, 20 and XI, 11)
the quite wrong inference has, however, been drawn
that his attitude towards the spirit-world was, if not
sceptical, at least agnostic. In the first passage a
disciple asks about wisdom. The wisdom here meant
is, of course, that of the ruler or member of the ruling
classes, and the point at issue is one frequently debated
in early Chinese literature: which should come first,
the claims of the people or those of the spirit-world?
In concrete terms, should the security of the whole
State, which depends ultimately on the goodwill of
the Spirits of grain, soil, rivers and hills, be first
assured by lavish offerings and sacrifices, even if such
a course involves such heavy taxation as to impose
great hardship on the common people? Or should the
claims of the people to what it is 'right and proper' (*i*)
for them to have be satisfied before public expenditure is lavished upon the protecting spirits? The reply
of Confucius is that the claims of the people should

[1] VII, 20.

come first; but that the spirits must be accorded an attention sufficient to 'keep them at a distance,' that is to say, prevent them from manifesting their ill-will by attacking human beings; for just as we regard sickness as due to the onslaught of microbes, the Chinese regarded it as due to demoniacal 'possession.'

The same question concerning the priority in budget-making of human and ghostly claims is discussed in the second passage. Tzu-lu asks about 'the service of spirits,' meaning, as has generally been recognized, the outlay of public expenditure on sacrifice and other ceremonies of placation. The Master's reply is, 'How can there be any proper service of spirits until living men have been properly served?' Tzu-lu then 'asked about the dead.' A much debated question was whether the dead are conscious; and it was suggested that if they are not, it must clearly be useless to sacrifice at any rate to that portion of the spirit-world which consists of the spirits of the dead, as opposed to those of hills, streams, the soil, etc. Confucius does not wish to commit himself to any statement about, for example, the consciousness or unconsciousness of the dead, and adroitly turns the question by replying, 'Until a man knows about the living,[1] how can he know the dead?' All that is meant by the reply (which is a rhetorical one and must not be analysed too logically) is that for the *chün-tzu*[2] questions about the existence led by the dead are of secondary importance as compared to those connected with the handling of living men.

There is not, as Western writers have often supposed, any allusion to an abstract metaphysical problem concerning the ultimate nature of Life. Nor are the two passages discussed above in any way isolated or exceptional. They are, on the contrary, characteristic of the general diversion of interest from the dead to

[1] Or 'knows about life.'
[2] See below, p. 34.

the living, from the spirit-world to that of everyday life, which marks the break-up of the old Chou culture, founded upon divination and sacrifice.[1]

T Ê [2]

This word corresponds closely to the Latin *virtus*. It means, just as *virtus* often does, the specific quality or 'virtue' latent in anything. It never (except by some accident of context) has in early Chinese the meaning of virtue as opposed to vice, but rather the meaning of 'virtue' in such expressions as 'in virtue of' or 'the virtue of this drug.' In individuals it is a force or power closely akin to what we call character and frequently contrasted with *li*, 'physical force.' To translate it by 'virtue,' as has often been done, can only end by misleading the reader, who even if forewarned will be certain to interpret the word in its ordinary sense (virtue as opposed to vice) and not in the much rarer sense corresponding to the Latin *virtus*. For this reason I have generally rendered *tê* by the term 'moral force,' particularly where it is contrasted with *li*, 'physical force.' We cannot, however, speak of a horse's *tê* as its 'moral force.' Here 'character' is the only possible equivalent; and in the case of human beings the term 'prestige' often comes close to what is meant by *tê*.

S H I H [3]

This word is often translated 'scholar'; but this is only a derived, metaphorical sense and the whole force of many passages in the *Analects* is lost if we do not understand that the term is a military one and means 'knight.' A *shih* was a person entitled to go to battle

---

[1] Cf. *The Way and Its Power*, pp. 24 seq.
[2] Cf. *The Book of Songs*, p. 346. See below, p. 52.
[3] See textual notes.

in a war-chariot, in contrast with the common soldiers
who followed on foot. Confucius, by a metaphor
similar to those embodied in the phraseology of the
Salvation Army, calls the stout-hearted defenders of
his Way 'Knights'; and hence in later Chinese the
term came to be applied to upholders of Confucianism
and finally to scholars and literary people in general.
The burden of most of the references to *shih* in the
Analects is that the Knight of the Way needs just the
same qualities of endurance and resolution as the
Soldier Knight. A saying such as 'A knight whose
thoughts are set on home is not worthy of the name
of knight'[1] refers in the first instance to real knights,
and is only applied by metaphor to the spiritual
warriors of Confucius's 'army.' If like Legge we
translate 'the scholar who cherishes his love of comfort . . . ,' we lose the whole point. As we shall see
later, Confucius was himself a knight in the literal
sense, and it is probable, as we have seen, that in his
later years he was senior knight, 'leader of the knights,'
responsible for their discipline.

CHÜN-TZU

Chün is the most general term for 'ruler,' and a
chün-tzu is a 'son of a ruler.' The term was applied to
descendants of the ruling house in any State, and so
came to mean 'gentleman,' 'member of the upper
classes.' But the gentleman is bound by a particular
code of morals and manners; so that the word *chün-
tzu* implies not merely superiority of birth but also
superiority of character and behaviour. Finally the
requisite of birth is waived. If an ox is of one colour
and thus fit for sacrifice, what does it matter that its
sire was brindled?[2] He who follows the Way of the

[1] XIV, 3.   [2] VI, 4.

chün-tzu is a *chün-tzu;* he who follows the way of 'small' (i.e. common) people is common. And what is the Way of the Gentleman? With the detailed code of his manners I shall deal presently, when discussing Book X. As to his deportment in general, it is defined for us by the disciple Tsêng[1] in terms that exactly correspond to the traditional Western conception of a gentleman: we recognize him by the fact that his movements are free from any brusqueness or violence, that his expression is one of complete openness and sincerity, that his speech is free from any low and vulgar or as we should say 'Cockney' tinge.

As regards his conduct, he must be extremely careful to make friends only with people of his own sort.[2] But he need never be lonely; for so long as he behaves as a gentleman should, he will be welcomed by his 'brothers' (i.e. by other gentlemen) 'everywhere within the Four Seas.'[3] The whole world is his club. The alliances of 'small people' are directed against others, are hostile and destructive in intent; but those of the gentlemen exist only for mutual satisfaction. He has no politics, but sides with the Right wherever he finds it.[4]

He must not lay himself open to the accusation of 'talking too much';[5] still less must he boast[6] or push himself forward or in any way display his superiority, except in matters of sport,[7] and even here he is restrained by the complicated dictates of fair play, by the elaborate etiquette which constitutes the 'rules of the game.' Nor must he exalt himself by the indirect

[1] VIII, 4. [2] I, 8. [3] XII, 5.
[4] IV, 10. [5] XVII, 17.
[6] XIV, 29. Here, as in other points, the Chinese code has a particular affinity with ours. 'Swank' in all its forms is far more severely condemned by the English gentleman than by the patrician, for example, of Latin countries. [7] III, 7.

method of denigrating other people, a method characteristic of 'small men.'[1]

His education, like that given till recently at gentlemen's schools in England, consists chiefly of moral training; he learns in order to build up his *tê* (character). To learn anything of actual utility, to have practical accomplishments, is contrary to the Way of the *chün-tzu*[2] and will lead to his merely becoming a 'tool,'[3] an instrument dedicated to one humdrum purpose. Such a general, moral education will produce a Knight of the Way ready to face all emergencies 'without fret or fear.'[4] His head will not be turned by success, nor his temper soured by adversity.[5] Success, however, is a theme seldom dealt with in the *Analects*; for it is well known that the Way 'does not prevail in the world,' and the merits of the true *chün-tzu* are not such as the world is likely to recognize or reward. 'Lack of recognition' is, indeed, one of Confucius's most frequent topics, and to feel no resentment (*yüan*) when repeatedly cashiered or neglected is the *chün-tzu's* highest virtue.

Moderation in conduct and opinion is a well-known hallmark of the true gentleman: 'The *chün-tzu* avoids the absolute, avoids the extreme.'[6] Mencius tells us that 'Confucius was one who abstained from extremes.'[7] 'To exceed is as bad as not to reach.'[8] This conception of virtue as a middle way between two extremes is one which we have no difficulty in understanding; for it is familiar to us as part of our popular heritage from Greek philosophy. It is, however, one which rapidly

---

[1] XII, 16. [2] IX, 6. [3] II, 12. [4] XII, 4. [5] I, 1.
[6] *Han Fei Tzu*, 33. (Roll XII); adapted in *Tao Tê Ching*, XXIX.
[7] *Mencius*, IV, 2. X.
[8] *Analects*, XI, 15. Cf. XIII, 21. I leave out of account the famous dictum (VI, 27) about the Golden Mean (*chung-yung*); for the original meaning of the passage is far from clear. See additional notes.

disappears so soon as purely magical, non-social virtues are held in esteem. The reputation of an Indian ascetic, for example, is in proportion to the 'excessiveness' of his behaviour; and a society which admired St. Simeon on his pillar would not easily have understood either the μηδὲν ἄγαν of the Classical Greeks or the 'middle conduct' (*chung hsing*) inculcated by Confucius.

That good lies between two extremes has been very generally accepted by those who have tried to view the world rationally. As a political principle it was the foundation of nineteenth-century Liberalism and in particular of English Liberalism. In many cases the doctrine is one which can hardly be disputed. Thus 'softness' (unwillingness to inflict pain or take life) carried to its logical conclusion involves extinction; and so, with equal sureness, does 'hardness' (indifference to the infliction of death and suffering). Unfortunately it is extremes and not compromises that most easily become associated with strong emotional impulse. The downfall of Liberalism has been due to the failure to associate the Middle Way with any strong trend of emotion. The success of Confucianism, its triumph over 'all the hundred schools' from the second century B.C. onwards, was due in a large measure to the fact that it contrived to endow compromise with an emotional glamour.

As regards the translation of the term *chün-tzu* 1 see no alternative but to use the word 'gentleman,' though the effect is occasionally somewhat absurd in English. One needs a word which primarily signifies superiority of birth, but also implies moral superiority. Neither Legge's 'superior man,' nor Soothill's various equivalents ('man of the higher type,' 'wise man,' etc.) fulfil this condition. The late Sir Reginald Johnston proposed 'the princely man'; but this seems to me (I may be peculiar in my interpretation) to suggest lavish expenditure rather than superiority of birth or morals.[1]

HSIAO

This word seems originally to have meant piety towards the spirits of ancestors or dead parents.[2] In the *Analects* it still frequently has this meaning; but it is also applied to filial conduct towards living parents, and this is its usual meaning in current Chinese. In this change of meaning we may see, I think, another example of that general transference of interest from the dead to the living which marked the break-up of the old Chou civilization. There is, however, reason to believe that filial piety played a relatively small part in the teaching of the earliest Confucians. By far the larger number of references to it in the *Analects* occur in Books I and II which do not, I think, belong to the earliest strata of the work. But it seems clear that during the fourth century B.C. a place of extreme importance had already been allotted by the Confucians to *hsiao* in its extended sense of piety towards living parents. For it was with reference to this virtue that the followers of Confucius came into conflict with those of Mo Tzu, who taught that affection and solicitude ought to be equally extended to all mankind and not reserved in a special degree for parents or relations. Towards the end of the third century B.C. *hsiao* became, at any rate in certain Confucian schools, the summit of all virtues, and in the *Canon of Filial Piety* which

---

[1] This was written before Sir Reginald Johnston in his *Confucianism and Modern China* adopted 'gentleman' as the most exact equivalent to *Chün-tzu*.

[2] In the *Book of Songs* hsiao refers almost exclusively to piety towards the dead. Out of twelve instances nine can only be taken in this sense; the other three are non-committal.

may have existed[1] in some form in the third century, but did not, I think, reach its present form till at least a century later, *hsiao* is surrounded by the mysterious halo that attends the term *jên* in the *Analects*.

But it seems that the compilers of the *Canon of Filial Piety* were hard put to it to get their material. For in one place[2] they have reproduced a panegyric upon the potency of ritual observance, preserved in the *Tso Chuan* chronicle,[3] and by altering the word *li* ('ritual') to *hsiao* they have turned it into a eulogy of filial piety.

W Ê N [4]

The original meaning of the word *wên* is criss-cross lines, markings, pattern. It also means a written character, an ideogram. This, however, is scarcely a separate meaning from that of pattern, for in early China certain patterns served equally as ideograms, both being conventionalizations of pictures. Thus the character for 'eye' also figures as a decoration on Chou bronzes. *Wên*, again, means what is decorated as opposed to what is plain, ornament as opposed to structure, and hence the things that vary and beautify human life, as opposed to life's concrete needs. In particular, *wên* denotes the arts of peace (music, dancing, literature) as opposed to those of war. The arts of peace, however, everything that we should call culture, have a *tê* that is useful for offensive purposes. They attract the inhabitants of neighbouring countries; and it must be remembered the States of ancient China were just as anxious to attract immigration as modern European States are to repel it. For vast areas still remained to

---

[1] The allusion to the *Canon of Filial Piety* in *Lü Shih Ch'un Ch'iu* is probably an intrusion of commentary into text.   [2] Paragraph 7.
[3] Chao Kung, 25th year.   [4] Cf. *The Book of Songs*, p. 346.

be opened up for agriculture; there was room for everyone, and fresh inhabitants meant fresh recruits for the
army. 'If the distant do not submit, cultivate the power
of *wên* to bring them to you.'[1] It is clear then that *wên*
means something very like our own word culture and
served many of the same purposes. The prestige (*tê*)
of culture is to-day used by us for military purposes.
During the War, for example, efforts were made by
both sides to win over neutrals by displays of culture,[2]
such as the sending of theatrical companies, pictures
and the like. The power of *wên* is also used, as in
ancient China, to attract immigrants, but only those
of the temporary kind called tourists.

For Confucius the *wên* (culture) *par excellence* was
that established by the founders of the Chou dynasty.
To gather up the fragments of this culture and pass
them on to posterity was the sacred mission entrusted
to him by Heaven.[3] His native State, Lu, was generally
regarded as the main depository of Chou culture;[4] but
we find him, on a visit to Ch'i, ready to admit the
superiority of a musical performance there to anything
of the kind he had known in Lu,[5] and it was only
'after his return from Wei'[6] that the correct ritual use
of the ancestral hymns and Court songs was properly
established.

The term *wên* is, however, often used in the *Analects*
in a narrower sense than that of civilization or culture.
We have seen that one of its primary senses is that of
'a written character,' and it occurs once[7] in the *Analects*
with this meaning. *Wên-hsüeh* (letter-study) is the
ordinary Chinese term for literature or literary pur-

---

[1] XVI, 1.
[2] 'Just as military preparations must not be revealed, so too culture
must not be concealed.' *Kuo Yü*, ch. 2.   [3] IX, 5.
[4] Cf. *Tso Chuan*, Chao Kung, 2nd year.
[5] VII, 13.   [6] IX, 14.   [7] XV, 25.

suits, and it already has this meaning in the *Analects*. Moreover, when we are told that one in whom 'substance preponderates over ornament' (*wên*) will degerate into a mere savage; while one in whom ornament prevails over substance degenerates into a mere scribe, it is obvious that the *wên* in question is literature and not culture in general.

The earlier English translators were embarrassed by the term *wên*, because although they knew that it corresponded in a general way to our word 'culture,' they were entirely unfamiliar with the practical efficacies (*tê*) with which the Chinese associated the word. Legge, indeed, in one passage translates *wên* 'the Cause of truth,' not being able to convince himself that Confucius could have been interested in transmitting anything so frivolous as a mere 'culture.'

T'IEN

Apart from cases where Heaven (*t'ien*) merely means 'the sky' (for example in the common phrase *t'ien-hsia*, 'that which is under heaven,' i.e. the whole world),[1] it clearly corresponds to our word Heaven and to the German *Himmel* in the sense of Providence, Nature, God. Heaven is the dispenser of life and death, wealth and rank (XII, 5). The *chün-tzu* must learn to know the will (*ming*) of Heaven and submit to it patiently, a hard lesson that Confucius himself did not master till the age of fifty (II, 4). Concerning 'the ways of Heaven' he was unwilling to discourse (V, 12); but its name lingered on his lips in certain ancient formulae, such as those of oath-taking and of submission to fate in times of affliction. His 'Heaven has bereft me!' at the time of Yen Hui's death and his 'It is (Heaven's) will that we should lose him,' at the death-bed of Po

[1] Or again in the 'climbing to the sky' of XIX, 25.

Niu, correspond to the Moslem *kismet* and to our own
'God's will be done.' Confucius is made sometimes to
speak as though he regarded himself as under the
special protection of Providence, just as he certainly
regarded himself as charged with a peculiar mission
as transmitter of the rapidly disappearing Chou culture.[1] But I fancy that phrases such as 'Heaven
implanted *tê* in me; what can such a one as Huan T'ui
do to me?' (VII, 22) are, like 'Heaven has bereft me,'
etc., pious formulae, signifying confidence in God's
protection.

T'ien then corresponds for the most part to our
Heaven and, as with us, occurs chiefly in pious,
traditional formulae. There is, however, at any rate
one passage where the translation 'Nature' would not
be out of place: 'Does Nature (*t'ien*) speak? No; but
the four seasons are regulated by it; the crops grow
by it' (XVII, 19). The Chinese conception of Heaven
is, then, a very familiar one. The only question that
arises is why a word meaning 'sky' should also have
the connotations God, Providence, etc.? The problem
is clearly one which cannot be attacked from the
Chinese side alone.

The Sanskrit *deva*, the Greek θεός, the Latin *deus*
—indeed the words for 'God' in most Indo-European
languages—are sometimes alleged to be connected
with roots meaning 'sky.' This is far from certain. It
is only between Chinese and Germanic that we get a
complete parallel in the use of *t'ien* and Heaven
(*Himmel*). Is the original meaning of *t'ien* 'sky' and
hence God, because God lives in the sky; or was it
the other way round? To the term Heaven as used in
the average early Chinese text exactly corresponds the
term *Shang Ti* used constantly in the *Book of Songs*,
and occasionally elsewhere. *Shang* means upper, top-

[1] IX, 5.

most, supreme; *Ti* means[1] 'ancestor' in the sense in
which the Ancestors sometimes figure in the religions
of the South Seas or Africa. A *Ti* is not simply an
ancestor, i.e. a grandfather, great-grandfather or the
like. It is not a word of relationship, but means a royal
ancestor, the deified spirit of a former king. The *Ti*
dwell in the Court of Heaven; and it seems to me that
t'ien, 'Heaven,' is used in Chinese as a collective term
meaning 'those who dwell in Heaven,' just as the
'House of Lords' frequently means those who sit in
that House.[2] The older term *Shang Ti*, found side by
side with *t'ien* in the *Book of Songs* and used apparently
in exactly the same sense, originally meant, I think,
the Supreme Ancestor, in the sense of the first of the
line of Royal Ancestors. But it is commonly taken in
the sense 'The *Ti* that is above,' i.e. in the sky, and
alternates with *T'ien Ti*, 'Heavenly Ti.' The fuller
expressions 'Supreme *Ti*' and 'Heavenly *Ti*' do not
occur in the *Analects*; but in the collection of ancient
fragments which constitutes Book XX, the word *Ti*
is used by itself in the sense of Heaven or God, in a
very personal sense, for *Ti* is spoken of as having
servants and a heart.

HSIN

This character is written *jên* ('man') at the side of
yen ('word'), and is generally translated 'good faith,'
'faithfulness,' 'truth,' etc. In early Chinese it almost
always refers to keeping promises, fulfilling undertakings. It does not mean telling the truth; nor do all
early peoples regard telling the truth as good in itself.
What early Chinese literature, as also that of the

---

[1] i.e. in actual use. I am not concerned with the philosophic glosses
of the early dictionaries and commentaries.

[2] Cf. *The Way and Its Power*, p. 21.

Hebrews, condemns is 'bearing false witness,' i.e.
telling lies that lead to harm. Other sorts of lie are
ritually enjoined; for example, that of saying one is ill
instead of bluntly refusing an invitation or declining
to see a visitor. The necessity of this sort of lie is
recognized by 'society' in Europe; but not by the
Church. Confucius once (XVII, 20) told a lie of this
kind, and Soothill wrote (in 1910) concerning it,
'That such laxity on the part of China's noblest
Exemplar has fostered that disregard for truth for
which this nation is so notorious, can hardly be denied.'
In this instance a man of the world would have understood Confucius better than a clergyman has done. In
the passage concerned Confucius shows not 'laxity,'
but on the contrary a strict attention to manners.

SSU

The mere fact that the physical sensations connected
by the Chinese with 'thinking' were evidently very
different from our own, should warn us against believing
that what they meant by *ssu* (the word ordinarily
translated 'think') was identical with what we mean by
'to think.' The Chinese located thought as going on
in the middle of the body. We locate it in the head,
and though this may be due to self-suggestion, we
definitely connect it with sensations in the head and
not in the belly.

There is evidence that in its origin the word *ssu*
meant to observe outside things. A *ssu-t'ing* was an
observation-post in the market, from which the overseer could observe which stall-holders were cheating.[1]
So it came to mean to fix the attention not only on
something exterior but also on a mental image, as for

[1] There is, of course, the possibility that *ssu* is here merely a
phonetic substitute for some other character.

example, that of a person from whom one is separated; hence 'to be in love.' This use occurs once in the *Analects* (IX, 30): 'It is not that I do not think of you. . . .' There are nine other passages where *ssu* occurs, and in all but two the meaning implied is that of 'directing one's attention,' or something very close to it. When one sees people who are better than oneself, one should turn one's attention to equalling them (IV, 17). One should not act till one has looked into the matter three times (V, 19). When one sees a chance of gain, one should divert one's attention to whether it can be pursued without violation of what is right (XIV, 13).[1] One should occupy one's attention with what belongs to one's own rank in society (XIV, 28). There are 'nine points' which should occupy a gentleman's attention (XVI, 10). One should question searchingly and pay close attention to what one is told (XIX, 6).

It may be rather forced to use the word 'attention' in some of these cases; but what I want to emphasize is that in each case we are dealing with a process that is only at a short remove from concrete observation. Never is there any suggestion of a long interior process of cogitation or ratiocination, in which a whole series of thoughts are evolved one out of the other, producing on the physical plane a headache and on the intellectual, an abstract theory. We must think of *ssu* rather as a fixing of the attention (located in the middle of the belly) on an impression recently imbibed from without and destined to be immediately re-exteriorized in action.

These considerations will help us to understand the two remaining passages in which *ssu*, 'to think,' is used. 'If one learns but does not think, one is lost; if one thinks but does not learn, one is in danger' (II, 15).

[1] XIX, 1, is practically a repetition of this.

'I once ate nothing all day and did not go to bed all night in order to think. It was no use. Far better, to learn' (XV, 30).

'Learning,' as I clearly show in my note on the passage (see below, p. 199), means copying the ancients. It may be objected that the meaning of both passages is evident, and that I am making a great fuss about nothing. They are, however, certainly open to mis-understanding. Chu Hsi (died A.D. 1200) paraphrases *ssu* as 'seeking within the heart,' evoking a whole complex of ideas—the 'good knowledge' of Mencius, the 'inward power' of Lao Tzu, the *bodhi* of the Zen Buddhists—which are entirely foreign to the *Analects*. Mencius, the Quietists, the Buddhists all believed that a well of wisdom lay buried deep in the human breast. But Confucius believed nothing of the kind, and all suggestions that *ssu* in these passages means some kind of *yoga*, seem to me utterly unfounded. Moreover, I think that the average European reader of the current translations, coming across the maxim 'Learning without thought is useless' (Legge, Soothill), might easily imagine that 'thought' meant a process of logical reasoning, a sustained interior argumentation, full of 'therefores' and 'becauses.' There is, as a matter of fact, hardly a single example of these conjunctions in the *Analects*. The 'all day and all night' of XV, 30, is simply a way of saying 'you may think (i.e. survey the matter in hand as the overseer surveys the market) till you are blue in the face. You are wasting time. It is much better to find out what the ancients did under similar circumstances.' The theme of II, 15 is slightly different: Learning and turning over in your mind what you have learnt are equally important. Here again, however, the sort of 'thought' that we write with a capital, contrast with Action, and associate with a wrinkled brow, is not in the least what is meant.

WANG

Chou legend centres round its two first kings (*wang*), Wên and Wu. *Wên* in this name probably meant 'mighty';[1] Wu means 'warrior.' But in Confucius's time *wên*, as we have seen, meant the arts of peace as opposed to those of war, and a theory had grown up that every great armed conquest was preceded by a period of cultural preparation, a building up of *tê* (moral force) as distinct from the *li* (physical force) of the warrior, which unless backed by *wên* (culture) cannot prevail. King Wên, the first Chou monarch, was naturally credited with the initial, cultural achievements and King Wu (the Warrior) with the military triumphs which established the Chou hegemony.

To Confucius, however, it was neither Wên nor Wu, but Wu's brother Tan, Duke of Chou, who was the real hero of the Chou conquest. This point of view was a purely local one. The Duke of Chou is barely mentioned in the *Book of Songs*.[2] But legend regarded him as the founder of the Ducal House in Lu; and Confucius, as a professed Conservative and Legitimist, dwelt fondly on the memory of this local Ancestor and felt a profound discouragement when the Duke of Chou no longer appeared to him in his dreams.[3]

The coming of Divine Sages and World Monarchs, in China as elsewhere, was heralded by portents. Confucius watched in vain for the appearance of such signs: 'the phoenix does not arrive and the river gives forth no chart.'[4] Birds have everywhere been regarded as intermediaries between Heaven and Earth. The sudden appearances and movements of birds were interpreted

---

[1] As it presumably does when it occurs as a stock epithet of 'ancestor.' *Wên*, 'pattern' is probably quite a different word.

[2] There are only two *Songs* (232 and 251) which mention him.

[3] VII, 5.   [4] IX, 8.

as ominous, in China as in the West. The sacred *fêng* (phoenix), half-bird, half-snake, acclaimed the holy kingship of Shun; it was a winged messenger, part man, part bird that heralded the coming of the western Saviour.

The legend of the river-omen existed in two forms, which were merely local variants of the same belief. The portent referred to in the *Analects* is the 'River Chart,'[1] which is brought out of the river (usually understood to mean the Yellow River) by an animal that is a mixture of horse and dragon. The variant legend concerns the 'Writings from the Lo River,' which are brought out of the Lo river (in Honan) by a Divine Tortoise. But the 'River Chart' is also sometimes spoken of as being brought by the Tortoise; indeed, the confusion between the two legends lasts till the thirteenth century.

There are two explanations as to what the Chart and the Writings consisted of. One is, that they contained the divinatory diagrams of the *Book of Changes*, that is to say the eight trigrams arrived at by arranging two symbols in every possible group of three. The other is, that they were magic arrangements of numbers. The two theories are closely related; for the process[2] of shuffling the forty-nine stalks in order to discover which divinatory diagram concerned one, was bound up both with ideas of numerical symbolism and with the natural properties of numbers. At the beginning of the Sung dynasty the theory was that the River Chart was the 'magic square'

$$
\begin{array}{ccc}
4 & 9 & 2 \\
3 & 5 & 7 \\
8 & 1 & 6
\end{array}
$$

[1] *T'u* means 'plan,' 'plot,' 'scheme'; it may be cognate to *t'u*, 'land,' and mean originally 'to plot out land.'

[2] Well described in Richard Wilhelm's book on the *I Ching*, which is about to appear in an English version.

in which the columns, whether added horizontally, vertically or diagonally always come to fifteen. Many Sung writers[1] are quite definite on this point. The River Chart with its nine chambers, they say, 'has five for its centre, carries nine on its head, treads on one, has three at the left, and seven at the right, has two and four on top, and six and eight below.'

But the magic square had behind it a long history. It was believed, certainly in the second century B.C. and probably much earlier, that the Nine chambers of the Ming T'ang (the ruier's audience-hall) had in ancient times been an architectural embodiment of the magic square.[2] It would then, I think, be fairly safe to assume that Confucius regarded the River Chart as a magic arrangement of symbols or numbers, and that he very likely identified it with the 'magic square' (492, 357, etc.) alluded to above.

WANG AND PO

In the *Analects* and in subsequent Chinese literature we find the term *wang* (king) used in a very special sense, that of a Saviour King who, unlike the monarchs of the world around us, rules by *tê*, by magico-moral force alone. The coming of such a Saviour was looked forward to with Messianic fervour. Were a True King to come, says Confucius, in the space of a single generation Goodness would become universal.[3] With the Saviour King is always contrasted the *Po* (verb, *pa*, 'to be a *po*'). The word originally means 'elder,' 'senior,' and in the early days of the Chou dynasty when the various conquered domains were ruled by descendants of the conquering House it was applied to the senior

---

[1] See *T'u Shu* encyclopaedia, XXI, 51, and charts on fols. III, 12 and IV, 12.

[2] *Ta Tai Li Chi*, 67. [3] XIII, 12.

among the feudal barons. After the central authority of the Chou declined it was applied to any local ruler who succeeded in acquiring an ascendancy over the rest, with a view (in theory at any rate) to re-establishing the pontifical authority of the Chou monarch. The greatest of the *Po* were Huan of Ch'i (middle of the seventh century) and Wên of Chin (second half of the seventh century). A *Po* acts by *li* (physical force) and not by *tê*. His achievements cannot lead to the reign of universal Goodness. The material consequences of such a hegemony may be immense. The two great *Po* saved China from complete immersion by the barbarians: but for the efforts of Huan 'we should be wearing our hair loose and folding our garments to the left.'[1] But the *Po* is guided by opportunism alone, his Way is not that of the Former Kings, his achievements are in the political not in the moral sphere. His fellow barons may reluctantly yield to his superior strength; but he cannot inspire 'everywhere under Heaven' that longing for spontaneous submission which overcame even the wild tribes of the west and north when the Saviour King T'ang appeared: 'when he advanced towards the East, the savages of the West were jealous; when he advanced towards the South, the barbarians of the North were jealous, saying "Why did he not advance upon us first?" Everywhere the people turned their gaze towards him, as men gaze towards a rainbow in days of drought.'[2]

[1] XIV, 18.   [2] *Mencius*, I, 2. XI.

WRITTEN TRADITION [1]

No doubt what Confucius knew of the Former Kings and of the 'antiquity' which he loved so well was derived partly from oral, partly from written sources. We must not, however, in dealing with societies where both sorts of tradition exist, attempt to make too sharp a distinction between the two. Wherever texts exist at all, even if they are accessible only to a small minority, the two sorts of tradition are bound to infiltrate one another. A Mongol peasant who tells the story of Buddha's life may have learnt most of the episodes orally from other members of the tribe, who also learnt most of them orally. But he may very well have learnt other episodes from a Lama who has read them in a book. And the same Lama, should he write a book, would be likely enough to incorporate in his story folk-lore elements belonging to an oral tradition. A Majorcan peasant who tells one stories about the Moors has probably never read a book about the Moors or, indeed, any book at all. But much of what he tells could ultimately be traced to printed texts.

Knowledge, in ancient Chinese phraseology, consists in 'hearing much.' In the chronicles, when the judgments of a famous man upon episodes of the past (events, say, of the seventh and sixth centuries) are recorded, he is invariably spoken of as 'hearing about' the event, even if it occurred centuries before his time; seldom, as reading about it. Confucius continually quotes ancient sayings, many of them in the form of didactic verse. How many of these are drawn from written collections we have no means of knowing. The one written work which almost certainly existed in his time and to which we may reasonably suppose he had at least occasional access was the *Book of Songs*.

[1] This section too may be omitted by the general reader.

Concerning this most important of all Chou texts I will say no more here, but refer the reader to my recently published *The Book of Songs*.[1] A far more thorny and complicated problem is presented by another book to which the *Analects* sometimes refer. This is the collection of documents known as *Shu Ching*. The European reader is familiar, through the translations of Legge and Couvreur, with a version of this text containing fifty-six books or chapters. Of these all but twenty-eight were strung together from very miscellaneous sources in the third century A.D. The sources used were mainly though not exclusively pre-Han, and the view is sometimes taken that even though the compilation of these forged books was late, their matter is early and therefore relevant to the study of Chou tradition. This is not really so; for isolated sentences have been detached from their context and strung together in such a way as completely to falsify the meaning. It may be convenient to the reader if I here give a list of the books which are not the work of a third-century forger:

(1) Yao Tien (second half now printed as Shun Tien)
(2) Kao Yao Mo (second half now printed as I Chi)
(3) Yü Kung
(4) Kan Shih
(5) T'ang Shih
(6) P'an Kêng
(7) Kao Tsung Yung Jih
(8) Hsi Po K'an Li
(9) Wei Tzu
(10) Mu Shih
(11) Hung Fan

[1] Allen and Unwin, 1937. Vol. I. Translations, Vol. II. Textual Notes.

(12) Chin T'êng
(13) Ta Kao
(14) K'ang Kao
(15) Chiu Kao
(16) Tzu Ts'ai
(17) Shao Kao
(18) Lo Kao
(19) To Shih
(20) Wu I
(21) Chün Shih
(22) To Fang
(23) Li Chêng
(24) Ku Ming (second half now printed as K'ang
  Wang Chih Kao)
(25) Pi Shih
(26) Lü Hsing
(27) Wên Hou Chih Ming
(28) Ch'in Shih

Those which have any chance of being contemporary documents are (13) to (28), excluding (26). (13), (15) and (21) are put in a class apart by Ho Ting-shêng,[1] as according most completely with the language and ideas of the inscriptions. In no document of the *Shu Ching*, however, does the use of pronouns (*wo*, 'I,' *êrh*, 'you,' etc.) concord with Western Chou inscriptions. P'an Kêng (6) is linguistically very close to (13)–(23) and was probably written as propaganda in favour of the transference of the Capital to the East at the close of the Western Chou period (*c.* 770 B C.?). The rest are later texts which were dressed up in superficial resemblance to the style of the Books, in order to gain credence and authority. The *Analects* quote exclusively from Books that are now lost (only

[1] National Sun Yat-sen University: *Linguistic and Historical Review* (in Chinese). V, 49 (1928).

the third-century A.D. forgeries of them exist); save in the one instance of XIV, 43 which is practically a quotation from Wu I (20). In general, however, the genuinely archaic books, being merely archival documents, are less quoted in Confucian literature than the later more moralistic compilations, intended at the outset for edification.

Confucius has been represented by some European writers as a bookish man. Soothill even went so far as to suggest that he had 'the scholar's indifferent digestion.' We have, however, no reason to suppose that his reading went beyond the *Songs* and *Shu Ching*, possibly some ritual texts and collections of moral sayings, and perhaps the Court annals of his own State.[1] His youth (of which we know little) was certainly not spent in poring over books, but presumably in hunting and fighting, the occupations common to his class. In the chronicles we find his disciples (for example, Jan Ch'iu and Fan Ch'ih) riding out to battle together; and again we have no reason to suppose that the Master's active years were spent differently from theirs.

RITUAL

It is very unlikely that any ritual texts existed until the decline of Chou civilization. So long as the rites were practised, it was unnecessary to fix them in writing. Probably the first books of ritual were composed for the benefit of such offshoots of the Chou ruling caste as were settled in the remoter conquered territories, and were in danger of becoming out of contact with the central culture. Whether Confucius knew any such texts or derived his knowledge of ritual solely from oral maxims is uncertain. All of the ritual books that we possess contain ancient material;

[1] This is very doubtful. Official annals were only accessible to high officers of state.

but all[1] of them were certainly composed long after the time of Confucius.

The Confucius of the *Analects* is not much concerned with the details of ritual, either public or domestic. Correct observance of small social rites, what we call 'good manners,' belongs, of course, equally to the Chinese and to our conception of the gentleman, as does also the insistence upon 'giving a fair chance' both to one's competitors in sport[2] and to one's victims in the chase.[3] But the actual text of the *Analects* is concerned with the general principles of conduct, with morality rather than manners; and so little guidance on the details of behaviour could the composers of the work find in the traditional sayings of the Master that they were obliged to insert in it, in order to meet the demands of a later Confucianism that was preoccupied above all with the details of ritual, a long ritual text, dealing in reality with the behaviour of gentlemen in general, but adapted and amplified in such a way as to read as though it were a description of Confucius's own behaviour. This text (Book X), though we cannot (as many western writers have done) use it as biographical material, throws so much light on early Confucian ideas that it will be worth while to consider its contents in detail. The first characteristic about it that strikes us is the profusion of reduplicative words (similar to such English formations as 'sing-song,' 'hurly-burly' and the like). In fulfilling religious rites it is not sufficient merely to say the correct words or perform the correct actions. Each rite requires also an appropriate

---

[1] Some Western scholars make an exception of the *I Li*, which is mainly concerned with the domestic ritual of everyday life. But this book, too, shows, for example, in the sections on mourning, the same tendency to build up theoretical schematizations rather than to describe actual practices, which marks the other ritual works.

[2] III, 7.   [3] For fishing and shooting, see VII, 26.

'attitude,' one of reverence, eagerness, reluctance, joy, gloom and so on.'[1] It is these attitudes (*jung*) that are defined by the expressive reduplicatives mentioned above. Such definitions are not confined to behaviour on ritual occasions. In VII, 4, we find the Master's attitude when sitting quietly at home described by a pair of typical 'expressive reduplicatives.' There was, in fact, no circumstance in life for which a particular attitude was not seemly and appropriate. In this respect we do not differ substantially from the Chinese. Anyone who knows how to behave adopts a special attitude when in church, one of reverence and constraint; he listens to the observations of his superiors in a special attitude of alert attention, his tenderly admirative attitude when taking the hand of an influential hostess is as different as possible from that which he adopts when shaking hands with a tennis opponent. A gentleman who adopted the wrong attitude on any one of these or a hundred other occasions would show grave ill-breeding. The assumption, for example, of a playful attitude when handing round the collecting-box in church or of the 'tenderly admirative' attitude when interviewing a male superior would be sufficient to close the most promising social or public career.

It might be objected that our 'attitudes' are of a spontaneous, instinctive kind—that they arise 'naturally' out of the situations to which they belong. But in point of fact they only seem to us natural and inevitable because we are used to them. The English church-going attitude, so far from arising naturally from the feelings connected with a place of worship, is peculiar to Anglicanism. It is far more extreme, in its contrast with the attitudes of everyday life, far more stylized and artificial than that practised in other Protestant countries (the 'off-hand' attitude of the

[1] See *The Way and Its Power*, p. 160.

Dutch when in church has often impressed English
travellers); in a southern Catholic church the contrast
is even less noticeable, with the Moslem (whose religion
functions equally inside and outside the Mosque) it
hardly exists at all.

The difference, in respect of 'attitudes,' between us
and the ancient Chinese is that we learn them and
practise them unconsciously; whereas with the Chinese
they were a subject of conscious interest and attention.
A high standard was set, gentility implied a fastidious
expertise in the niceties of bearing, a whole armoury
of gesture and attitude was developed, beside which
our humble stock (hat-raising, hand-shaking and the
like) seems meagre indeed.

The commonest method of symbolizing one's own
'smallness' as contrasted with the 'greatness' of another
is to shrink oneself. Even we, with our impoverished
vocabulary of attitude, maintain various forms of ceremonial 'shrinking,' such as bowing, nodding, kneeling.
The Chinese *chün-tzu* knew a far wider range of
bendings and contractions, many of which (but by no
means all) are mentioned in Book X of the *Analects*.
He 'made himself small' now by, as we should say,
grogging at the knees, now by squeezing himself as
though creeping through a hole, now by stooping
across the bar of his chariot, now by bending at the
waist.

Anthropologists are or were in the habit of trying
to discover the 'real reason' why particular injunctions
or prohibitions were imposed among primitives. If the
reason given by the people themselves seemed to them
trivial or unintelligible they set it down as a rationaliza-
tion or, alternatively, attributed it to secretiveness
regarding the 'real reason.'

The truth, however, is that there is no 'real reason'
for ritual acts. In any community where the perform-

ance of such acts is linked to a general system of
thought, they will be explained in terms of that system.
If the system changes, as frequently happens, without
disturbing these ritual acts, they will be reinterpreted
in terms of the new system. Where such acts or some
of them have not been linked, at any rate in the mind
of the person questioned, to any system of thought,
they sink to the role of mere etiquette and will be
explained as 'customary,' as being 'good manners,'
'the thing to do,' or the like. The ultimate origin of
the act or abstentions concerned is a matter for the
psychologist, who is at present only able to furnish
very speculative and provisional answers.

If, however, we find among people in many parts
of the world a prohibition against treading on[1] or lying
across thresholds, we can at least say that some of the
reasons given for this prohibition belong to ways of
thought that are older than others. Huai-nan Tzu,[2] in
the second century B.C., gives two alternative reasons
for not lying with the head across a threshold, (1)
because ghosts inhabit the threshold; (2) because one
will catch cold from the draught. It is not difficult to
decide which of these two reasons belongs to the earlier
way of thinking; and it might seem at first sight as
though in this case we had tracked down the prohibition to its source; had found not only an initial but a
'real' reason. For it is well known that in primitive
societies the dead were often buried under the threshold,
and this practice seems to give an adequate explanation
of the threshold 'taboo.'[3] But we are still confronted
with the question, why were ghosts believed in and
why were they feared? Once more we are in the realm
not of anthropology but of psychological speculation.

The *Analects* simply record that on entering the

[1] Book X, 4.   [2] P'ien 13, 2 fols. from end.
[3] See Frazer, *Folklore in the Old Testament*, Vol. III, p. 11.

ruler's palace a gentleman does not step on the threshold
and the commentators can tell us no more than that it
was not ritually correct to do so. It seems not unreason-
able to suppose that in this case an old religious 'taboo'
(i.e. a prohibition formally connected with a set of
obligatory beliefs) has passed into the domain of
etiquette, of things that are done because they are
done. It was the task of the ritual theorists in the third
century B.C. to detrivialize ritual, to arrest its lapse
into the domain of mere etiquette or good manners,
by reintegrating it into the current system of thought.
The Jews have made similar efforts to reinterpret
religious taboos in terms of scientific hygiene.

Matter very like parts of the *Analects* is contained in
the *Āpastamba Dharma Sūtra*, a Sanskrit work probably
contemporary with the *Analects*, and in the *Mārkandeya
Purāna*, which is certainly subsequent to the Christian
era. In Chapter XXXIV of the latter work we read that
the 'master of a household' must not sleep with his
head to the north or the west; compare *Analects*, X, 16.
He must not eat stale rice (*Analects*, X, 8, 2) and must
not converse 'while impure owing to the fact that he
is taking food' (*Analects*, X, 8, 8). The injunction
against eating food bought in the market (*Analects*,
X, 8, 5) is, of course, inevitable in the case of anyone
whose eating is subject to strict taboos, and applied
also to Brahmins and Buddhist monks. We also read
in the *Purāna* that the 'householder' must not sit with
his feet stretched out (XXXIV, 44), which reminds
us of *Analects*, XIV, 46, where a disciple is chastised
for sitting in a sprawling position.

DRESS

It would be surprising if any code of upper-class
behaviour did not deal with the subject of dress, and

equally surprising if the dress-regulations contained in the *Analects*[1] meant much more to us than our own upper-class dress-regulations (with a white stiff shirt a gentleman wears a white tie if his waistcoat is white, a black tie if his waistcoat is black; with a white waistl coat he wears a long coat, with a black waistcoat he wears a short coat, etc.) would mean to a resurrected Confucius. To understand early Chinese dress-ritue- would demand a detailed knowledge of early Chinesa social history, such as we are far indeed from possessing. There are, however, certain general analogies to the dress-rules that we are bound by; and I have tried to point out some of these analogies in my notes on the relevant passages. It is my impression that the 'knightly' origin of some regulations had been forgotten. I would hazard the guess that the shortness of the right sleeve was not (as the commentators tell us) intended (origi- nally, at any rate) to facilitate the use of the right hand in general, but in particular to leave it free to defend the *chün-tzu's* honour with the sword.[2] It is possible that the regulation about bed-coverings has a similar origin. They are to be one and a half times (and not twice) as long as the sleeper, lest trapped in a complete bag of bed-clothes, he may be unable if attacked to defend himself with alacrity. But this is only a speculation.

THE DEAD

No practices have been subject to a more constant reinterpretation than those connected with mourning and burial. In some places,[3] for example, the plugging of all the orifices of the corpse is regarded as a device for preventing the soul escaping and doing harm to

[1] X, 6.

[2] Or dagger. Swords do not seem to belong to Western Chou culture.

[3] See Sir James Frazer, *Fear of the Dead*, Vol. II, p. 109.

the community. In China mortuary jades, used in just the same way, were looked upon as a means of fortifying the 'life' of the departed in his new abode. We find among mankind in general, indeed, two sharply contrasted attitudes towards the dead. In some societies they are feared; in others they are reverenced. The first attitude can exist without any admixture of the second. But the attitude of reverence and love seldom exists without some admixture of fear. Those, for example, who honour and love the dead by day walk none too boldly through a graveyard by night.

Now it is perfectly possible that both these attitudes are expressions of the same fundamental feeling. Certain psychologists call this feeling a 'sense of guilt,' and imply that somewhere at the bottom of our hearts we feel that it was we who slew those whom we profess to love. Be that as it may, we find among men as we know them these two sharply contrasted conscious attitudes, and there is not I think the slightest doubt that the attitude of fear is the more primitive. For example, in societies where the two attitudes exist side by side, it is always the less developed members of the community who fear the dead—who refuse, for example, to cross the cemetery by night.

In China the attitude towards the dead was, among the upper classes, at any rate, one solely of love and reverence; and all the rites of burial, mourning and sacrifice to immediate forefathers were interpreted in this sense. It does not, however, by any means follow that these rites and practices had always been so interpreted or that any of them had their origin in the attitude of tenderness and regret. The personal name of the dead was not allowed to be mentioned.[1] If his

---

[1] The evidence of the inscriptions is that the Chou conquerors themselves did not practise this taboo. It had however, become general long before Confucius's time·

fame had not spread beyond the family circle he was known as 'the departed father,' 'the late uncle,' or the like; if he were a person of public importance, destined to become as we say, 'known to history,' he received a 'posthumous name,' descriptive of his virtues:[1] the Steadfast, the Cultured, the Pious. This avoidance of the personal name was interpreted as due to 'respect' for the dead. But it is difficult not to regard it merely as a particular example of the general rule that to name a spirit is to compel its presence; and we may be fairly sure that there was once a time in China when, if the dead were not named, it was through fear lest they should suddenly appear.

As with us, an important feature of funeral rites was the eulogy (*lei*) pronounced over the dead. Later *lei* are, like ours, for the most part merely laudatory, but in that quoted by Tzu-lu in the *Analects* is manifest the desire not merely to placate the dead but to disclaim responsibility, to remind him that the living 'did everything they could': 'we prayed for you (i.e. during your illness) upwards and downwards, to the spirits of Heaven and to the spirits of earth below.'[2]

MOURNING

The mourner leads a life apart, wears special clothes, eats special food, abstains from physical pleasures, retires from public life, and so on. One explanation of why he does these things is that he has been contaminated by contact with death; he has become a sinister person and must be segregated in order to go through

[1] Or of his vices? It is a disputed question whether certain 'posthumous names' are to be taken in a bad sense. Was Li Wang (died 828 B.C.) the Cruel King or the Dignified King? Many Western sovereigns are, of course, 'known to history' by bad names. e.g. Bloody Mary and Theophylact the Unbearable.   [2] VII, 34.

a process of 'disinfection.' A quite different interpretation of the mourner's behaviour is given in ancient
China. If he leads an abnormal life it is not because
he is ritually unclean and must, so to speak, be cured.
It is because he would not 'feel at ease'[1] in his ordinary
clothes, on his ordinary mat, eating his usual food,
doing his habitual work. And if someone brought into
contact with a mourner must behave towards him in a
propitiatory fashion, and even for the time being follow
the mourner's regime,[2] it is not (as in some communi-
ties) because the mourner may well try to transfer
some of his uncleanness to those with whom he comes
in contact, and this secondary taint requires to be
removed by the same means as the original one; on
the contrary, these precautions are due in Chinese
theory to respect for the mourner's feelings. But there
are practices which fit in badly with this explanation;
for example, the prohibition, mentioned in other books
besides the *Analects*[3], against singing on the same day
that one has wailed at a funeral.

Preparation for sacrifice, to which Book X devotes
a long section, bears a strong resemblance to mourning.
The sacrificer segregates himself, alters all his habits,
denies himself every indulgence; this time certainly
not in order to rid himself of a taint caused by contact
with the dead, but to purify himself, to spiritualize
himself in such a way as to be fit for contact with the
spirit world and at the same time to impress the spirits
with the earnestness of the appeals he is about to make.

Spirits are fastidious; it cannot be expected that
they will accept the sacrifice and come in person to
partake of it, if the sacrificer is in a condition which
even his earthly wives or concubines would object to,
if he smells of wine or garlic. This idea, I think,

[1] XVII, 21.   [2] VII, 9; IX, 9; X, 16.
[3] VII, 9.

underlies the prohibitions against eating onions, garlic, ginger[1] and so on, that we find not only in the regime of the sacrificer, who is a temporary priest; but also in that of the permanent priests of Buddhism.

THE MAGIC EFFICACY OF RITUAL

The word *li* ('ritual') is expressed in writing by a picture of a ritual vessel. The original meaning is said to be 'arranging ritual vessels'; and this may very well be true, for it appears to be cognate to a number of words meaning 'to arrange in proper order,' 'to put in sequence,' etc. But as used in early China *li* would cover everything from the opening of the great doors of St. Peter's down to saying 'Bless you!' when someone sneezes.[2] Modern writers have said that Confucius, in common with the early Chinese in general, attributed a magic influence to ritual. In a sense this is true. The influence of saying 'God bless you!' can hardly be considered otherwise than a magic one; and no doubt Confucius attributed a like influence to all the small prescriptions and conventions that we should put under the heading of good manners. But the rites to which Confucius attributed a true magic efficacy in the fullest sense were, naturally enough, not those that he saw practised around him in everyday life, nor the usurped rites illicitly carried on by the dictators of Lu;[3] but those enacted by the ideal monarchs of the legendary past, by Yao and Shun, by Yü the Great, by Wên

[1] The 'He does not eschew ginger-food' (i.e. food sprinkled with ginger), of Book X, takes for granted that the mourner does eschew the eating of ginger as a separate dish. It follows that if pungent herbs, etc., are avoided when we wish to attract spirits they will be used when we wish to repel spirits. It is therefore not surprising that peasants in many parts of Europe hang garlic at their doors to drive away evil spirits.

[2] There are other words for 'deportment,' 'seemliness,' and so on. But *li* is the generic word which covers them all.   [3] III, 1 and 2.

and Wu of Chou, and above all by the Duke of Chou, patron saint of Lu.

Wherever the idea of divine kingship prevails we find coupled with it the conviction that upon the correct performance of kingly ritual depends the whole welfare of the State, the fertility of its lands, the fruitfulness of its trees, the fecundity both of its women and of its herds and flocks. The Divine King (*T'ien wang*) in ancient China was the Emperor (the 'Son of Heaven') and the State rulers merely inherited a fraction of his divinity. In Confucius's time there was no longer a Son of Heaven. The King of Chou still used this title, but the mere fact that the local rulers no longer deferred to him showed that he had lost his heavenly 'appointment.' The Imperial rites, too, had long ago fallen into abeyance; with the parody of them that was enacted in his native State Confucius had no patience: 'At the Ancestral Sacrifice, as for all that comes after the libation—I had rather not witness it!'[1]

Not only were the rites incorrectly performed, but their *shuo* (explanation) was lost,[2] and with it the magic power that enabled Divine Kings to 'deal with all things under Heaven as easily as I lay my finger here.'[3]

That countries could really adopt with success a home policy of government by the magic of ritual (as opposed to government by penalties) and a foreign policy of 'giving way' (*jang*) as opposed to one of push and grab (*chin-ch'ü*) is a fundamental part of Confucius's Way. If a king could for a single day fully and completely carry out the kingly ritual, the whole country would 'surrender' to his Goodness.

---

[1] III, 10.

[2] i.e. They had become divorced from the circle of ideas to which they originally belonged, and had not been successfully reinterpreted. A rite divorced from its *Shuo* has as little efficacy as a scripture apart from its traditional interpretation (also called *Shuo*).   [3] III, 11.

'Keep order among them by chastisement and they will flee from you; keep order among them by ritual and they will come to you of their own accord.'[1]

I do not think Confucius attributed this magic power to any rites save those practised by the divinely appointed ruler. It is true that the correct practice of ritual by 'those above' (as opposed to 'those below,' i.e. the *min*, 'masses') also exercises a profound influence upon the populace. In a country where the *chün-tzu* are punctilious in their ritual observances[2] the small people will be punctilious in the discharge of their duties towards their superiors,[3] and will be easy to rule.[4] It is for the upper classes to 'set a good example,' as we say; to exert a good influence. In regard to this function of the *chün-tzu* I do not think that the Confucian conception was very different from ours. The idea that human institutions should be harmonized (*ho*) with the operations of Nature, should for example be arranged in categories, corresponding to the seasons, the planets, the points of the compass, though it is referred to by Master Yu in one entirely isolated passage,[5] does not belong to the teaching of Confucius in the *Analects*.

The Chinese have a special word for things done 'after a fashion,' in a hugger-mugger way, but not according to the proper ritual.[6] Such things are said to be fluked (*kou*). What is done in this way may seem for the moment to 'work,' just as a hastily patched tyre may carry us for a mile or two as comfortably as a properly mended one. But the *chün-tzu's* code, like that of the old-fashioned artisan, compels him to 'make a good job' of whatever he undertakes. A temporary success secured by irregular means gives him

---

[1] II, 3.   [2] Including, of course, etiquette and manners.
[3] XIII, 4.   [4] XIV, 44.   [5] I, 12.
[6] See additional note on XIII, 3.

no satisfaction; it is stolen (*t'ou*), not honestly come by.[1]
True, the social virtues (loyalty, promise-keeping,
respect for elders, courage in the cause of right) come
first, are the groundwork upon which *li* (ritual) must
be built.[2] 'A man that is not good, what can he have
to do with ritual?'[3] But right conduct does not proceed
automatically from right feelings. It is virtuous to
respect Heaven; but if (to take a Western equivalent)
one took off one's shoes in church instead of one's
hat as a sign of respect, *pu hsing*: 'it would not work.'
The domain of Chinese ritual, of obligatory acts and
abstentions was a vast one. Three hundred rules of
major ritual and three thousand minor observances
had, according to the usual computation,[4] to be mas-
tered. The expression 'to know,' used by itself, means
'to know the rites,' and he who lacked this *savoir faire*
could not be regarded as a gentleman. It might,
indeed, seem to us that the *chün-tzu*, faced with the
necessity of learning 3,300 injunctions,[5] was in some
danger of turning into precisely what is everywhere
held to be inconsistent with his status—was in danger,
that is to say, of turning into a qualified specialist.
But it was with the relation of ritual as a whole to
morality and not with the details of etiquette and
precedence that the early Confucians were chiefly concerned. Master Tsêng, indeed, even goes so far as to

---

[1] The word 'steal' is often coupled with or substituted for *kou*.
[2] *Li hou yeh*, 'Ritual is secondary.' III, 8. [3] III, 3.
[4] e.g. *Chung-yung*, XXVII, 3 and *Li Chi*, X.
[5] Some of them seem to us superfluous: 'If when you are calling
on another gentleman, he begins to yawn and stretch himself, twiddles
his hair-pins, fiddles with the knob of his sword, shuffles his feet and
asks how the time is going, you will not be at fault in proposing to
retire.' (*Li Chi*, XVII.) This is less absurd than it sounds; for the
wording implies that the visitor is inferior in age or status, and in such
cases (as in our own Court etiquette) it was for the host and not the
guest to terminate the interview.

say that the ordering of ritual vessels is a matter for
the special officers put in charge of them, and does not
fall within the *chün-tzu's* proper sphere.[1]

MUSIC AND DANCING (YO)

Our view of music as an agreeable arrangement of
sounds,[2] listened to solely for enjoyment, and of
dancing as a means of social distraction combined
with mild bodily exercise, is a very abnormal one.
Everywhere during the greater part of man's history
and by a large portion of the world's inhabitants even
to-day these related arts are regarded in a way wholly
different from the way in which we regard them.
Music, in the view not only of primitives, but in that
of almost all non-European peoples, exercises a magic
power not only over the heart of man (as we in Europe
would to some extent admit), but also over the forces
of nature. Everyone familiar with early Chinese books
knows the story, existing in countless variants, of Duke
P'ing of Chin[3] and the baleful music—how drawn by
the magic of an evil tune eight huge black birds
swooped from the south and danced on his terrace,
black clouds blotted out the sky, a tempest tore down
the hangings of his palace, broke the ritual vessels,
hurled down the tiles from the roof; the king fell sick,
and for three years no blade of grass grew in Chin,
no tree bore fruit.

A similar view of the magic power of music over
the forces of nature still prevails in India; it is by music
and dancing that rain is produced all over Africa, just
as it was in ancient China. I do not think that Con-

---

[1] VIII, 4.

[2] Obviously there are in our use of music some remnants of an
earlier conception; particularly its use in connection with war.

[3] The incident is placed by legend in about 533 B.C.

fucius would have questioned the possibility of music possessing such power; but it was to the music of the Divine Sages and not to the 'songs of Wei and Chêng' that he attributed it; and this 'music of the ancients' had all but disappeared. The music of the Succession Dance (*Shao*), which Confucius characterizes as 'perfectly beautiful' apparently did not exist in Lu. Later legend regarded it as the accession music of the Divine Sage Shun; but it also figures as a Chou dance, and we do not know whether Confucius regarded any of the magical music of the Sages as surviving in his time.

When he heard the Succession music, he 'did not notice what he was eating' for three months afterwards. This gives the impression that Confucius's whole being was profoundly stirred by the performance, much in the same way as the young Bach was moved by the organ-playing of Buxtehude. And, indeed, if we could register the exact physiological reactions in the two cases, we might well find that they were very much the same. But we should be mistaken if we supposed that Confucius's conscious attitude towards music, his 'interpretation' of its place in life, concorded in the least with that of a European musician. To him, as to the ancient Greeks, it was important above all as an instrument of education.[1] It promotes virtue; it is an intrinsic part of the Way that causes gentlemen to love other gentlemen and makes small men easy to rule.[2]

[1] VIII, 8.
[2] XIII, 3.

APPENDIX I

The Interpretations

THERE are two main interpretations of the *Analects*, the 'old' and the 'new.' The old interpretation is that of the *Lun Yü Chi Chieh*, 'Collected Explanations of the *Lun Yü*,' presented to the throne by a committee of scholars about A.D. 240. The chief commentators whose explanations were here collected are Pao Hsien (6 B.C.–A.D. 65), Ma Jung, Chêng Hsüan, Wang Su, the noted literary forger (A.D. 195–256) and Chou-shêng Lieh, who is interesting to us from the fact that he was a native of Tun-huang, the scene of Sir Aurel Stein's and Professor Pelliot's epoch-making archaeological discoveries. A commentary falsely attributed to K'ung An-kuo (c. 130–90 B.C.) was also used. It seems likely that the editors did not originally indicate which explanations were extracted from which commentaries. Possessors of the book added the names as best they could, and there was subsequently a good deal of confusion as to which commentary any particular gloss really came from; for the commentaries themselves fell out of use and disappeared. It seemed, indeed, in the highest degree unlikely that any of them would be recovered. But as has already been mentioned, a considerable part of Chêng Hsüan's commentary was found at Tun-huang. Many of the glosses that the current *Lun Yü Chi Chieh* attributes to him occur *verbatim* in the Tun-huang fragments; but there are also many discrepancies.

The main object of the old interpreters[1] was to make

---

[1] What follows, refers in the main to the *Chi Chieh*; Huang K'an (died A.D. 545) is already considerably more expatiatory; his sub-commentary on the *Chi Chieh* was lost in China, but rediscovered

the text easily comprehensible to current readers. They do not use it as a peg either for pure philology or for moral edification. To this end they explain allusions to persons and events by reference to the annals and to the much-expanded legend of Confucius and his disciples, as it existed in their time. For the rest, they confine themselves to translating archaisms into the language of their own day, and to bringing allusions to rituals and usages into line with current ritual theories. Almost all the information they supply is such as anyone familiar with extant early literature could even to-day easily supply for himself. They are valuable in that they show the new interpretation to have had no ancient authority. But they seldom help anyone with a complete knowledge of early Chinese literature a step further towards understanding the real difficulties of the text.

The old interpretation, in all its essentials at any rate, held the field until the second half of the twelfth century. Hitherto the *Analects* had been a scripture among other scriptures, studied by those who were adept in ancient literature. But in the Sung dynasty it became a school-book, and finally not merely *a* school-book, but *the* school-book, basis of all education. This transformation was due almost entirely to the efforts of one very remarkable man, Chu Hsi (A.D. 1130–1200). Chu Hsi was occupied with the *Analects* during the greater part of his life. His labours were embodied in a series of books, culminating in the *Lun Yü Chi Chu* of 1177. But we possess very minute

in Japan in 1720 by Nemoto Hakushu, who published it at Yedo in 1750, with a preface by the well-known scholar Fukube Genkyo. It was reprinted in China in the nineteenth century. Fragments have also been recovered at Tun-huang, and these show that the current text is a contamination of the Huang K'an commentary with later commentaries.

records of his conversations,[1] and we see him down till his last years still wrestling with the problems that the *Chi Chu* had provisionally disposed of, meeting criticisms of that work and constantly modifying his published opinions.

Chu Hsi, like Confucius, was a 'transmitter rather than an originator.' His main object was to popularize the new approach to the Confucian Classics taught by the brothers Ch'êng.[2]

Neo-Confucianism, as we call the school to which the Ch'êng brothers belonged, had its origins in the ninth century.[3] If it seems to us to spring into the world unheralded upon the rise of the Sung, it is only because of the hiatus due to the disturbed state of China in the long period of anarchy between T'ang and Sung. The method of this school, as applied to the Classics, was a complete reinterpretation in terms of the syncretist philosophy (deeply influenced by Taoism and Zen Buddhism) which had gradually grown up since the ninth century.

Chu Hsi has been called a great scholar, but no one would call him so who had any experience of the difference between scholarship and theology. For though Chu Hsi was not a theologian in the literal sense of the term, though he is concerned with a Truth rather than with a God, his methods are at every point those of the theologian, not those of the scholar. It was not his aim to discover, as a scholar would have done, what the Classics meant when they were written. He assumed that there was one Truth, embodied equally in the teachings of the brothers Ch'êng and

[1] Those referring to the *Analects* are conveniently collected in chapters 10 to 19 of the *Chu Tzu Ch'üan Shu*.

[2] Ch'êng Hao (A.D. 1032–1085), Ch'êng I (1033–1107).

[3] The mental furniture of the average chün-tzu in the ninth century was derived impartially from Confucianism, Taoism and Buddhism.

in the sayings of Confucius. In the teachings of the brothers this Truth lay on the surface; in the *Analects* it lay hidden behind the words, and was not easily accessible even to those who had fully embraced it in its more exoteric manifestations. Chu Hsi's task was to make this hidden Truth, ensconced in the Classical books, accessible to everybody. To him every sentence vibrated with this Truth. The old interpreters allowed the reader to go his own way, only coming to his assistance occasionally where an archaism or allusion was likely to hold him up. Chu Hsi is always at our elbow, ready to save us from the 'obfuscation' of thinking that the text really means what it says. Again and again Confucius confesses to ignorance and imperfection. Chu Hsi is at hand to tell us that this is only ritual modesty; 'How could a Sage really err, how could a Sage truly not know?'; or to construe the sentence differently, so that 'You and I are not equal to him' (V, 8) becomes 'I grant you are not equal to him'; or to make a Sage figure as a Sage should, so that 'sent on a mission' becomes 'sent on a mission by Confucius' (VI, 3). He is there to save us from supposing that a Sage ever spoke the dialect of his native State (VII, 17); and all the time, by perpetual paraphrase and adaptation, he brings the recalcitrant text into line with Truth, so that in the end the *Analects* become as orthodox a Neo-Confucian treatise as any that proceeded from the class-room of the brothers Ch'êng. Chu Hsi was a great popular educator, a great evangelist; but in no sense was he a scholar.

The following discourse of Yu Tso (flourished *c.* A.D. 1100) on *Analects*, XII, 1, contained in his *Lun Yü Tsa Chieh*, is a good example of the mixed Taoist-Buddhist interpretation of the *Analects*, which prevailed in Sung times:

Goodness is the heart of man. All that the word

Goodness means is 'getting access to one's real heart.' In its true and original state the heart did not experience pleasure, anger, grief or delight. But once a man begins to pursue his own private ends, harassed by rage and desire, he ceases to be in any proper sense a man. If on the other hand, he can overcome the personal cravings of his human heart and return to the impersonal state that belongs to the heart of Tao, then he will regard others just as he regards himself, will regard things just as he regards men, and the true original state of this man's nature will be manifested. Henceforward he will be seen to treat his parents as parents should be treated, to show consideration to his inferiors and affection towards all creatures, all of which will follow spontaneously from workings of his real, unspoiled heart. That is what is meant by the saying 'Goodness is overcoming one's personal self and returning to *li*.'[1] For *li* simply means the natural state of the heart. It is a question of getting the heart back to its original state; that one thing and no more. It is not a question of recognizing a duty as a duty, and doing it; or of recognizing a creature as a creature, and loving it. Nor is it a matter of piling day on day or month on month before one can attain to the end desired. If a man can for a single day return to the original state, go back to the always-so,[2] then the ten thousand things will be for him all of like form and condition, and wherever he goes there will be Goodness. That is why the Master said, 'If for a single day a man can overcome his personal self and return to *li*, everything under Heaven for that man turns into Goodness.'

[1] Literally 'ritual'; but in the language of the Sung philosophers it had come to mean 'the natural.'

[2] The vocabulary belongs to Taoism; the conception, to the Sudden Illumination branch of Zen Buddhism.

Chu Hsi himself is, as a rule, careful to avoid interpretations too markedly Buddhist or Taoist in character. He does not, however, refrain from using expositions wholly bound up with Sung scholasticism and having no connexion whatever with doctrines which could possibly have existed in the time of Confucius. For example, on *Analects*, 1, 2, he reproduces a passage from Ch'êng Hao which insists that while Goodness is inborn, family piety is not; for it is well known that 'nature' consists 'solely of four constituents, Goodness, Conscience, Reverence and Knowledge.' All this is not merely alien to but directly contradicts the teaching of the *Analects*. Confucius would, for example, have been surprised indeed to learn that Goodness, the quality he so persistently refused to accord even to his most favoured disciples, was common to all men; and that inborn knowledge, which he himself expressly disclaimed,[1] was to be reckoned as an inevitable part of human equipment.

The methods of critical philology were first applied to the text by scholars such as Yüan Yüan (1764–1849), Wang Nien-sun (1744–1832),[2] Wang Yin-chih (1766–1834), Yü Yüeh (1821–1906). The only European writer who has used these native studies to any purpose is Chavannes, in dealing with the biography of Confucius in *Mémoires Historiques*, Vol. V. All existing translations of the *Analects* rely entirely on the 'scriptural' interpretation of Chu Hsi. It is the Chu Hsi interpretation which, except in small academic

[1] VII, 19.

[2] Valuable commentaries on passages in the *Analects* will be found scattered about his *Tu Shu Tsa Chih*, and in the *Ching I Shu Wen* of his son Wang Yin-chih. Much of the best work of the eighteenth and nineteenth century scholars is collected in the *Huang Ch'ing Ching Chieh* ('Classical Commentaries of the Ch'ing Dynasty') and its continuation *Huang Ch'ing Ching Chieh Hsü Pien*, referred to henceforward as H.C.C.C. and H.P.

circles, is still accepted unquestioningly everywhere in the Far East and which, in so far as Confucius has not been replaced by Sun Yat-sen, still forms the basis of moral education. Translations such as those of Legge, Soothill, Couvreur and Richard Wilhelm have therefore by no means lost their value; at the same time, there is room for a version such as mine, which attempts to tell the European reader not what the book means to the Far East of to-day, but what it meant to those who compiled it. I have used the work of the eighteenth century and nineteenth century native scholars, and appreciated it. But in many ways, especially as regards phonology, it is completely out of date; and my chief guide throughout has been a knowledge of the rest of early Chinese literature.

The references to *Chou Li* are to the *Chou Li Chêng I* of Sun I-jang. The transliteration used throughout is that of Wade, save for the omission of the short mark over *u* following *ss* and *tz*, and the occasional use of *Yi* for *I* where confusion with the English first person singular was likely. The substitution of an apostrophe for the 'rough breathing,' to mark aspirated consonants, is a concession to the preferences of the printer.

APPENDIX II

Biographical Dates

INTEREST tends to centre upon certain kinds of biographical data to the exclusion of others. Western scholars think it extremely important to discover exactly when people were born and exactly when they died. About various other kinds of biographical data we have no curiosity at all. Chinese legend finds it consequent to record the exact height of its heroes,[1] and the American writer, Ella Wheeler Wilcox, reflecting presumably a fairly general interest in the subject, records[2] that one of her characters 'did not weigh over 110 pounds at most.' A European biographer is not expected to give exact data about height or weight; but he is prepared to spend months in discovering whether his subject was born on the first or the second of July, and no one would consider that he was wasting his time.

The Chinese were not lacking in a sense of chronology. But they applied it exclusively to public events and persons connected with public events. It you take up an ordinary Chinese biographical dictionary, such as the fat green one published by the Commercial Press, you will find that exact dates are given only in in the case of persons who held high official positions and whose lives were intertwined with high affairs of State. Otherwise we are generally only told to what dynasty a person belonged, which is fairly vague, considering that dynasties often lasted for several hundred years. At the most, we are told during what period (and the Ch'ien Lung period, for example,

[1] See Granet, *La Pensée Chinoise*, pp. 202 seq.
[2] *The Worlds and I*, p. 273.

lasted sixty years) he passed his official examinations.

The Confucius of the *Analects* did not hold any high official rank. That his real dates should really have been handed down is against all probability. We do not, for example, know the dates of other great teachers, such as Mo Tzu, Chuang Tzu, Mencius. I do not personally doubt that the currently accepted dates (551–479 b.c.) and the slight variants upon them still current in the Han dynasty were supplied at a time when legend had turned Confucius into a great statesman, a person of public importance, the dates of whose birth and death were matters that concerned the State. What his family must in any case have known is the day of the year upon which his anniversary was kept. If it was known that he died on the twenty-sixth day of the sixty-day cycle, in the fourth month, it could be discovered which years had a day answering to this description, and of the possible years one could be fastened upon as the official date. M. Maspero has suggested that the actual date may quite likely have been a quarter of a century later than the accepted one.

THE ANALECTS

THE ANALECTS
(*Lun Yü*)

BOOK I

1.   The Master said, To learn and at due times to repeat what one has learnt, is that not after all[1] a pleasure? That friends should come to one from afar,[2] is this not after all delightful? To remain unsoured even though one's merits are unrecognized by others, is that not after all what is expected of a gentleman?

2.   Master Yu[3] said, Those who in private life behave well towards their parents and elder brothers, in public life seldom show a disposition to resist the authority of their superiors. And as for such men starting a revolution, no instance of it has ever occurred. It is upon the trunk[4] that a gentleman works. When that is firmly set up, the Way grows. And surely proper behaviour towards parents and elder brothers is the trunk of Goodness?

[1] See textual notes. The 'after all' implies 'even though one does not hold office.'

[2] Several of the disciples belonged to other States (e.g. Wei and Ch'i); but there is no evidence that they came to Lu on account of Confucius. Unless, however, there is here some allusion that escapes us, the phrase must refer to the visits of admirers from abroad, perhaps friends made during the Master's journeys in Honan.

[3] See p. 20.

[4] i.e. upon what is fundamental, as opposed to 'the twigs,' i.e. small arts and accomplishments, which the gentleman leaves to his inferiors.

3. The Master said, 'Clever talk and a pretentious manner'[1] are seldom found in the Good.

4. Master Tsêng[2] said, Every day I examine myself on these three points: in acting on behalf of others, have I always been loyal to their interests? In intercourse with my friends, have I always been true to my word? Have I failed to repeat[3] the precepts that have been handed down to me?

5. The Master said, A country of a thousand war-chariots cannot be administered unless the ruler attends strictly to business, punctually observes his promises, is economical in expenditure, shows affection towards his subjects in general, and uses the labour of the peasantry only at the proper times of year.[4]

6. The Master said, A young man's duty is to behave well to his parents at home and to his elders abroad, to be cautious in giving promises and punctual in keeping them, to have kindly feelings towards everyone, but seek the intimacy of the Good. If, when all that is done, he has any energy to spare, then let him study the polite arts.[5]

7. Tzu-hsia said, A man who

> Treats his betters as betters,
> Wears an air of respect,
> Who into serving father and mother
> Knows how to put his whole strength,

[1] Traditional phrase. Cf. *Shu Ching*, Kao Yao Mo.
[2] See p. 20.　　　　　　　　　　　[3] And so keep in memory.
[4] i.e. not when they ought to be working in the fields. Bad rulers, on the contrary, listen to music or go hunting when they ought to be attending to business, continually employ labour on ostentatious building-schemes, etc.
[5] i.e. learn to recite the *Songs*, practise archery, deportment, and the like.

Who in the service of his prince will lay
down his life,
Who in intercourse with friends is true
to his word——

others may say of him that he still lacks education,[1]
but I for my part should certainly call him an edu-
cated man.

8. The Master said, If a gentleman is frivolous,[2]
he will lose the respect of his inferiors and lack firm
ground[3] upon which to build up his education. First
and foremost he must learn to be faithful to his
superiors, to keep promises, to refuse the friendship
of all who are not like him.[4] And if he finds he has
made a mistake, then he must not be afraid of admitting
the fact and amending his ways.

9. Master Tsêng said, When proper respect towards
the dead is shown at the End and continued after they
are far away the moral force (*tê*)[5] of a people has reached
its highest point.

10. Tzu-Ch'in[6] said to Tzu-kung,[7] When our
Master arrives in a fresh country he always manages
to find out about its policy.[8] Does he do this by asking

[1] i.e. knowledge of ritual, precedents, the correct use on social
occasions of verses from the *Songs*, etc.
[2] i.e. irresponsible and unreliable in his dealings with others.
[3] The sentence runs awkwardly and is probably corrupt.
[4] i.e. of those who still reckon in terms of 'profit and loss,' and have
not taken *jên* (Goodness) as their standard.
[5] Cf. Introduction, p. 33.
[6] Disciple of Confucius. See XVI, 13 and XIX, 25.
[7] See Introduction, p. 20.
[8] Not, of course, about the details of administration, but about the
secret, general maxims which inspire the ruler.

questions, or do people tell him of their own accord?
Tzu-kung said, Our Master gets things by being
cordial, frank, courteous, temperate, deferential. That
is our Master's way of enquiring—a very different
matter,¹ certainly, from the way in which enquiries
are generally made.

11.   The Master said, While a man's father is alive,
you can only see his intentions; it is when his father
dies that you discover whether or not he is capable of
carrying them out. If for the whole three years of
mourning he manages to carry on the household
exactly as in his father's day, then he is a good son
indeed.²

12.   Master Yu said, In the usages of ritual it is
harmony³ that is prized; the Way of the Former Kings
from this⁴ got its beauty. Both small matters and great
depend upon it. If things go amiss, he who knows the
harmony⁵ will be able to attune them. But if harmony
itself is not modulated by ritual, things will still go
amiss.⁶

13.   Master Yu said,
        In your promises cleave to what is right,
        And you will be able to fulfil your word.
        In your obeisances cleave to ritual,
        And you will keep dishonour at bay.

---

¹ The double particle *ch'i-chu*, peculiar to the *Analects* and *Kung-
yang Chuan*, does not seem to differ in meaning from the ordinary
modal *ch'i*.   ² See Introduction, p. 38.
³ Harmony between man and nature; playing the musical mode
that harmonizes with the season, wearing seasonable clothes, eating
seasonable food, and the like.   ⁴ i.e. from harmony.
⁵ i.e. the act that harmonizes with the moment.
⁶ See Introduction, p 66.

Marry one who has not betrayed her own kin,
And you may safely present her to your
Ancestors.[1]

14. The Master said, A gentleman who never goes
on eating till he is sated, who does not demand comfort
in his home, who is diligent in business and cautious
in speech, who associates with those that possess the
Way and thereby corrects his own faults—such a one
may indeed be said to have a taste for learning.

15. Tzu-kung said, 'Poor without cadging, rich
without swagger.' What of that?[2] The Master said,
Not bad. But better still, 'Poor, yet delighting in the
Way;[3] rich, yet a student of ritual.' Tzu-kung said,
The saying of the *Songs*,[4]

As thing cut, as thing filed,
As thing chiselled, as thing polished

refers, I suppose, to what you have just said? The
Master said, Ssu, now I can really begin to talk to
you about the *Songs*, for when I allude to sayings of
the past, you see what bearing they have on what was
to come after.

16. The Master said, (the good man) does not
grieve that other people do not recognize his merits.
His only anxiety is lest he should fail to recognize
theirs.

[1] Lines 2, 4, and 6 rhyme. For the last rhyme, which belongs to
a well-established type, see Karlgren, *The Rimes in the Sung section
of the Shi King*. For the presentation of the bride to the husband's
ancestors, see *The Book of Songs*, p. 90.

[2] i.e. what of it as a motto?   [3] See textual notes.

[4] *The Book of Songs* p. 46, which describes the elegance of a lover.
Tzu-kung interprets it as describing the pains the gentleman has taken
to improve his character, and suggests that Confucius prefers the second
maxim ('Poor, yet delighting . . .') because it implies a greater effort
of self-improvement.

BOOK II

1.   The Master said, He who rules by moral force (*tê*) is like the pole-star, which remains in its place while all the lesser stars do homage to it.

2.   The Master said, If out of the three hundred *Songs* I had to take one phrase to cover all my teaching, I would say 'Let there be no evil in your thoughts.'[1]

3.   The Master said, Govern the people by regulations, keep order among them by chastisements, and they will flee from you, and lose all self-respect. Govern them by moral force, keep order among them by ritual[2] and they will keep their self-respect and come to you of their own accord.[3]

4.   The Master said, At fifteen I set my heart upon learning. At thirty, I had planted my feet firm upon the ground. At forty, I no longer suffered from perplexities. At fifty, I knew what were the biddings of Heaven. At sixty, I heard them with docile ear. At seventy, I could follow the dictates of my own heart; for what I desired no longer overstepped the boundaries of right.

5.   Mêng I Tzu[4] asked about the treatment of parents. The Master said, Never disobey! When Fan

---

[1] *The Book of Songs*, p. 275, l. 7, where however *ssu* does not mean 'thoughts,' but is an exclamation, 'oh,' 'ah,' or the like; but in applying ancient texts it is the words themselves that matter, not the context; and these words can be reapplied in any sense which they are conceivably capable of bearing.

[2] See Introduction, p. 66.   [3] See textual notes.

[4] A young grandee of Lu, whose father sent him to study with Confucius. He died in 481 B.C.

Ch'ih[1] was driving his carriage for him, the Master said, Mêng asked me about the treatment of parents and I said, Never disobey! Fan Ch'ih said, In what sense did you mean it? The Master said, While they are alive, serve them according to ritual. When they die, bury them according to ritual and sacrifice to them according to ritual.[2]

6. Mêng Wu Po[3] asked about the treatment of parents. The Master said, Behave in such a way that your father and mother have no anxiety about you, except concerning your health.

7. Tzu-yu[4] asked about the treatment of parents. The Master said, 'Filial sons' nowadays are people who see to it that their parents get enough to eat. But even dogs and horses are cared for to that extent. If there is no feeling of respect, wherein lies the difference?

8. Tzu-hsia[5] asked about the treatment of parents. The Master said, It is the demeanour[6] that is difficult. Filial piety does not consist merely in young people undertaking the hard work, when anything has to be done, or serving their elders first with wine and food. It is something much more than that.

---

[1] A disciple.

[2] Evidently by 'disobey' Confucius meant 'disobey the rituals.' The reply was intended to puzzle the enquirer and make him think. In *Mencius*, III, 1, II, 2, 'While they are alive . . .', etc., is given as a saying of Master Tsêng. Here and elsewhere 'sacrifice' means offerings in general and not only animal-sacrifice.

[3] Son of Mêng I Tzu.   [4] A disciple; see Introduction, p. 20.

[5] See Introduction, p. 20.

[6] This is Chêng Hsüan's interpretation. Pao Hsien (6 B.C.–65 A.D.) takes *sê* to mean the expression of one's parents, which must be watched for hints of approval or disapproval.

9.　　The Master said, I can talk to Yen Hui[1] a whole day without his ever differing from me. One would think he was stupid. But if I enquire into his private conduct when he is not with me I find that it fully demonstrates what I have taught him. No, Hui is by no means stupid.

10.　　The Master said, Look closely into his aims, observe the means by which he pursues them, discover what brings him content—and can the man's real worth[2] remain hidden from you, can it remain hidden from you?

11.　　The Master said, He who by reanimating[3] the Old can gain knowledge of the New is fit to be a teacher.

12.　　The Master said, A gentleman is not an implement.[4]

13.　　Tzu-kung asked about the true gentleman. The

---

　[1] The favourite disciple. His early death is several times referred to in this book. It would be possible to put this passage in the past and suppose it to have been spoken after Yen Hui's death; but I see no reason to do so.

　[2] i.e. whether he is fit to be entrusted with office. There is no need to have seen him actually handling practical issues. Cf. *Mencius*, IV, I, XV.

　[3] Literally, 'warming up.' The business of the teacher is to give fresh life to the Scriptures by reinterpreting them so that they apply to the problems of modern life. All scriptures (Homer, the *Koran*, our own Bible) have been used in this way. I have seen 'The poor ye have always with you' used as an argument against slum-clearance. We have read above how Tzu-kung showed himself to be a true teacher by 'reanimating' a passage from the *Songs*.

　[4] i.e. a specialist, a tool used for a special purpose. He need only have general, moral qualifications.

Master said, He does not preach what he practises till he has practised what he preaches.

14. The Master said, A gentleman can see a question from all sides without bias. The small man¹ is biased and can see a question only from one side.

15. The Master said, 'He who learns but does not think,² is lost.' He who thinks but does not learn is in great danger.³

16. The Master said, He who sets to work upon a different strand destroys the whole fabric.⁴

17. The Master said, Yu,⁵ shall I teach you what knowledge is? When you know a thing, to recognize that you know it, and when you do not know a thing, to recognize that you do not know it. That is knowledge.⁶

18. Tzu-chang was studying the *Song* Han-lu.⁷ The

¹ Cf. Introduction, p. 35 . For the maxim, Cf. *Kuo Yü*, 8.
² For 'thinking,' see Introduction, p. 44.
³ I imagine that the first clause is a proverbial saying, and that Confucius meets it with the second clause. The proverb says: 'To learn without thinking is fatal.' Confucius says: To think but not to learn (i.e. study the Way of the ancients) is equally dangerous.
⁴ The metaphor is one of weaving or netting. 'Strand' (*tuan*) is a sprout, something that sticks out, and so 'the loose end of a thread.' The moral Way as opposed to the opportunist Way of the World must be followed consistently. It is no use working at it in disconnected patches.
⁵ Familiar name of the disciple Tzu-lu, see Introduction, p. 20.
⁶ That knowledge consists in knowing that one does not know is a frequent theme in early Chinese texts. Cf. *Tao Tê Ching*, ch. LXXI.
⁷ *The Book of Songs*, p. 213. It puns on Han-lu, the name of a mountain, and *han-lu* 'seeking princely rewards, preferment.'

Master said, Hear much, but maintain silence¹ as regards doubtful points and be cautious in speaking of the rest; then you will seldom get into trouble. See much, but ignore what it is dangerous to have seen, and be cautious in acting upon the rest; then you will seldom want to undo your acts. He who seldom gets into trouble about what he has said and seldom does anything that he afterwards wishes he had not done, will be sure incidentally² to get his reward.

19. Duke Ai³ asked, What can I do in order to get the support of the common people? Master K'ung⁴ replied, If you 'raise up the straight and set them on top of the crooked,' the commoners will support you. But if you raise the crooked and set them on top of the straight, the commoners will not support you.

20. Chi K'ang-tzu⁵ asked whether there were any form of encouragement by which he could induce the common people to be respectful and loyal. The Master said, Approach them with dignity, and they will respect you. Show piety towards your parents and kindness towards your children, and they will be loyal to you. Promote those who are worthy, train those who are incompetent; that is the best form of encouragement.

21. Someone, when talking to Master K'ung, said, How is it that you are not in the public service? The

¹ Literally, 'leave a gap,' a metaphor derived from the language of copyists and scribes. Cf. XV, 25.
² See additional notes. From 'Hear much' to 'acts' is in rhyme, but would be awkward to print as verse.
3 Duke of Lu from 494–468.   4 i.e. Confucius.
5 Head of the three families who were *de facto* rulers of Lu. Died 469 B.C.

Master said, The Book[1] says: 'Be filial, only be filial and friendly towards your brothers, and you will be contributing to government.' There are other sorts of service quite different from what you[2] mean by 'service.'

22. The Master said, I do not see what use a man can be put to, whose word cannot be trusted. How can a waggon be made to go if it has no yoke-bar or a carriage, if it has no collar-bar?

23. Tzu-chang[3] asked whether the state of things[4] ten generations hence could be foretold. The Master said, We know in what ways the Yin modified ritual when they followed upon the Hsia.[5] We know in what ways the Chou[6] modified ritual when they followed upon the Yin.[7] And hence we can foretell what the successors of Chou will be like, even supposing they do not appear till a hundred generations from now.

24. The Master said, Just as to sacrifice to ancestors other than one's own is presumption, so to see what is right and not do it is cowardice.

---

[1] i.e. what Europeans call the *Book of History*. The passage does not occur in the genuine books (see Introduction, p. 53). What it meant in its original context no doubt was 'Be pious to your ancestors . . . be generous in rewarding your officers of State.' Confucius 'reanimates' the ancient text, in order to prove that a virtuous private life makes a real contribution towards the public welfare.

[2] *Ch'i* corresponds to the Latin *iste*.

[3] See Introduction, p. 20.   [4] As regards ritual.

[5] Supposed to have ruled in the 3rd and 2nd millennia B.C.

[6] The dynasty which still had a nominal hegemony in the time of Confucius.

[7] The fall of Yin took place in the eleventh century B.C. It was on the site of one of their capitals that the famous 'Honan oracle-bones' were found.

BOOK III

1. Master K'ung said of the head of the Chi family[1] when he had eight teams[2] of dancers performing in his courtyard, If this man can be endured, who cannot be endured!

2. The Three Families used the *Yung Song*[3] during the removal of the sacrificial vessels. The Master said,

> *By rulers and lords attended,*
> *The Son of Heaven, mysterious——*

What possible application can such words have in the hall of the Three Families?

3. The Master said, A man who is not Good, what can he have to do with ritual? A man who is not Good, what can he have to do with music?

4. Lin Fang asked for some main principles in connexion with ritual. The Master said, A very big question. In ritual at large it is a safe rule always to be too sparing rather than too lavish; and in the particular case of mourning-rites, they should be dictated by grief rather than by fear.[4]

5. The Master said, The barbarians of the East

---

[1] One of the Three Families that had usurped most of the powers of the Duke of Lu.   [2] See additional notes.
[3] 'He comes in solemn state . . .' *The Book of Songs*, p. 231. Its use was obviously only appropriate at the Emperor's Court. It would have been out of place at the Duke's palace, and was still more so in the hall of the Three Families.   [4] See textual notes.

and North have retained their princes. They are not
in such a state of decay as we in China.[1]

6.   The head of the Chi family was going to make the
offerings on Mount T'ai.[2] The Master said to Jan Ch'iu,[3]
Cannot you save him from this? Jan Ch'iu replied, I
cannot. The Master said, Alas, we can hardly suppose
Mount T'ai to be ignorant of matters that even Lin
Fang enquires into![4]

7.   The Master said, Gentlemen never compete. You
will say that in archery they do so. But even then they
bow and make way for one another when they are
going up to the archery-ground, when they are coming
down and at the subsequent drinking-bout. Thus even
when competing, they still remain gentlemen.

8.   Tzu-hsia asked, saying, What is the meaning of

> *Oh the sweet smile dimpling,*
> *The lovely eyes so black and white!*
> *Plain silk that you would take for coloured stuff.*[5]

The Master said, The painting comes after the plain
groundwork.[6] Tzu-hsia said, Then ritual comes after-

---

[1] Where in several States the ruling families had been ousted by
usurpers.
[2] To the spirit of the mountain, a thing which the Duke alone had
the right to do. The offering is said to have consisted of jade objects.
[3] Who was in the service of the Chi family.
[4] The mountain must surely know enough of ritual to be aware
that no sacrifice but the Duke's could be accepted.

[5] So dazzling is the contrast that the effect is that of painted stuff
rather than of a design in black and white. The first two lines occur
in *Song* 86, where however they are not followed by the third line.
[6] Confucius reinterprets the third line of verse in the sense 'It is
on plain silk that one makes coloured designs,' or the like. In scriptural
reinterpretation the fact that the new meaning does not fit in with the
original context is of no consequence.

wards?[1] The Master said, Shang[2] it is who bears me up. At last I have someone with whom I can discuss the Songs!

9.   The Master said, How can we talk about the ritual of the Hsia? The State of Ch'i[3] supplies no adequate evidence. How can we talk about the ritual of Yin? The State of Sung supplies no adequate evidence. For there is a lack both of documents and of learned men. But for this lack we should be able to obtain evidence from these two States.

10.   The Master said, At the Ancestral Sacrifice, as for all that comes after the libation, I had far rather not witness it![4]

11.   Someone asked for an explanation of the Ancestral Sacrifice. The Master said, I do not know. Anyone who knew the explanation could deal with all things under Heaven as easily as I lay[5] this here; and he laid his finger upon the palm of his hand.[6]

[1] Can only be built upon Goodness.

[2] Familiar names of Tzu-hsia. For a further discussion of this passage, see additional notes.

[3] In Honan, where descendants of the Hsia still carried on the sacrifices. Confucius laments that these States had not preserved the documents and rites of their ancestors. The interrogative particles seem to have been accidentally omitted.

[4] In interpreting such passages as this we have to be careful not to read them in the light of later and to a large extent Utopian, theoretical books of ritual. Confucius was obviously displeased by the way in which the *Ti* (Ancestor-sacrifice) was carried out in Lu; presumably because it was too closely modelled on Imperial ritual; more than that we cannot say. See above p. 65.

[5] See textual notes.

[6] For the magical effect of ritual in controlling men and things, see Introduction, p. 64. For the anecdote, cf. *Chung Yung*, XIX, 6, and *K'ung Tzu Chia Yü*, 27. (Lun Li).

12. Of the saying, 'The word "sacrifice" is like[1] the word "present"; one should sacrifice to a spirit as though[2] that spirit was present,' the Master said, If I am not present at the sacrifice, it is as though there were no sacrifice.[3]

13. Wang-sun Chia[4] asked about the meaning of the saying,

> Better pay court to the stove
> Than pay court to the Shrine.[5]

The Master said, It is not true. He who has put himself in the wrong with Heaven has no means of expiation left.

14. The Master said, Chou could survey the two preceding dynasties. How great a wealth of culture! And we follow upon Chou.[6]

15. When the Master entered the Grand Temple[7]

---

[1] See textual notes.

[2] i.e. with the same demeanour and expression. Cf. *Li Chi*, XIII, end, 'In general, in sacrifice demeanour and expression should be as though one were in the presence of the person who is being sacrificed to.'

[3] i.e. do not worry about 'spirits being present' and the like. What matters is the state of mind of the sacrificer. If he is not heart and soul 'there,' the sacrifice is useless. On the purely subjective value of sacrifice, see *Hsün Tzu*, P'ien XIX, end.

[4] Commander-in-chief in the State of Wei, mentioned under the year 502 B.C. in the *Tso Chuan*.

[5] This rhymed saying means that it is better to be on good terms with the hearth-god and have a full belly than waste one's food on the Ancestors, who cannot enjoy it. Confucius, who is usually able to reinterpret old maxims in a new, moral sense, finds himself obliged to reject this cynical piece of peasant-lore *in toto*.

[6] i.e. we in Lu have all three dynasties, Hsia, Yin, and Chou to look back upon and imitate.

[7] Erected in honour of the first Duke of Chou.

he asked questions about everything there. Someone said, Do not tell me that this son of a villager from Tsou[1] is expert in matters of ritual. When he went to the Grand Temple, he had to ask about everything. The Master hearing of this said, Just so! such is the ritual.[2]

16.   The Master said, the saying

In archery it is not the hide that counts,
For some men have more strength than others,

is the way of the Ancients.[3]

17.   Tzu-kung wanted to do away with the presentation[4] of a sacrificial sheep at the announcement[5] of each new moon. The Master said, Ssu! You grudge sheep, but I grudge ritual.

18.   The Master said, Were anyone to-day to serve his prince according to the full prescriptions of ritual, he would be thought a sycophant.

19.   Duke Ting (died 495 B.C.) asked for a precept concerning a ruler's use of his ministers and a minister's

---

[1] A village with which Confucius's family had been connected.

[2] i.e. precisely by doing so I showed my knowledge of ritual; for the asking of such questions is prescribed by ritual. For questions of this sort, see additional notes.

[3] i.e. it is not piercing the hide stretched as a target that counts. In this ancient rhymed saying Confusius saw a maxim which metaphorically resumed the whole way of the Ancient Sages, who ruled by Goodness, not by force. For the first of the two lines, cf. *I Li*, Couvreur's translation, p. 173. Cf. also *Chou Li,* where *chu p'i* seems merely to mean 'hitting the target.' See additional notes.

[4] By the Duke to his State officers. This is the explanation of Liu T'ai-kung (1751–1805). See H.C.C.C. 798.

[5] To the Ancestors, who are kept informed of everything that goes on below.

service to his ruler. Master K'ung replied saying, A ruler in employing his ministers should be guided solely by the prescriptions of ritual. Ministers in serving their ruler, solely by devotion to his cause.

20. The Master said, The Ospreys![1] Pleasure not carried to the point of debauch; grief not carried to the point of self-injury.

21. Duke Ai asked Tsai Yü[2] about the Holy Ground. Tsai Yü replied, The Hsia sovereigns marked theirs with a pine, the men of Yin used a cypress, the men of Chou used a chestnut-tree, saying, 'This will cause the common people to be in fear and trembling.'[3] The Master hearing of it said, What is over and done with, one does not discuss. What has already taken its course, one does not criticize; what already belongs to the past, one does not censure.[4]

22. The Master said, Kuan Chung[5] was in reality a man of very narrow capacities. Someone said, Surely

---

[1] *The Book of Songs*, No. 87, which begins by describing a lover's grief at being separated from his lady and ends by describing their joyful union. Confucius sees in it a general guide to conduct, whether in joy or affliction. The opening words are : '*Kuan, kuan* cry the ospreys.'

[2] A disciple in whom Confucius was much disappointed.

[3] Pun on *li* a chestnut-tree and *li* 'to be in awe.'

[4] The usual explanation of this passage makes Confucius's comment refer to Tsai Yü's pun 'which might lead the Duke to severe measures' in dealing with his people (Legge, p. 26). The comment, however, is phrased in such a way that it must be taken as referring to the remote and not to the immediate past. It is perhaps unfortunate, Confucius suggests, that the founders of the Chou dynasty chose a tree with so inauspicious a name; but it was ill-bred of Tsai Yü to criticize them in conversation with Duke Ai of Lu, who was their direct descendant.

[5] Kuan Tzu, seventh century B.C., the statesman who built up the power of the Ch'i kingdom. Confucius regarded him as having merely increased the political prestige of his country without raising its moral status. See Introduction, p. 50.

he displayed an example of frugality? The Master said, Kuan had three lots of wives,[1] his State officers performed no double duties. How can he be cited as an example of frugality? That may be, the other said; but surely he had a great knowledge of ritual? The Master said, Only the ruler of a State may build a screen to mask his gate; but Kuan had such a screen. Only the ruler of a State, when meeting another such ruler, may use cup-mounds;[2] but Kuan used one. If even Kuan is to be cited as an expert in ritual, who is not an expert in ritual?

23. When talking to the Grand Master[3] of Lu about music, the Master said, Their music[4] in so far as one can find out about it began with a strict unison. Soon the musicians were given more liberty;[5] but the tone remained harmonious, brilliant, consistent, right on till the close.

24. The guardian of the frontier-mound at I[6] asked to be presented to the Master, saying, No gentleman arriving at this frontier has ever yet failed to accord me an interview. The Master's followers presented him. On going out the man said, Sirs, you must not be disheartened by his failure. It is now a very long while[7] since the Way prevailed in the world. I feel sure that Heaven intends to use your Master as a wooden bell.[8]

[1] Each consisting of a wife and two 'understudies' (bridesmaids); only a feudal lord was entitled to such an establishment.
[2] A mound upon which to stand pledge-cups; see textual notes.
[3] The *maestro*, music-master, who was always a blind man.
[4] The music of the ancients.   [5] To improvise.
[6] On the borders of the State of Wei.
[7] Sages appear at regular intervals. One is now due.
[8] A rattle, used to arouse the populace in times of night-danger, and in general by heralds and town-criers; cf. *Li Chi*, Yüeh-ling. (Couvreur's translation, I, 343).

25. The Master spoke of the Succession Dance[1] as being[2] perfect beauty and at the same time perfect goodness; but of the War Dance as being perfect beauty, but not perfect goodness.

26. The Master said, High office filled by men of narrow views, ritual performed without reverence, the forms of mourning observed without grief—these are things I cannot bear to see!

[1] This dance (at any rate according to the later Confucian theory) mimed the peaceful accession of the legendary Emperor Shun; the War Dance mimed the accession by conquest of the Emperor Wu, who overthrew the Yin. See above, p. 93.

[2] Or as we should say, 'as embodying.'

BOOK IV

1.   The Master said, It is Goodness that gives to a neighbourhood its beauty.[1] One who is free to choose, yet does not prefer to dwell among the Good—how can he be accorded the name of wise?[2]

2.   The Master said, Without Goodness a man

> Cannot for long endure adversity,
> Cannot for long enjoy prosperity.

The Good Man rests content with Goodness; he that is merely wise pursues Goodness in the belief that it pays to do so.

3, 4.   Of the adage[3] 'Only a Good Man knows how to like people, knows how to dislike them,' the Master said, He whose heart is in the smallest degree set upon Goodness will dislike no one.

5.   Wealth and rank are what every man desires; but if they can only be retained to the detriment of the Way he professes, he must relinquish them. Poverty and obscurity are what every man detests; but if they can only be avoided to the detriment of the Way he

---

[1] Cf. *Mencius*, II, i, VII, 2.

[2] A justification of the maxim, 'When right does not prevail in a kingdom, then leave it,' and of Confucius's own prolonged travels.

[3] Cf. *Ta Hsüeh* ('The Great Learning'), commentary, X, 15. 'Only the Good man is considered capable of loving (*ai*) men, capable of hating them.' In the *Kuo Yü* (ch. 18), however, the saying is quite differently interpreted: 'Only a good man is safe to like and safe to dislike. . . . For if you like him, he will not take undue advantage of it; and if you dislike him, he will not resent it.' The words 'The Master said' at the beginning of paragraph 3 should be omitted, and paragraphs 3 and 4 taken together.

professes, he must accept them. The gentleman who ever parts company with Goodness does not fulfil that name. Never for a moment[1] does a gentleman quit the way of Goodness. He is never so harried but that he cleaves to this; never so tottering but that he cleaves to this.

6.   The Master said, I for my part[2] have never yet seen one who really cared for Goodness, nor one who really abhorred wickedness. One who really cared for Goodness would never let any other consideration come first. One who abhorred wickedness would be so constantly doing Good that wickedness would never have a chance to get at him. Has anyone ever managed to do Good with his whole might even as long as the space of a single day? I think not. Yet I for my part have never seen anyone give up such an attempt because he had not the *strength* to go on. It may well have happened, but I for my part have never seen it.[3]

7.   The Master said, Every man's faults belong to a set.[4] If one looks out for faults it is only as a means of recognizing Goodness.

8.   The Master said, In the morning, hear the Way; in the evening, die content![5].

9.   The Master said, A Knight whose heart is set upon the Way, but who is ashamed of wearing shabby

---

[1] Literally, 'for as long as it takes to eat' one bowl of rice. A common impression, simply meaning a very little while.

[2] *Wo* as a nominative is more emphatic than *wu.*

[3] It is the will not the way that is wanting.

[4] i.e. a set of qualities which includes virtues.

[5] The well-known saying *Vedi Napoli e poi mori* follows the same pattern. The meaning is, you will have missed nothing.

clothes and eating coarse food, is not worth calling into counsel.

10.   The Master said, A gentleman in his dealings with the world has neither enmities nor affections;[1] but wherever he sees Right he ranges himself beside it.

11.   The Master said, Where gentlemen set their hearts upon moral force (*tê*),[2] the commoners set theirs upon the soil.[3] Where gentlemen think only of punishments, the commoners think only of exemptions.[4]

12.   The Master said, Those[5] whose measures are dictated by mere expediency will arouse continual discontent.

13.   The Master said, If it is really possible to govern countries by ritual and yielding, there is no more[6] to be said. But if it is not really possible, of what use is ritual?[7]

14.   The Master said, He[8] does not mind not being

---

[1] Reading uncertain, but general sense quite clear. See textual notes.
[2] As opposed to physical compulsion. See additional notes.
[3] They *an t'u,* 'are content with the soil,' and prepared to defend it.
[4] *Hui* means amnesties, immunities, exemptions, as opposed to what is 'lawful and proper.'
[5] The rulers and upper classes in general.   [6] See textual notes.
[7] The saying can be paraphrased as follows: If I and my followers are right in saying that countries can be governed solely by correct carrying out of ritual and its basic principle of 'giving way to others,' there is obviously no case to be made out for any other form of government. If on the other hand we are wrong, then ritual is useless. To say, as people often do, that ritual is all very well so long as it is not used as an instrument of government, is wholly to misunderstand the purpose of ritual.
[8] The gentleman. But we might translate 'I do not mind,' etc.

in office; all he minds about is whether he has qualities that entitle him to office. He does not mind failing to get recognition; he is too busy doing the things that entitle him to recognition.

15.   The Master said, Shên! My Way has one (thread) that runs right through it. Master Tsêng said, Yes. When the Master had gone out, the disciples asked, saying What did he mean? Master Tsêng said, Our Master's Way is simply this: Loyalty, consideration.[1]

16.   The Master said, A gentleman takes as much trouble to discover what is right as lesser men take to discover what will pay.

17.   The Master said, In the presence of a good man, think all the time how you may learn to equal him. In the presence of a bad man, turn your gaze within![2]

18.   The Master said, In serving his father and mother a man may gently remonstrate with them. But if he sees that he has failed to change their opinion, he should resume an attitude of deference and not thwart them; may feel discouraged,[3] but not resentful.

19.   The Master said, While father and mother are

---

[1] Loyalty to superiors; consideration for the feelings of others, 'not doing to them anything one would not like to have done to oneself,' as defined below, XV, 23. 'Loyalty and Consideration' is one of the Nine Virtues enumerated by the *I Chou Shu*, 29, I verso. Cf. also XV, 2 below.

[2] 'Within yourself scrutinize yourself.' *êrh* is the second person singular pronoun, not the conjunction?   [3] See textual notes.

alive, a good son does not wander far afield; or if he does so, goes only where he has said he was going.[1]

20. The Master said, If for the whole three years of mourning a son manages to carry on the household exactly as in his father's day, then he is a good son indeed.[2]

21. The Master said, It is always better for a man to know the age of his parents. In the one case[3] such knowledge will be a comfort to him; in the other,[4] it will fill him with a salutary dread.

22. The Master said, In old days a man kept a hold on his words, fearing the disgrace that would ensue should he himself fail to keep pace with them.

23. The Master said, Those who err on the side of strictness are few indeed!

24. The Master said, A gentleman covets the reputation of being slow in word but prompt in deed.[5]

25. The Master said, Moral force (*tê*) never dwells in solitude; it will always bring neighbours.[6]

26. Tzu-yu said, In the service of one's prince repeated scolding[7] can only lead to loss of favour; in friendship, it can only lead to estrangement.

[1] Particularly in order that if they die he may be able to come back and perform the rites of mourning.
[2] Cf. I, 11.
[3] If he knows that they are not so old as one might think.
[4] If he realizes that they are very old.
[5] Cf. *The Way and Its Power*, p. 198.
[6] Whenever one individual or one country substitutes *tê* for physical compulsion, other individuals or other countries inevitably follow suit.
[7] Cf. XII, 23 and additional notes.

BOOK V

1.   The Master said of Kung Yeh Ch'ang, Though he has suffered imprisonment, he is not an unfit person to choose as a husband; for it was not through any fault of his own. He married him to his daughter.

The Master said of Nan Jung,[1] In a country ruled according to the Way, he would not be overlooked; in a country not ruled according to the Way, he would manage to avoid capital punishment or mutilation. He married him to his elder brother's[2] daughter.

2.   Of Tzu-chien[3] he said, A gentleman indeed is such a one as he! If the land of Lu were indeed without gentlemen, how could he have learnt this?

3.   Tzu-kung asked saying, What do you think of me? The Master said, You are a vessel.[4] Tzu-kung said, What sort of vessel? The Master said, A sacrificial vase of jade![5]

4.   Someone said, Jan Yung is Good, but he is a poor talker. The Master said, What need has he to be a good talker? Those who down others with clap-trap are seldom popular. Whether he is Good, I do not know. But I see no need for him to be a good talker.

[1] The commentators identify Nan Jung with Nan-kung Kuo, son of Mêng I Tzu, head of the powerful Mêng Family. This is, however, no ground for this identification, nor any reason to suppose that Confucius ever formed so exalted a family connection.

[2] According to later tradition Confucius's elder brother was a cripple and for this reason his duties devolved on Confucius.

[3] The disciple Fu Tzu-chien, who figures in later legend as model governor of the town of Shan-fu. See additional notes.

[4] A man of particular capacities, but lacking the general state of electness known as *Jên* (Goodness).

[5] i.e. the highest sort of vessel.

5.   The Master gave Ch'i-tiao K'ai leave to take office, but he replied, 'I have not yet sufficiently perfected myself in the virtue of good faith.' The Master was delighted.

6.   The Master said, The Way makes no progress. I shall get upon a raft and float out to sea.¹ I am sure Yu would come with me. Tzu-lu on hearing of this was in high spirits. The Master said, That is Yu indeed! He sets far too much store by feats of physical daring. It seems as though I should never get hold of the right sort of people.²

7.   Mêng Wu Po³ asked whether Tzu-lu was Good. The Master said, I do not know. On his repeating the question the Master said, In a country of a thousand war-chariots Yu could be trusted to carry out the recruiting. But whether he is Good I do not know. 'What about Ch'iu?'⁴ The Master said, In a city of a thousand families or a baronial family with a hundred chariots he might do well as Warden. But whether he is Good, I do not know. 'What about Ch'ih?'⁵ The Master said, Girt with his sash, standing in his place at Court he might well be charged to converse with

---

    ¹ What Confucius proposes is, of course, to go and settle among the barbarians. Cf. III, 5 and IX, 13. A certain idealization of the 'noble savage' is to be found fairly often in early Chinese literature; cf. the eulogy of the barbarians put into the mouth of a Chinese whose ancestors had settled among them, *Shih Chi V*, and the maxim 'When the Emperor no longer functions, learning must be sought among the Four Barbarians,' north, west, east, and south (*Tso Chuan*, Chao kung seventeenth year).
    ² Literally, 'get material.' Cf. *I Chou Shu* VIII, 1 verso. Yu (familiar name of Tzu-lu) figures in later legend as a converted swashbuckler, who constantly shocked Confucius by his pugnacity.
    ³ See above, II, 6.   ⁴ The disciple Jan Ch'iu.
    ⁵ The disciple Kung-hsi Hua.

strangers and guests. But whether he is Good, I do not know.[1]

8.   The Master in discussing Tzu-kung said to him, Which do you yourself think is the better, you or Hui?[2] He answered saying, I dare not so much as look at Hui. For Hui has but to hear one part in ten, in order to understand the whole ten. Whereas if I hear one part, I understand no more than two parts. The Master said, Not equal to him—you and I are not equal to him![3]

9.   Tsai Yü[4] used to sleep during the day. The Master said, Rotten wood cannot be carved, nor a wall of dried dung be trowelled.[5] What use is there in my scolding him any more?
    The Master said, There was a time when I merely listened attentively to what people said, and took for granted that they would carry out their words. Now I am obliged not only to give ear to what they say, but also to keep an eye on what they do. It was my dealings with Tsai Yü that brought about the change.

10.   The Master said, I have never yet seen a man who was truly steadfast.[6] Someone answered saying, 'Shên Ch'êng.' The Master said, Ch'êng! He is at the mercy of his desires. How can *he* be called steadfast?

---

[1] Jan Ch'iu is known to history as a faithful henchman of the Lu dictator. Kung-hsi Hua's ambition was to perfect himself in the etiquette of State ceremonies. See XI, 25.   [2] See above, II, 9.
[3] See p. 74.   [4] See III, 21.
[5] i.e. patterned with the trowel. To translate 'be plastered' destroys the parallelism.
[6] Impervious to outside influences, intimidations, etc.

11.   Tzu-kung said, What I do not want others to
do to me, I have no desire to do to others. The Master
said, Oh Ssu! You have not quite got to that point
yet.

12.   Tzu-kung said, Our Master's views concerning
culture¹ and the outward insignia² of goodness, we are
permitted to hear; but about Man's nature³ and the
ways of Heaven⁴ he will not tell us anything at all.

13.   When Tzu-lu heard any precept and was still
trying unsuccessfully to put it into practice, his one
fear was that he might hear some fresh precept.

14.   Tzu-kung asked saying, Why was K'ung Wên
Tzu called Wên ('The Cultured')?⁵ The Master said,
Because he was diligent⁶ and so fond of learning that
he was not ashamed to pick up knowledge even from
his inferiors.

15.   Of Tzu-ch'an⁷ the Master said that in him
were to be found four of the virtues that belong to the

---

¹ See Introduction, p. 39.

² *Chang* ('insignia') means literally 'emblems' (usually represen-
tations of birds, beasts or plants) figuring on banners or dresses to show
the rank of the owner. Hence metaphorically, the outward manifestations of an inner virtue.

³ As it is before it has been embellished with 'culture.'

⁴ T'ien Tao. The Tao taught by Confucius only concerned human
behaviour ('the ways of man'); he did not expound a corresponding
Heavenly Tao, governing the conduct of unseen powers and divinities.

⁵ i.e. why was he accorded this posthumous title? See Introduction,
p. 39. He was a statesman of the Wei State who died between 484
and 480 B.C. He figures in the chronicles as a disloyal and self-seeking
minister.

⁶ There is perhaps a play on *wên* and *min* ('diligent'); the two
words were pronounced very similarly in ancient Chinese.

⁷ Minister in the Chêng State; died 522 B.C.

Way of the true gentleman. In his private conduct he was courteous, in serving his master he was punctilious, in providing for the needs of the people he gave them even more than their due; in exacting service from the people, he was just.

16. The Master said, Yen P'ing Chung is[1] a good example of what one's intercourse with one's fellow-men should be. However long he has known anyone he always maintains the same scrupulous courtesy.

17. The Master said, Tsang Wên Chung[2] kept a Ts'ai tortoise[3] in a hall with the hill-pattern on its pillar tops and the duckweed pattern on its king-posts.[4] Of what sort, pray, was his knowledge?[5]

18. Tzu-chang asked saying, The Grand Minister Tzu-wên[6] was appointed to this office on three separate occasions, but did not on any of these three occasions display the least sign of elation. Three times he was deposed; but never showed the least sign of disappoint-ment. Each time, he duly informed his successor con-

---

[1] Or 'was.' The Ch'i minister Yen Tzu, famous for his wise counsels, died in 500 B.C.

[2] Minister of Lu in the seventh century B.C.

[3] The country of Ts'ai was famous for its tortoises.

[4] Such decoration was proper only to the Emperor's ancestral temple and palace. Cf. *I Chou Shu* 48, end. Kuan Tzu (*Li Chi*, Tsa Ch'i, Couvreur's translation, II, 187) is accused of decorating his palace in the same way.

[5] i.e. his knowledge of ritual. For a tortoise kept on a special terrace and smeared daily with the blood of four bulls, see *Kuan Tzu*, P'ien 75. Strictly speaking only rulers kept tortoises for use in divination (*Li Chi* X); ministers used the yarrow-stalks. But we find Tsang's grandson still in possession of a Ts'ai tortoise (*Tso Chuan*, Duke Hsiang twenty-third year); so perhaps the family claimed an hereditary privilege.

[6] Middle of the seventh century B.C.

cerning the administration of State affairs during his
tenure of office. What should you say of him? The
Master said, He was certainly faithful to his prince's
interests. Tzu-chang said, Would you not call him
Good? The Master said, I am not sure. I see nothing
in that to merit the title Good.

(Tzu-chang said) When Ts'ui Tzu assassinated the
sovereign of Ch'i,[1] Ch'ên Wên Tzu[2] who held a fief
of ten war chariots gave it up and went away. On
arriving in another State, he said, 'I can see they
are no better here than our minister Ts'ui Tzu';
and he went away. On arriving in the next country,
he said, 'I can see they are no better here than our
minister Ts'ui Tzu'; and went away. What should
you say of him? The Master said, He was certainly
scrupulous. Tzu-chang said, Would you not call him
Good? The Master said, I am not sure. I see nothing
in that to merit the title Good.

19.   Chi Wên Tzu[3] used to think thrice before
acting. The Master hearing of it said, Twice is quite
enough.[4]

20.   The Master said, Ning Wu Tzu[5] 'so long as
the Way prevailed in his country showed wisdom;
but when the Way no longer prevailed, he showed his
folly.'[6] To such wisdom as his we may all attain; but
not to such folly!

---

[1] In 548 B.C. The Duke of Ch'i had seduced his wife.
[2] Another Ch'i minister.   [3] Died 568 B.C.
[4] Ch'êng Hao (A.D. 1032–1085) says that if one thinks more than
twice, self-interest begins to come into play.
[5] A minister of Wei (seventh century B.C.), famous for his blind
devotion to his prince, whose enemies had incarcerated him in a deep
dungeon. Here Ning managed to feed his prince through a tube.
[6] Such was the judgment of the world.

21.   When the Master was in Ch'ên[1] he said, Let us go back, let us go back! The little ones[2] at home are headstrong and careless. They are perfecting themselves in all the showy insignia of culture without any idea how to use them.

22.   The Master said, Po I and Shu Ch'i[3] never bore old ills in mind and had but the faintest feelings of rancour.

23.   The Master said, How can we call even Wei-shêng Kao upright? When someone asked him for vinegar he went and begged it from the people next door, and then gave it as though it were his own gift.[4]

24.   The Master said, Clever talk, a pretentious

---

[1] About 492 B.C.?   [2] Disciples.
[3] Legendary brothers, almost always bracketed together in this way. The 'old ills' were the misdeeds of the last Yin ruler. When he was attacked by the Chou tribe, the brothers refused to take up arms against their sovereign, despite his great wickedness. Their lack of *yüan* ('rancour') was a classical theme; cf. VII, 14. This was shown by their attitude after each in turn had resigned his rights of accession to the rulership of the small State to which they belonged. Having proposed this act of 'cession' (*jang*), they carried it out loyally and uncomplainingly.
[4] Wei-shêng Kao (see *Chuang Tzu* XXIX, 1, *Chan Kuo Ts'ê*, Yen stories, Pt. 1, *Huai-nan Tzu* XVII, end) is the legendary paragon of truthfulness. Confucius adopts the same formula as the rhyme:

> *The Germans in Greek*
> *Are sadly to seek.*
> *All except Hermann;*
> *And Hermann is a German.*

How rare, how almost non-existent a quality uprightness must be, Confucius bitterly says, if even into the legend of the most upright of all men there has crept an instance of falsity!

Translators have supposed Wei-shêng Kao to have been some actual contemporary of Confucius, whose conduct the Master was criticizing. This misses the whole point.

manner and a reverence that is only of the feet[1]—Tso Ch'iu Ming[2] was incapable of stooping to them, and I too could never stoop to them. Having to conceal one's indignation and keep on friendly terms with the people against whom one feels it—Tso Ch'iu Ming was incapable of stooping to such conduct, and I too am incapable of stooping to such conduct.[3]

25.   Once when Yen Hui and Tzu-lu were waiting upon him the Master said, Suppose each of you were to tell his wish. Tzu-lu said, I should like to have carriages and horses, clothes and fur rugs,[4] share them with my friends and feel no annoyance if they were returned to me the worse for wear. Yen Hui said, I should like never to boast of my good qualities nor make a fuss about the trouble I take on behalf of others. Tzu-lu said, A thing I should like is to hear the Master's wish. The Master said, In dealing with the aged, to be of comfort to them; in dealing with friends, to be of good faith with them; in dealing with the young, to cherish them.

26.   The Master said, In vain have I looked for a single man capable of seeing his own faults and bringing the charge home against himself.

27.   The Master said, In an hamlet of ten houses you may be sure of finding someone quite as loyal and true to his word as I. But I doubt if you would find anyone with such a love of learning.[5]

---

[1] Cf. *Ta Tai Li Chi*, 49, where 'foot reverence' is coupled with 'mouth holiness.'   [2] See additional notes.

[3] And am therefore unfitted for Court life, where such behaviour is the sole way to preferment.   [4] See textual notes.

[5] i.e. self-improvement in the most general sense. Not book-learning.

BOOK VI

1. The Master said, Now Yung,[1] for example. I should not mind setting him with his face to the south.[2] Jan Yung then asked about Tzu-sang Po-tzu.[3] The Master said, He too would do. He is lax.[4] Jan Yung said, I can understand that such a man might do as a ruler, provided he were scrupulous in his own conduct and lax only in his dealings[5] with the people. But you would admit that a man who was lax in his own conduct as well as in government would be too lax.[6] The Master said, What Yung says is quite true.

2. Duke Ai asked which of the disciples had a love of learning. Master K'ung answered him saying, There was Yen Hui. He had a great love of learning. He never vented his wrath upon the innocent nor let others suffer for his faults. Unfortunately the span of life allotted to him by Heaven was short, and he died. At present there are none or at any rate I have heard of none who are fond of learning.[7]

3. When Kung-hsi Hua was sent on a mission to Ch'i, Master Jan asked[8] that Hua's mother might be granted an allowance of grain. The Master said, Give her a cauldron[9] full. Jan said that was not enough. The Master said, Give her a measure.[10] Master Jan

---

[1] The disciple Jan Yung.   [2] Trying him as a ruler.
[3] Cf. the Tzu-sang of *Chuang Tzu* VI, 11.
[4] This is a paradox, *chien* ('lax') being generally used in a bad sense.
[5] i.e. in the exaction of taxes, corvées, and the like. I punctuate after *ching*, not after *chien*.
[6] i.e. too lax to 'set with his face to the south.'   [7] Cf. XI, 6.
[8] i.e. asked the government (the Chi Family), in whose service he was.
[9] A merely nominal amount. Confucius disapproved of her being given any at all.   [10] A good deal more; but still not a great deal.

gave her five bundles.¹ The Master said, When Ch'ih²
went to Ch'i he drove sleek horses and was wrapped
in light furs. There is a saying, A gentleman helps out
the necessitous; he does not make the rich richer still.

When Yüan Ssu was made a governor, he was given
an allowance of nine hundred measures of grain, but
declined it. The Master said, Surely you could find
people who would be glad of it among your neighbours
or in your village?

4.   The Master said of Jan Yung, If the offspring
of a brindled³ ox is ruddy-coated⁴ and has grown its
horns, however much people might hesitate to use it,⁵
would the hills and streams really reject it?

5.   The Master said, Hui is⁶ capable of occupying
his whole mind for three months on end with no
thought but that of Goodness. The others can do so,
some for a day, some even for a month; but that is all.⁷

6.   Chi K'ang-tzu⁸ asked whether Tzu-lu was the
right sort of person to put into office. The Master

¹ Ten times (?) more than a measure. Jan entirely disregards Confucius's advice.
² i.e. Kung-hsi Hua. He ought to have left behind sufficient
provision for his mother.
³ i.e. one unsuitable for sacrifice.
⁴ All over. Only animals of one colour could be used for sacrifice.
⁵ In sacrificing to the hills and streams. The implication is that Jan
Yung was of humble origin. This, says Confucius, ought not to pre-
judice us against him.
⁶ There is nothing to indicate whether this was said before or after
Yen Hui's premature death.
⁷ On the strength of sayings such as this, the Taoists claimed Yen
Hui as an exponent of *tso-wang* ('sitting with blank mind'), the Chinese
equivalent of *yoga*.
⁸ Became head of the actual administration of Lu in 492 B.C.

said, Yu is efficient. It goes without saying that he is capable of holding office. Chi K'ang-tzu said, How about Tzu-kung? Would he be the right sort of person to put into office? The Master said, He can turn his merits to account.[1] It goes without saying, that he is capable of holding office. Chi K'ang-tzu said, How about Jan Ch'iu? Would he be the right sort of person to put into office? The Master said, He is versatile. It goes without saying that he is capable of holding office.

7. The Chi Family[2] wanted to make Min Tzu-ch'ien governor of Pi.[3] Min Tzu-ch'ien said, Invent a polite excuse for me. If that is not accepted and they try to get at me again, I shall certainly install myself on the far side of the Wên.[4]

8. When Jan Kêng was ill, the Master went to enquire after him, and grasping his hand through the window said, It is all over with him! Heaven has so ordained it——[5] But that such a man should have such an illness! That such a man should have such an illness![6]

9. The Master said, Incomparable indeed was Hui! A handful[7] of rice to eat, a gourdful of water to drink, living in a mean street—others would have found it unendurably depressing, but to Hui's cheerfulness it

---

[1] For *ta*, see additional notes.
[2] i.e. the government. He would not serve a usurper.
[3] The great stronghold of the Chi Family.
[4] i.e. I shall take refuge in the neighbouring land of Ch'i, where I cannot be got at. He was faithful to the legitimate ruler, the Duke of Lu.   [5] And we must not repine.
[6] Later tradition very naturally explains the passage by saying that Jan Kêng's illness was leprosy. This fits in with the concluding words and also explains why Confucius did not enter the house.
[7] Literally, a split bamboo-sectionful.

made no difference at all. Incomparable indeed was
Hui![1]

10.   Jan Ch'iu said, It is not that your Way does
not commend itself to me, but that it demands powers
I do not possess. The Master said, He whose strength
gives out collapses during the course of the journey
(the Way); but you deliberately draw the line.[2]

11.   The Master said to Tzu-hsia, 'You must practise the *ju*[3] of gentlemen, not that of the common
people.

12.   When Tzu-yu was Warden of the castle of Wu,
the Master said, Have you managed to get hold of
the right sort of people there? Tzu-yu said, There is
someone called T'an-t'ai Mieh-ming who 'walks on
no by-paths.'[4] He has not once come to my house
except on public business.

13.   The Master said, Mêng Chih-fan is no boaster.
When his people were routed[5] he was the last to flee;
but when they neared the city-gate, he whipped up his

---

[1] Cf. *Mencius*, IV, 2, XXIX.

[2] Metaphor of marking boundary-lines of estates or the like.

[3] A word of very uncertain meaning. Perhaps 'unwarlikeness.' See
additional notes. The meaning of the saying may be 'The unwarlikeness
of gentlemen means a preference for *tê* (moral force), that of inferior
people is mere cowardice.'
   Ju came ultimately to be the general name for followers of the
Confucian Way.

[4] i.e. strictly follows our Way. There is probably some further
point in this story, that is lost to us owing to our knowing so little
about T'an-t'ai Mieh-ming.

[5] At a battle with Ch'i outside the Lu capital in 484 B.C. To belittle
his own achievements (the opposite of boasting) is the duty of a gallant
gentleman. So a modern airman who had stayed behind to fight a rear
action might say, 'I was in a funk all the time, but I couldn't get away;
my engine was missing fire.'

horses, saying, It was not courage that kept me behind. My horses were slow.

14.   The Master said, Without the eloquence of the priest[1] T'o and the beauty of Prince Ch'ao of Sung it is hard nowadays to get through.

15.   The Master said, Who expects to be able to go out of a house except by the door? How is it then that no one follows this Way of ours?[2]

16.   The Master said, When natural substance prevails over ornamentation,[3] you get the boorishness of the rustic. When ornamentation prevails over natural substance, you get the pedantry of the scribe. Only when ornament and substance are duly blended do you get the true gentleman.

17.   The Master said, Man's very life is honesty, in that without it he will be lucky indeed if he escapes with his life.[4]

18.   The Master said, To prefer it[5] is better than only to know it. To delight in it is better than merely to prefer it.

19.   The Master said, To men who have risen at all above the middling sort, one may talk of things higher yet. But to men who are at all below the middling sort it is useless to talk of things that are above them.[6]

---

[1] The *chu* ('priest') recited invocations addressed to the ancestors. Both T'o and Chao flourished about 500 B.C.

[2] Though it is the obvious and only legitimate way out of all our difficulties.   [3] i.e. when nature prevails over culture.

[4] I punctuate after *chih*, not after *yeh*.   [5] The Way.

[6] that belong to a higher stage of learning.

20.   Fan Ch'ih asked about wisdom.[1] The Master said, He who devotes himself to securing for his subjects what it is right they should have, who by respect for the Spirits keeps them at a distance,[2] may be termed wise. He asked about Goodness. The Master said, Goodness cannot be obtained till what is difficult[3] has been duly done. He who has done this may be called Good.

21.   The Master said, The wise man delights in water, the Good man delights in mountains. For the wise move; but the Good stay still. The wise are happy; but the Good, secure.[4]

22.   A single change could bring Ch'i to the level of Lu; and a single change would bring Lu to the Way.

23.   The Master said, A horn-gourd that is neither horn nor gourd! A pretty horn-gourd indeed, a pretty horn-gourd indeed.[5]

[1] i.e. to what rulers the title 'Wise' could be accorded.

[2] When the Spirits of hills and streams do not receive their proper share of ritual and sacrifice they do not 'keep their distance,' but 'possess' human beings, causing madness, sickness, pestilence, etc.

[3] This only becomes intelligible when we refer to XIV, 2, where we see that the 'difficult thing' is to rid oneself of love of mastery, vanity, resentment, and covetousness.

[4] For the origin of this saying, which has here taken on a form distorted by quietist influences, see additional note and Introduction, p. 29.

[5] A particular sort of bronze goblet was called *ku*, which is written 'horn' beside 'gourd,' though the object in question is not shaped like a gourd and is not a drinking-horn. The saying is, of course, a metaphorical way of lamenting over the political state of China, 'ruled over' by an Emperor who had no temporal power and local sovereigns whose rights had been usurped by their ministers.

24.   Tsai Yü asked saying, I take it a Good Man, even if he were told that another Good Man[1] were at the bottom of a well, would go to join him? The Master said, Why should you think so? 'A gentleman can be broken, but cannot be dented;[2] may be deceived, but cannot be led astray.'[3]

24 (Paraphrased).   Tsai Yü, half playfully asked whether, since the Good always go to where other Good Men are, a Good Man would leap into a well on hearing that there was another Good Man at the bottom of it. Confucius, responding in the same playful spirit, quotes a maxim about the true gentleman, solely for the sake of the reference in it to *hsien*, which means 'throw down' into a pit or well, but also has the sense 'to pit,' 'to dent.'

25.   The Master said, A gentleman who is widely versed in letters and at the same time knows how to submit his learning to the restraints of ritual is not likely, I think, to go far wrong.

26.   When the Master went to see Nan-tzu,[4] Tzu-lu was not pleased. Whereupon the Master made a solemn declaration[5] concerning his visit, saying, Whatsoever I have done amiss, may Heaven avert it,[6] may Heaven avert it!

27.   The Master said, How transcendent is the

---

[1] See textual notes.

[2] Cf. *Shuo Yüan*, XVII: The gentleman (like jade) can be broken, but not bent.

[3] i.e. deceived as to facts; but cannot be enticed into wrong conduct. Cf. *Mencius*, V, I, II, 4; Legge, p. 224.

[4] The wicked concubine of Duke Ling of Wei.

[5] See additional notes.

[6] See textual notes.

moral power of the Middle Use![1] That it is but rarely found among the common people is a fact long admitted.[2]

28.   Tzu-kung said, If a ruler not only conferred wide benefits upon the common people, but also compassed the salvation of the whole State, what would you say of him? Surely, you would call him Good? The Master said, It would no longer be a matter of 'Good.' He would without doubt be a Divine Sage.[3] Even Yao and Shun could hardly criticize him.[4] As for Goodness—you yourself desire rank and standing; then help others to get rank and standing. You want to turn your own merits to account; then help others to turn theirs to account—in fact, the ability to take one's own feelings as a guide—that is the sort of thing that lies in the direction of Goodness.[5]

---

[1] Confucius's Way was essentially one of moderation: 'to exceed is as bad as to fall short.' See additional notes and Introduction, p. 37.

[2] *Chiu i* constantly has an idiomatic sense of this sort, and does not mean simply 'a long while.' Cf. *Doctrine of the Mean*, III. Legge, p. 251.

[3] See introduction, p. 17.

[4] Cf. XIV, 45, and *Han Shih Wai Chuan*, VII, 9.

[5] For *fang*, 'direction,' cf. XI, 25.

BOOK VII

1, 2, 3.   The Master said, I have 'transmitted what was taught to me without making up anything of my own.'[1] I have been faithful to and loved the Ancients. In these respects, I make bold to think, not even our old P'êng[2] can have excelled me. The Master said, I have listened in silence and noted what was said, I have never grown tired of learning nor wearied of teaching others what I have learnt. These at least are merits which I can confidently claim.[3] The Master said, The thought that 'I have left my moral power (*tê*) untended, my learning unperfected, that I have heard of righteous men, but been unable to go to them; have heard of evil men, but been unable to reform them'[4]—it is these thoughts that disquiet me.

4.   In his leisure hours the Master's manner was very free-and-easy, and his expression alert and cheerful.

5.   The Master said, How utterly have things gone to the bad with me! It is long now indeed since I dreamed that I saw the Duke of Chou.[5]

6.   The Master said, Set your heart upon the Way,

---

[1] Cf. *Mo Tzu*, P'ien 46. 'A gentleman does not make anything up; he merely transmits.'

[2] The Chinese Nestor. It is the special business of old men to transmit traditions.

[3] For the idiom *ho yu*, 'there is no further trouble about,' see above, IV, 13,

[4] The passage in inverted commas consists of two rhymed couplets, and is probably traditional. For the rhymes, see Liu Pao-nan; and textual notes.   [5] See Introduction, p. 17.

support yourself by its power, lean upon Goodness, seek distraction in the arts.[1]

7.   The Master said, From the very poorest upwards —beginning even with the man who could bring no better present than a bundle of dried flesh[2]—none has ever come to me without receiving instruction.

8.   The Master said, Only one who bursts with eagerness do I instruct; only one who bubbles with excitement, do I enlighten. If I hold up one corner and a man cannot come back to me with the other three,[3] I do not continue the lesson.

9.   If at a meal the Master found himself seated next to someone who was in mourning, he did not eat his fill. When he had wailed at a funeral, during the rest of the day he did not sing.[4]

10.   The Master said to Yen Hui, The maxim

When wanted, then go;
When set aside; then hide.

is one that you and I could certainly fulfil. Tzu-lu said, Supposing you had command of the Three Hosts,[5] whom would you take to help you? The Master said, The man who was ready to 'beard a tiger or rush a river'[6] without caring whether he lived or died—that sort of man I should not take. I should certainly take

---

[1] Music, archery and the like.   [2] See additional notes.

[3] Metaphor from laying out of field-plots?

[4] Both of these are common ritual prescriptions. Cf. *Li Chi* III, fol. 6 and I, fol. 6.   [5] i.e. the whole army.

[6] Cf. *The Book of Songs*, No. 295, verse 6. The reply is clearly intended as a snub to the impulsive Tzu-lu. The song is one which I omit in my translation.

someone who approached difficulties with due caution and who preferred to succeed by strategy.

11. The Master said, If any means of escaping poverty presented itself that did not involve doing wrong, I would adopt it, even though my employment were only that of the gentleman who holds the whip.¹ But so long as it is a question of illegitimate means, I shall continue to pursue the quests that I love.²

12. The rites to which the Master gave the greatest attention were those connected with purification before sacrifice, with war and with sickness.3

13. When he was in Ch'i the Master heard the Succession,4 and for three months did not know the taste of meat.5 He said, 'I did not picture to myself that any music existed which could reach such perfection as this.6

14. Jan Ch'iu said, Is our Master on the side of the Prince of Wei?7 Tzu-kung said, Yes, I must ask him about that. He went in and said, What sort of

---

¹ i.e. the most menial. 'Gentleman,' *shih*, in such contexts is used with a slightly ironical intention, as one might say in French, le monsieur qui . . . .' Cf. *Chuang Tzu* XV, 1.   ² The study of the Ancients.

3 A special sacrifice was held before the departure of military expeditions, and the sacrificial meat was distributed among the soldiers. The populace flocked to the Ancestral Shrines, wailing to the Ancestors for assistance. Sickness was exorcized by sacrifices to hills and streams.

4 See III, 25.   5 i.e. did not notice what he was eating.

6 The older commentators take 'this' to mean the land of Ch'i, i.e. 'I did not expect to find such music here in Ch'i.' This may be right.

7 When Duke Ling died in the summer of 493 B.C., the throne passed to his grandson, his son having previously abdicated his rights to the accession. Soon, however, the son went back on his word and attempted to oust the grandson from the throne.

people were Po I and Shu Ch'i?¹ The Master said,
They were good men who lived in the days of old.
Tzu-kung said, Did they repine? The Master said,
They sought Goodness and got Goodness. Why should
they repine? On coming out Tzu-kung said, Our
Master is not on his side.

15.   The Master said, He who seeks only coarse
food to eat, water to drink and a bent arm for pillow,
will without looking for it find happiness to boot.² Any
thought of accepting wealth and rank by means that
I know to be wrong is as remote from me as the
clouds that float above.

16.   The Master said, Give me a few more years,
so that I may have spent a whole fifty in study,³ and
I believe that after all I should be fairly free from error.

17.   The occasions upon which the Master used
correct pronunciation⁴ were when reciting the *Songs* or

¹ See above, V, 22. The contrast is between Po I and Shu Ch'i
on the one hand (they are always spoken of as though they were to
all intents and purposes a single person) and Duke Ling's son on
the other. The two 'good men of old' harboured no rancour after their
act of cession; whereas Ling's son became discontented with his
lot. Tzu-kung sounds Confucius indirectly upon his attitude, because
the Master was at this time living in Wei and would have been loath
to make an open pronouncement on the question.

² For the idiom, see II, 18.

3 See textual notes. In common with most scholars, I follow the
Lu version here. The Ku version introduces a reference to the *Book
of Changes*. But there is no reason to suppose that the *Changes* had in
Confucius's time been philosophized, or that he regarded it as anything
but a book of divination.

4 Whereas in daily life he used the Lu dialect. See above,
p. 74. Similarly the Swiss, for example, use their own dialect in daily
life, but Hochdeutsch in church services or in reciting a poem by
Schiller. Cf. *Hsün Tzu*, P'ien 4, A man of Yüeh is at ease in Yüeh
speech, a man of Ch'u in Ch'u speech; gentlemen, in the 'correct pronunciation,' *ya*, the same term as is used here. See further, additional notes.

the *Books* and when practising ritual acts. At all such times he used the correct pronunciation.

18.   The 'Duke of Shê'[1] asked Tzu-lu about Master K'ung (Confucius). Tzu-lu did not reply. The Master said, Why did you not say 'This is the character of the man: so intent upon enlightening the eager that he forgets his hunger, and so happy in doing so, that he forgets the bitterness of his lot and does not realize that old age is at hand.[2] That is what he is.

19.   The Master said, I for my part[3] am not one of those who have innate knowledge. I am simply one who loves the past and who is diligent in investigating it.

20.   The Master never talked of prodigies, feats of strength, disorders[4] or spirits.

21.   The Master said, Even when walking in a party of no more than three I can always be certain of learning from those I am with. There will be good qualities that I can select for imitation and bad ones that will teach me what requires correction in myself.

22.   The Master said, Heaven begat the power (*tê*) that is in me. What have I to fear from such a one as Huan T'ui?[5]

[1] An adventurer, known originally as Shên Chu-liang; first mentioned in 523 and still alive in 475. The title 'Duke of Shê' was one which he had invented for himself.

[2] According to the traditional chronology Confucius was sixty-two at the time when this was said.

[3] *Wo*, emphatic as opposed to the simple nominative *wu*. Cf. *Hu Shih Wên Ts'un*, Vol. II, p. 13. Cf. p. 103 above.

[4] Disorders of nature; such as snow in summer, owls hooting by day, or the like.

[5] Minister of War in Sung. Cf. *Tso Chuan*, Duke Ai fourteenth year.

23.   The Master said, My friends, I know you think that there is something I am keeping from you. There is nothing at all that I keep from you. I take no steps about which I do not consult you, my friends. Were it otherwise, I should not be Ch'iu.¹

24.   The Master took four subjects for his teaching: culture, conduct of affairs, loyalty to superiors and the keeping of promises.

25.   The Master said, A Divine Sage² I cannot hope ever to meet; the most I can hope for is to meet a true gentleman. The Master said, A faultless man I cannot hope ever to meet; the most I can hope for is to meet a man of fixed principles. Yet where all around I see Nothing pretending to be Something,³ Emptiness pretending to be Fulness, Penury pretending to be Affluence, even a man of fixed principles will be none too easy to find.

26.   The Master fished with a line but not with a net; when fowling he did not aim at a roosting bird.⁴

27.   The Master said, There may well be those who can do without knowledge; but I for my part am certainly not one of them. To hear much, pick out what is good and follow it, to see much and take due

---

¹ Familiar name of Confucius. There is no evidence that Confucius is here disclaiming the possession of an esoteric doctrine. The wording (*hsing*, 'steps,' '*démarches*') suggests that practical steps (with a view to office, patronage or the like) are all that is intended.

² See Introduction, p. 17.

³ An impotent cipher pretending to be a Duke, powerless tools of adventurers such as Yang Huo pretending to be Ministers.

⁴ See Introduction, p. 35. For 'fowling,' see *The Book of Songs*, p. 36.

note of it,[1] is the lower[2] of the two kinds of knowledge.

28. At Hu village[3] the people were difficult to talk to.[4] But an uncapped[5] boy presented himself for an interview. The disciples were in two minds about showing him in. But the Master said, In sanctioning his entry here I am sanctioning nothing he may do when he retires. We must not be too particular. If anyone purifies[6] himself in order to come to us, let us accept this purification. We are not responsible for what he does when he goes away.

29. The Master said, Is Goodness indeed so far away? If we really wanted Goodness, we should find that it was at our very side.

30. The Minister of Crime in Ch'ên asked whether Duke Chao of Lu knew the rites. Master K'ung said, He knew the rites. When Master K'ung had withdrawn, the Minister motioned Wu-ma Ch'i[7] to come

---

[1] As I do.

[2] The higher being innate knowledge, which Confucius disclaims above, VII, 19. He thus (ironically) places himself at two removes from the hypothetical people who can dispense with knowledge, the three stages being, (1) those who do not need knowledge; (2) those who have innate knowledge; (3) those who accumulate it by hard work.

[3] Unknown. Probably one of the places Confucius passed through during his travels.   [4] About the Way. Cf. XV, 7.

[5] The 'capping' of boys marked their initiation into manhood.

[6] A suppliant of any kind (whether asking a Master for teaching or Heaven for good crops) purifies himself by fasting and abstinence in order to enhance the power of his prayer. For abstinence before entertaining a teacher, cf. *Kuan Tzu*, P'ien 19, where the purification consists in washing in water from a new well, making a burnt offering, and ten days' abstinence and fasting.

[7] Later regarded as a disciple of Confucius.

forward and said, I have heard the saying 'A gentleman is never partial.' But it seems that some gentlemen are very partial indeed. His Highness[1] married into the royal family of Wu who belong to the same clan as himself, calling her Wu Mêng Tzu.[2] If his Highness knew the rites, who does not know the rites? Wu-ma Ch'i repeated this to the Master, who said, I am a fortunate man. If by any chance I make a mistake, people are certain to hear of it![3]

31. When in the Master's presence anyone sang a song that he liked, he did not join in at once, but asked for it to be repeated and then joined in.

32. The Master said, As far as taking trouble goes,[4] I do not think I compare badly with other people. But as regards carrying out the duties of a gentleman in actual life, I have never yet had a chance to show what I could do.

33. The Master said, As to being a Divine Sage or even a Good Man, far be it from me to make any such claim. As for unwearying effort to learn and unflagging patience in teaching others,[5] those are merits that I do not hesitate to claim. Kung-hsi Hua said, The trouble is that we disciples cannot learn!

34. When the Master was very ill, Tzu-lu asked leave to perform the Rite of Expiation. The Master

---

1 Duke Chao, reigned from 541 to 510 B.C.

2 He broke the rule of exogamy and hoped to pass this off by speaking of her in a way that might lead people to think she belonged to another clan, the Tzu.

3 This is, of course, ironical. It would have been improper for Confucius to criticize his own late sovereign.

4 See textual notes. 5 Cf. *Mencius*, II, 1, II, 19.

said, Is there such a thing?[1] Tzu-lu answered saying,
There is. In one of the Dirges[2] it says, 'We performed
rites of expiation for you, calling upon the sky-spirits
above and the earth-spirits below.' The Master said,
My expiation began long ago![3]

35. The Master said, Just as lavishness leads easily
to presumption, so does frugality to meanness. But
meanness is a far less serious fault than presumption.[4]

36. The Master said, A true gentleman is calm and
at ease; the Small Man is fretful and ill at ease.

37. The Master's manner was affable yet firm,
commanding but not harsh, polite but easy.

[1] i.e. is there any ancient authority for such a rite?
[2] See Introduction, p. 62.
[3] What justifies me in the eyes of Heaven is the life I have led.
There is no need for any rite now. In a fragment of one of the lost
books of *Chuang Tzu* there is a parallel story in which Tzu-lu wants
to take the omens about Confucius's chance of recovery, and Confucius
says 'My omen-taking was done long ago!' See *T'ai P'ing Yü Lan* 849,
fol. 1 verso. The reference was kindly sent to me by Dr. Gustav
Haloun.
[4] Cf. III, 4. The lavishness of the Chi Family became presumption
when it led them to have eight rows of dancers (III, 1) and thereby
infringe upon a ducal prerogative.

BOOK VIII

1. The Master said, Of T'ai Po[1] it may indeed be said that he attained to the very highest pitch of moral power. No less than three times he renounced the sovereignty of all things under Heaven, without the people getting a chance to praise him for it.

2. The Master said, Courtesy not bounded by the prescriptions of ritual becomes tiresome. Caution not bounded by the prescriptions of ritual becomes timidity, daring becomes turbulence, inflexibility becomes harshness.[2]

The Master said,[3] When gentlemen deal generously with their own kin, the common people are incited to Goodness. When old dependents are not discarded, the common people will not be fickle.

3. When Master Tsêng was ill he summoned his disciples and said, Free my feet, free my hands. The *Song* says:

---

[1] T'ai Po was the eldest son of King Tan, legendary ancestor of the Chou sovereigns. He renounced the Throne in favour of his youngest brother. *Jang* ('renunciation') is the virtue that engenders the greatest quantity of *tê* (moral power). No renunciation can be greater than to renounce 'the sovereignty of all things under Heaven.' Moreover, a *yin tê* (secret accretion of 'power') is always more redoubtable than an open one. The secrecy seems to have been achieved by giving it out that T'ai Po's flight to the lands of Wu and Yüeh was undertaken in order to collect medicines for Old King Tan, who was ill. (Chêng Hsüan makes a rather forced effort to enumerate three separate occasions upon which T'ai Po renounced his claims.)

[2] See textual notes and compare XVII, 8.

[3] The Pelliot MS. supplies these words, which have dropped out of the current version.

> *In fear and trembling,*
> *With caution and care,*
> *As though on the brink of a chasm,*
> *As though treading thin ice.*

But I feel now that whatever may betide I have got through safely, my little ones.[1]

4. When Master Tsêng was ill, Mêng Ching Tzu[2] came to see him. Master Tsêng spoke to him saying, When a bird is about to die its song touches the heart.[3] When a man is about to die, his words are of note.[4] There are three things that a gentleman, in following the Way, places above all the rest: from every attitude, every gesture that he employs he must remove all trace of violence or arrogance; every look that he composes in his face must betoken good faith; from every word that he utters, from every intonation, he must remove all trace of coarseness or impropriety. As to the ordering of ritual vessels and the like, there are those whose business it is to attend to such matters.

5. Master Tsêng said, Clever, yet not ashamed to consult those less clever than himself; widely gifted,

---

[1] While a man was dying four people held his hands and feet, 'one for each limb' (*Li Chi*, XXII). After death, the hands and feet were freed (*Li I Chih*, supplement to the *Hou Han Shu*, Part III, fol. 1). Tsêng says that he has got through safely, his moral course is run; there is no need to hold his hands and feet, which was done 'in case the dying man should in his death-struggle get into some "non-ritual" attitude.' He interprets the *Song* 295 as describing the heavy responsibilities of the man who has 'taken Goodness for his load'; see below, VIII, 7. For the anthropological connotations of 'freeing hands and feet,' see additional notes.

[2] Son of Mêng Wu Po (see II, 6). He appears to have been still alive in 430 B.C.   [3] Cf. our belief concerning 'swan-songs.'

[4] For 'la prescience reconnue aux mourants, cf. A. Lods, *Israel*, p. 260.

yet not ashamed to consult those with few gifts; having, yet seeming not to have; full, yet seeming empty; offended against, yet never contesting—long ago I had a friend[1] whose ways were such as this.

6.   Master Tsêng said, The man to whom one could with equal confidence entrust an orphan not yet fully grown[2] or the sovereignty of a whole State,[3] whom the advent of no emergency however great could upset— would such a one be a true gentleman? He I think would be a true gentleman indeed.

7.   Master Tsêng said, The true Knight of the Way must perforce be both broad-shouldered and stout of heart; his burden is heavy and he has far to go. For Goodness is the burden he has taken upon himself; and must we not grant that it is a heavy one to bear? Only with death does his journey end; then must we not grant that he has far to go?

8.   The Master said, Let a man be first incited by the *Songs*, then given a firm footing by the study of ritual, and finally perfected by music.

9.   The Master said, The common people can be made to follow it;[4] they cannot be made to understand it.

10.   The Master said, One who is by nature daring and is suffering from poverty will not long be law-abiding. Indeed, any men, save those that are truly Good, if their sufferings are very great, will be likely to rebel.[5]

[1] It has been suggested that the friend in question was Yen Hui.
[2] Literally, an orphan of six feet (i.e. four of our feet).
[3] Literally, the command of a hundred leagues.   [4] i.e. the Way.
[5] Official interpretation, 'Men who are not truly Good, if you criticize them too severely, are likely to rebel.'

11.   The Master said, If a man has gifts as wonderful as those of the Duke of Chou, yet is arrogant and mean, all the rest is of no account.

12.   The Master said:

> One who will study for three years
> Without thought of reward[1]
> Would be hard indeed to find.

13.   The Master said, Be of unwavering good faith, love learning, if attacked[2] be ready to die for the good Way. Do not enter a State that pursues dangerous courses, nor stay in one where the people have rebelled. When the Way prevails under Heaven, then show yourself; when it does not prevail, then hide. When the Way prevails in your own land, count it a disgrace to be needy and obscure; when the Way does not prevail in your land, then count it a disgrace to be rich and honoured.

14.   The Master said, He who holds no rank in a State does not discuss its policies.

15.   The Master said, When Chih the Chief Musician led the climax of the *Ospreys*,[3] what a grand flood of sound filled one's ears!

16.   The Master said, Impetuous, but tricky! Ingenuous, but dishonest! Simple-minded, but capable of breaking promises![4] To such men I can give no recognition.

---

[1] i.e. of obtaining a paid appointment. See textual notes.
[2] Literally, 'on the defensive.'
[3] See III, 20. For Chih, see XVIII, 9.
[4] In old days (see XVII, 16) people at any rate had the merits of their faults.

17. The Master said, Learn as if you were following someone whom you could not catch up, as though it were someone you were frightened of losing.

18. The Master said, Sublime were Shun and Yü! All that is under Heaven was theirs, yet they remained aloof from it.

19. The Master said, Greatest, as lord and ruler, was Yao.[1] Sublime, indeed, was he. 'There is no greatness like the greatness of Heaven', yet Yao could copy it. So boundless was it[2] that the people could find no name for it;[3] yet sublime were his achievements, dazzling the insignia of his culture!

20. Shun had five ministers and all that is under Heaven was well ruled. King Wu[4] said, I have ten[5] ministers. Master K'ung said, True indeed is the saying that 'the right material is hard to find'; for the turn of the T'ang and Yü dynasties[6] was the time most famous for this.[7] (As for King Wu),[8] there was a woman among his ten, so that in reality there were only nine men. Yet of all that is under Heaven he held two parts in three, using them in submissive service to the dynasty of Yin.[9] The moral power (*tê*)

---

[1] For the legendary rulers Yao, Shun and Yü, see Introduction, p. 18. Cf. *Mencius*, III, 1, IV, 11.   [2] i.e. Yao's *tê*.

[3] So that it remained a *yin tê*, 'secret prestige.' Cf. above, VIII, 1.

[4] The Warrior King, founder of the Chou dynasty.

[5] His mother, and his nine brothers? See additional notes.

[6] i.e. the accession of Shun.

[7] i.e. for 'the right material,' for an abundance of good ministers. Yet even then there were only five.

[8] Some such words have dropped out of the text.

[9] And by this act of cession (*jang*) building up the *tê* required for his subsequent campaign. For the whole paragraph, see additional notes.

of Chou may, indeed, be called an absolutely perfect moral power!

21.   The Master said, In Yü I can find no semblance of a flaw. Abstemious in his own food and drink, he displayed the utmost devotion in his offerings to spirits and divinities.[1] Content with the plainest clothes for common wear, he saw to it that his sacrificial apron and ceremonial head-dress were of the utmost magnificence. His place of habitation was of the humblest, and all his energy went into draining and ditching.[2] In him I can find no semblance of a flaw.

[1] To ancestors, and spirits of hill, stream, etc.
[2] For Yü, see Introduction, p. 19. For the question of rhyme in this paragraph, see textual notes.

BOOK IX

1. The Master seldom spoke of profit or fate or Goodness.[1]

2. A villager from Ta-hsiang said, Master K'ung is no doubt a very great man and vastly learned. But he does nothing to bear out this reputation. The Master, hearing of it, said to his disciples, What shall I take up? Shall I take up chariot-driving? Or shall it be archery? I think I will take up driving![2]

3. The Master said, The hemp-thread crown is prescribed by ritual.[3] Nowadays people wear black silk,[4] which is economical; and I follow the general practice. Obeisance below the daïs is prescribed by ritual. Nowadays people make obeisance after mounting the daïs. This is presumptuous, and though to do so is contrary to the general practice, I make a point of bowing while still down below.

4. There were four things that the Master wholly eschewed: he took nothing for granted,[5] he was never over-positive, never obstinate, never egotistic.

---

[1] We may expand: Seldom spoke of matters from the point of view of what would pay best, but only from the point of view of what was right. He did not discuss whether Heaven determines all human actions (a question debated by the school of Mo Tzu in later days and evidently already raised in the time of Confucius). He refused to define Goodness or accord the title Good to any of his contemporaries.

[2] See additional notes.

[3] For wear at the ancestral sacrifice; made of threads twisted from a very thin yarn, very costly to manufacture.   [4] See textual notes.

[5] Chêng Hsüan (Pelliot MS.) reads the 'man' determinative at the side of *i* and interprets 'he never took anything for granted when he was not sure.' This is certainly right.

5. When the Master was trapped in K'uang,[1] he said, When King Wên perished, did that mean that culture (*wên*) ceased to exist?[2] If Heaven had really intended that such culture as his should disappear, a latter-day mortal would never have been able to link himself to it as I have done. And if Heaven does not intend to destroy such culture, what have I to fear from the people of K'uang?

6. The Grand Minister (of Wu?)[3] asked Tzu-kung saying, Is your Master a Divine Sage? If so, how comes it that he has many practical accomplishments?[4] Tzu-kung said, Heaven certainly intended[5] him to become a Sage; it is also true that he has many accomplishments. When the Master heard of it he said, The Grand Minister is quite right about me. When I was young I was in humble circumstances; that is why I have many practical accomplishments in regard to simple, everyday matters. Does it befit a gentleman to have many accomplishments? No, he is in no need of them at all.

Lao says that the Master said, It is because I have not been given a chance[6] that I have become so handy.

---

[1] A border town held at various times by Chêng, Wei, Sung and Lu. For the legend as to why he was maltreated here, see additional notes. For 'trapped,' see textual notes.

[2] Literally, 'was not in this.' Cf. the common Chinese phrase 'Suppose there were a man in this,' i.e. 'suppose the case of a man who . . . ' 'being in this' meaning 'existing.' Cf. *Mencius*, VI, 2, II, 3. 'Take the case of a man not strong enough to lift. . . .'

[3] Probably P'i (adult name, Tzu-yü), who is mentioned in connexion with Tzu-kung in 488 B.C.

[4] Gentlemen do not stoop to practical accomplishments; much less the Sage.   [5] But the wickedness of the world prevented it.

[6] In public life. Lao is usually identified with the Ch'in Chang mentioned in *Tso Chuan*, Duke Chao, 20th year, and the Tzu-lao of *Chuang Tzu* XXV, 6.

7   The Master said, Do I regard myself as a possessor of wisdom? Far from it. But if even a simple peasant comes in all sincereity and asks me a question, I am ready to thrash the matter out, with all its pros and cons, to the very end.

8.   The Master said, The phoenix does not come; the river gives forth no chart.[1] It is all over with me![2]

9.   Whenever he was visited by anyone dressed in the robes of mourning or wearing ceremonial head-dress, with gown and skirt, or a blind man, even if such a one were younger than himself, the Master on seeing him invariably rose to his feet, and if compelled to walk past him always quickened his step.[3]

10.   Yen Hui said with a deep sigh, The more I strain my gaze up towards it,[4] the higher it soars. The deeper I bore down into it, the harder it becomes. I see it in front; but suddenly it is behind. Step by step the Master skilfully lures one on. He has broadened me with culture, restrained me with ritual. Even if I wanted to stop, I could not. Just when I feel that I have exhausted every resource, something seems to rise up, standing out sharp and clear.[5] Yet though I long to pursue it, I can find no way of getting to it at all.

11.   When the Master was very ill, Tzu-lu caused

---

[1] The arrival of this magical bird and the sudden revelation of a magical chart were portents that heralded the rise of a Saviour Sage. See Introduction, p. 48.

[2] Heaven does not intend to let me play a Sage's part.

[3] A sign of respect.   [4] Goodness.

[5] Literally, 'overtoppingly,' like a mountain-top or the top of a tree.

some of the disciples to get themselves up as official retainers.[1] Coming to himself for a short while, the Master said, How like Yu, to go in for this sort of imposture! In pretending to have retainers when I have none, whom do I deceive? Do I deceive Heaven? Not only would I far rather die in the arms of you disciples than in the arms of retainers, but also as regards my funeral—even if I am not accorded a State Burial, it is not as though I were dying by the roadside.[2]

12.   Tzu-kung said, Suppose one had a lovely jewel, should one wrap it up, put it in a box and keep it, or try to get the best price one can for it? The Master said, Sell it! Most certainly sell it! I myself am one who is waiting for an offer.[3]

13.   The Master wanted to settle among the Nine Wild Tribes of the East.[4] Someone said, I am afraid you would find it hard to put up with their lack of refinement. The Master said, Were a true gentleman to settle among them there would soon be no trouble[5] about lack of refinement.

14.   The Master said, It was only after my return from Wei to Lu that music was revised, Court pieces

---

[1] Such as he would have been entitled to, had he held office.

[2] i.e. don't think I am worrying about whether I shall be buried with public honours. I know I can trust you to give me a decent burial; and that is all I ask for.

[3] The question at issue is, of course, whether a man of talent should try to obtain office. Confucius declares that he himself is only too anxious to 'sell his jewel' (i.e. accept office), should any opportunity present itself.

[4] For Confucius's ideas on the 'noble savage,' see above, p. 108.

[5] For *ho yu*, an idiom that cannot be translated literally, cf. VI, 6, VII, 2, IX, 15, and textual note on IV, 13.

and Ancestral Recitations being at last properly discriminated.[1]

15.   The Master said, I can claim that at Court I have duly served the Duke and his officers; at home, my father and elder brother. As regards matters of mourning, I am conscious of no neglect, nor have I ever been overcome with wine. Concerning these things at any rate my mind is quite at rest.[2]

16.   Once when the Master was standing by a stream, he said, Could one but go on and on[3] like this, never ceasing day or night!

17.   The Master said, I have never yet seen anyone whose desire to build up his moral power was as strong as sexual desire.

18.   The Master said, The case[4] is like that of someone raising a mound. If he stops working, the fact that it perhaps needed only one more basketful makes no difference; I stay where I am. Whereas even if he has not got beyond levelling the ground, but is still at work, the fact that he has only tilted one basketful of earth makes no difference. I go to help him.

19.   The Master said, It was Hui whom I could count on always to listen attentively to anything I said.

----

[1] The words of the Court pieces (*ya*) are contained in the second and third parts, the Recitations (*sung*) in the last of the four great divisions of the *Book of Songs*.

[2] Another instance of the idiomatic *ho yu*.

[3] In one's moral striving, cf. *Mencius*, IV, 2, XVIII.

[4] i.e. my attitude towards disciples in different stages of progress. A parallel passage in *Hsün Tzu* P'ien 28, makes the sense and construction of this passage quite clear.

20. The Master said of Yen Hui, Alas, I saw him go forward, but had no chance to see whither this progress would have led him in the end.[1]

21. The Master said, There are shoots whose lot it is to spring up but never to flower; others whose lot it is to flower, but never bear fruit.[2]

22. The Master said, Respect the young. How do you know that they will not one day be all that you are now? But if a man has reached forty or fifty and nothing has been heard of him, then I grant there is no need to respect him.

23. The Master said, The words of the *Fa Yü*[3] (Model Sayings) cannot fail to stir us;[4] but what matters is that they should change our ways. The words of the *Hsüan Chü*[5] cannot fail to commend themselves to us; but what matters is that we should carry them out.[6] For those who approve but do not carry out, who are stirred, but do not change, I can do nothing at all.

24. The Master said, First and foremost, be faithful to your superiors, keep all promises, refuse the friendship of all who are not like you; and if you have made a mistake, do not be afraid of admitting the fact and amending your ways.[7]

---

[1] This seems better than the traditional, 'I saw him make progress, and never saw him stand still.'

[2] This surely refers to Yen Hui's early death.

[3] Name of a collection of moral sayings? I suspect that it is the same as the *Fa Yen* twice quoted in *Chuang Tzu* (IV, 2, Wieger, pp. 236, 237). [4] See textual notes.

[5] Name of another collection of moral sayings, on the 'choice' and 'promotion' of the virtuous? See textual notes. [7] Cf. I, 8.

[6] See p. 262.

25.   The Master said, You may rob the Three Armies of their commander-in-chief, but you cannot deprive the humblest peasant of his opinion.

26.   The Master said, 'Wearing a shabby hemp-quilted gown, yet capable of standing unabashed with those who wore fox and badger.' That would apply quite well to Yu, would it not?

> Who harmed none, was foe to none,
> Did nothing that was not right.[1]

Afterwards Tzu-lu (Yu) kept on continually chanting those lines to himself. The Master said, Come now, the wisdom contained in them is not worth treasuring[2] to that extent!

27.   The Master said,[3] Only when the year grows cold do we see that the pine and cypress are the last[4] to fade.

28.   The Master said, he that is really Good can never be unhappy. He that is really wise can never be perplexed. He that is really brave is never afraid.[5]

---

[1] Confucius quotes these two lines from *Songs*, No. 67.

[2] Pun on two senses of *tsang* (1) excellent; (2) treasure, to treasure up, to store.   [3] He is, however, only repeating a proverb.

[4] *hou*, 'last,' should probably be *pu* or *wu* ('not'). A similar saying in *Lü Shih Ch'un Ch'iu* (74, 2) refers to the Master's ordeals in Ch'ên and Ts'ai. Cf. *Chuang Tzu* XXVIII, 8.

[5] Goodness, wisdom and courage are the Three Ways of the true gentleman. Cf. XIV, 30. Confucius always ranks courage below wisdom and wisdom below Goodness. In the original the first two clauses have become transposed. This is, however, a mere slip, as is shown by comparison with the parallel passage, XIV, 30. The *Chung Yung* ('Doctrine of the Mean'), XX, in reproducing the terms in the order wisdom, goodness, courage, merely betrays the influence of this corrupted passage.

29. The Master said, There are some whom one can join in study but whom one cannot join in progress along the Way; others whom one can join in progress along the Way, but beside whom one cannot take one's stand;[1] and others again beside whom one can take one's stand, but whom one cannot join in counsel.

30.   *The flowery branch of the wild cherry*
      How swiftly it flies back![2]
      It is not that I do not love you;
      But your house is far away.

The Master said, He did not really love her. Had he done so, he would not have worried about the distance.[3]

[1] i.e. with whom one cannot collaborate in office. Cf. X, 3 and XVI, 13.

[2] When one pulls it to pluck the blossom. Cf. *Songs*, 268, 1. Image of things that are torn apart after a momentary union. Evidently a verse from some song not included in our *Book of Songs*.

[3] Men fail to attain to Goodness because they do not care for it sufficiently, not because Goodness 'is far away.' I think the old interpretation, which treats 29 and 30 as one paragraph, is definitely wrong.

BOOK X

1.   At home in his native village his manner is simple and unassuming, as though he did not trust himself to speak. But in the ancestral temple and at Court he speaks readily, though always choosing his words with care.

2.   At Court when conversing with the Under Ministers his attitude is friendly and affable; when conversing with the Upper Ministers, it is restrained and formal. When the ruler is present it is wary, but not cramped.

3.   When the ruler summons him to receive a guest, a look of confusion comes over his face and his legs seem to give beneath his weight. When saluting his colleagues he passes his right hand to the left, letting his robe hang down in front and behind; and as he advances with quickened step, his attitude is one of majestic dignity.
   When the guest has gone, he reports the close of the visit, saying, 'The guest is no longer looking back.'

4.   On entering the Palace Gate he seems to shrink[2] into himself, as though there were not room. If he halts, it must never be in the middle of the gate, nor in going through does he ever tread on the threshold.[3] As he passes the Stance[4] a look of confusion comes

---

   [1] 'The gentleman's. See Introduction, p. 55. In the text this has been altered to 'Master K'ung.' Throughout this Book the reader should refer constantly to the textual notes.
   [2] For shrinking, bowing, crawling, etc., see Introduction, p. 57.
   [3] For the 'unluckiness' of thresholds, see Introduction, p. 58.
   [4] The place where the ruler takes up his stand when seeing off important guests?

over his face, his legs seem to give way under him and words seem to fail him. While, holding up the hem of his skirt, he ascends the Audience Hall, he seems to double up and keeps in his breath, so that you would think he was not breathing at all. On coming out, after descending the first step his expression relaxes into one of satisfaction and relief. At the bottom of the steps he quickens his pace, advancing with an air of majestic dignity. On regaining his place he resumes his attitude of wariness and hesitation.

5. When carrying the tablet of jade,[1] he seems to double up, as though borne down by its weight. He holds it at the highest as though he were making a bow,[2] at the lowest, as though he were proffering a gift. His expression, too, changes to one of dread and his feet seem to recoil, as though he were avoiding something. When presenting ritual-presents, his expression is placid. At the private audience his attitude is gay and animated.

6. A gentleman[3] does not wear facings of purple or mauve, nor in undress does he use pink or roan.[4] In hot weather he wears an unlined gown of fine thread loosely woven, but puts on an outside garment before going out-of-doors.[5] With a black robe he wears black lambskin; with a robe of undyed silk, fawn. With a

---

[1] Symbol of the ruler's feudal investiture; the *kuei.*

[2] On a level with his forehead.

[3] Here the compilers have forgotten to alter *chün-tzu* (gentleman) to K'ung Tzu (Confucius).

[4] Usually translated 'purple.' But the term is applied to the coats of horses and cannot mean anything that we should call purple. These colours were reserved for times of fasting and mourning.

[5] To do otherwise, would be like going out into the town in one's shirt-sleeves.

yellow robe, fox fur.¹ On his undress robe the fur cuffs
are long; but the right is shorter than the left.² His
bedclothes must be half as long again as a man's
height.³ The thicker kinds of fox and badger are for
home wear. Except when in mourning, he wears all
his girdle-ornaments.⁴ Apart from his Court apron,
all his skirts are wider at the bottom than at the waist.
Lambskin dyed black and a hat of dark-dyed silk must
not be worn when making visits of condolence.⁵ At the
Announcement⁶ of the New Moon he must go to
Court in full Court dress.

7, 8.   When preparing himself for sacrifice he must
wear the Bright Robe,⁷ and it must be of linen. He
must change his food and also the place where he
commonly sits. But there is no objection to his rice
being of the finest quality, nor to his meat being finely
minced. Rice affected by the weather or turned he
must not eat, nor fish that is not sound, nor meat that
is high. He must not eat anything discoloured or that
smells bad. He must not eat what is overcooked nor
what is undercooked, nor anything that is out of
season. He must not eat what has been crookedly cut,

¹ Cf. our black tie with black waistcoat.

² To give him freedom of movement (pseudo K'ung An-kuo).

³ He does not, of course, undress, but simply draws the bedclothes
over him. According to Chu Hsi this refers only to one preparing for
sacrifice.

⁴ Which are lucky talismans; or (in a more sophisticated vein of
explanation) symbolic ornaments indicating his rank. Those of an
ordinary gentleman were of jade.

⁵ i.e., 'plain' articles must be worn, approximating to those worn by
the mourner. For these rules of dress, cf. *Li Chi*, XIII, fol. 3, and
Introduction, p. 59.

⁶ See textual notes, and above, p. 98.

⁷ *Ming I*, the 'spirit robe' used during the period of purification.
Cf. *Ming Ch'i*, 'spirit gear,' the objects buried along with the dead in
a tomb.

nor any dish that lacks its proper seasoning. The meat that he eats must at the very most not be enough to make his breath smell of meat rather than of rice. As regards wine, no limit is laid down; but he must not be disorderly. He may not drink wine bought at a shop or eat dried meat from the market. He need not refrain from such articles of food as have ginger sprinkled over them; but he must not eat much of such dishes.[1]

After a sacrifice in the ducal palace, the flesh must not be kept overnight. No sacrificial flesh may be kept beyond the third day. If it is kept beyond the third day, it may no longer be eaten. While it is being eaten, there must be no conversation, nor any word spoken while lying down after the repast. Any article of food, whether coarse rice, vegetables, broth or melon, that has been used as an offering must be handled with due solemnity.

9.   He must not sit on a mat that is not straight.[2]

10.   When the men of his village are drinking wine he leaves the feast directly the village-elders have left. When the men of his village hold their Expulsion Rite,[3] he puts on his Court dress and stands on the eastern steps.[4]

11.   When sending a messenger to enquire after someone in another country, he prostrates himself twice while speeding the messenger on his way. When

---

[1] All the above refers to periods of preparation for sacrifice. See Introduction, p. 63.   [2] While eating sacrificial flesh?

[3] The driving away of evil spirits at the close of the year; see additional and textual notes.

[4] The place occupied by one who is presiding over a ceremony.

K'ang-tzu[1] sent him some medicine he prostrated himself and accepted it; but said, As I am not acquainted with its properties, I cannot venture to taste it.[2]

1 2.   When the stables were burnt down, on returning from Court, he said, Was anyone hurt? He did not ask about the horses.

1 3.   When his prince sends him a present of food, he[3] must straighten his mat and be the first to taste what has been sent. When what his prince sends is a present of uncooked meat, he must cook it and make a sacrificial offering. When his prince sends a live animal, he must rear it.[4] When he is waiting upon his prince at meal-times, while his prince is making the sacrificial offering, he (the gentleman) tastes the dishes. If he is ill and his prince comes to see him, he has himself laid with his head to the East with his Court robes thrown over him and his sash drawn across the bed. When the prince commands his presence he goes straight to the palace without waiting for his carriage to be yoked.[5]

14.   On entering the Ancestral Temple, he asks about every detail.[6]

1 5.   If a friend dies and there are no relatives to fall back on, he says, 'The funeral is my affair.' On

---

[1] Head of the all-powerful Chi family. This sentence and the next paragraph obviously refer to Confucius himself.

[2] A *chün-tzu* takes no medicine except that administered to him by a doctor whose father and grandfather have served the family. Compare the attachment of the English *chün-tzu* to the 'old family doctor.'

[3] The gentleman?   [4] Not use it for food.

[5] Cf. *Mencius*, V, 2, VII, 9.   [6] Cf. III, 15.

receiving a present from a friend, even a carriage and horses, he does not prostrate himself. He does so only in the case of sacrificial meat being sent.

16.   In bed he avoids lying in the posture of a corpse.[1] When at home he does not use ritual attitudes. When appearing before[2] anyone in mourning, however well he knows him, he must put on an altered expression, and when appearing before anyone in sacrificial garb, or a blind man, even informally, he must be sure to adopt the appropriate attitude. On meeting anyone in deep mourning he must bow across the bar of his chariot; he also bows to people carrying planks.[3] When confronted with a particularly choice dainty at a banquet, his countenance should change and he should rise to his feet. Upon hearing a sudden clap of thunder or a violent gust of wind, he must change countenance.

17.   When mounting a carriage, he must stand facing it squarely and holding the mounting-cord. When riding he confines his gaze,[4] does not speak rapidly or point with his hands.[5]

18.   (The gentleman) rises and goes at the first sign,[6] and does not 'settle till he has hovered.'[7] (A song) says:

---

[1] i.e. with his face to the North, where lies the land of the Dead.

[2] Or 'when he sees.' For different ways of writing the expression for 'mourning garb,' see *Tz'u T'ung*, 434.

[3] Traditionally explained as meaning 'census tablets.'

[4] Does not look about promiscuously. See textual notes.

[5] Pointing is considered maleficent, unlucky, rude, as the case may be, in many parts of the world.

[6] Of evil intentions on the part of the ruler; cf. *Lü Shih Ch'un Ch'iu*, P'ien 101, fol. 1. 'The *chün-tzu* is like a bird; if he is startled he rises.'

[7] Is circumspect in choosing a new State in which to settle.

The hen-pheasant of the hill-bridge,
Knows how to bide its time, to bide its time!
When Tzu-lu made it an offering,
It sniffed three times before it rose.[1]

[1] This quatrain (if such it is intended to be) resembles in content the songs by means of which the people commented on current political events. It is natural to interpret it as referring to the circumspect conduct of Confucius when the Chi Family (through the agency of Tzu-lu) invited him to return to Lu. One makes an offering to birds or animals whose behaviour suggests that they are sent by Heaven as omens or portents. For an anecdote of Tzu-lu and a pheasant, see *Lü Shih Ch'un Ch'iu*, 44, 1.

BOOK XI

1. The Master said, 'Only common people wait till they are advanced in ritual and music [before taking office]. A gentleman can afford to get up his ritual and music later on.' Even if I accepted this saying, I should still be on the side of those who get on with their studies first.[1]

2A. The Master said, My adherents in Ch'ên and Ts'ai were none of them in public service.[2]

2B. Those who worked by moral power were Yen Hui, Min Tzu-ch'ien, Jan Kêng and Jan Yung. Those who spoke well were Tsai Yü and Tzu-kung. Those who surpassed in handling public business were Jan Ch'iu and Tzu-lu; in culture and learning, Tzu-yu and Tzu-hsia.[3]

3. The Master said, Hui was not any help to me; he accepted everything I said.

4. The Master said, Min Tzu-ch'ien is indeed a very good son. No one can take exception to what his parents or brothers have said of him.[4]

[1] This is the interpretation of Liu Pao-nan, founded on Chêng Hsüan. For the contrast between *chün-tzu* and *yeh-jên* cf. *Mencius*, III, 1, III, 14: 'If there were no *chün-tzu*, there would be no one to keep the common people (*yeh-jên*) in order; if there were no common people, there would be no one to produce food for the *chün-tzu*.'

[2] Cf. *Mencius*, VII, 2, XVIII, where Confucius's difficulties in Ch'ên and Ts'ai are attributed to his being out of touch with the ruling classes in those States. The current interpretation 'Not one of them now comes near my door,' taken as a complaint of their infidelity, is comparatively recent.

[3] This classification of the disciples is not put into the mouth of Confucius, as is clear from the form in which the names are given.

[4] For the legend of his piety, see additional notes.

5.   Nan Jung in reciting the *I* Song repeated the verse about the sceptre of white jade three times. (In consequence of which) Master K'ung gave him his elder brother's daughter to marry.[1]

6.   K'ang-tzu of the Chi Family asked which of the disciples had a love of learning. Master K'ung replied, There was Yen Hui. He was fond of learning, but unfortunately his allotted span was a short one, and he died. Now there is none.

7.   When Yen Hui died, his father Yen Lu begged for the Master's carriage, that he might use it to make the enclosure[2] for the coffin. The Master said, Gifted or not gifted,[3] you have spoken of your son and I will now speak of mine. When Li[4] died he had a coffin, but no enclosure. I did not go on foot in order that he might have an enclosure; for I rank next to the Great Officers[5] and am not permitted to go on foot.

8.   When Yen Hui died, the Master said, Alas, Heaven has bereft me, Heaven has bereft me![6]

9.   When Yen Hui died the Master wailed without

---

[1] The Song in question is No. 271; see verse 5: A flaw in a white jade sceptre may be polished away; but a flaw in words cannot be repaired. 'Gave him his brother's daughter,' cf. V. 1.

[2] See additional notes.

[3] Confucius thus apologizes for putting his son on a level with Yen Hui.

[4] The name means 'carp-fish.' Later tradition makes him die later than Yen Hui.

[5] It was the *shih* ('knights,' 'gentlemen,' those who fought in chariots and not afoot) who ranked after the Great Officers, and it is possible that Confucius ranked as 'leader of the *shih*.' See Introduction, p. 33.

[6] Recorded because Confucius rarely spoke of Heaven?

restraint. His followers said, Master, you are wailing without restraint! He said, Am I doing so? Well, if any man's death could justify abandoned wailing, it would surely be this man's!

10. When Yen Hui died, the disciples wanted to give him a grand burial. The Master said it would be wrong to do so; nevertheless they gave him a grand burial. The Master said, Hui dealt with me as though I were his father. But I have failed to deal with him as though he were my son.[1] The fault however is not mine. It is yours, my friends!

11. Tzu-lu asked how one should serve ghosts and spirits. The Master said, Till you have learnt to serve men, how can you serve ghosts? Tzu-lu then ventured upon a question about the dead. The Master said, Till you know about the living, how are you to know about the dead?[2]

12A. When Min Tzu-ch'ien stood by the Master's side in attendance upon him his attitude was one of polite restraint. That of Tzu-lu was one of impatient energy; that of Jan Ch'iu and of Tzu-kung was genial and affable.[3] The Master was pleased.

12B. [The Master said],[4] A man like Yu[5] never dies in his bed.

[1] Failed to assert my right to bury him in the way I thought suitable.
[2] e.g. whether they are conscious, which was a much debated problem. See Introduction, p. 32.
[3] See textual note on X, 2.
[4] There seems to be a hiatus in the text.
[5] Tzu-lu. For his death in 480 B.C. during the accession struggles in Wei, see *Tso Chuan*, Ai kung, 15th year. Confucius may well have said this on hearing of Tzu-lu's death. The words are usually regarded as a prophecy.

13.   When the men of Lu were dealing with the question of the Long Treasury, Min Tzu-ch'ien said, What about restoring it on the old lines? I see no necessity for rebuilding it on a new plan.¹ The Master said, That man is no talker; but when he does say anything, he invariably hits the mark.

14.   The Master said, Yu's zithern has no right to be in my house at all.² Whereupon the disciples ceased to respect Tzu-lu. The Master said, The truth about Yu is that he has got as far as the guest-hall, but has not yet entered the inner rooms.³

15.   Tzu-kung asked which was the better, Shih or Shang.⁴ The Master said, Shih goes too far and Shang does not go far enough. Tzu-kung said, If that is so, then Shih excels. The Master said, To go too far is as bad as not to go far enough.

16.   The head of the Chi Family was richer than the Duke of Chou;⁵ but Ch'iu⁶ when entrusted with the task of collecting his revenues for him, added to them and increased the yield. The Master said, He

¹ The point of the remark is very uncertain. See additional and textual notes.
² i.e. Tzu-lu has no right to call himself a follower of my Way. The *sê* was a 25-stringed zithern.
³ Tzu-lu had an abundance of courage, which is the elementary virtue of the gentleman. But he lacked the two other virtues: wisdom and Goodness.
⁴ i.e. Tzu-chang or Tzu-hsia.
⁵ Huang K'an (sixth century) says that this does not refer to Tan, legendary founder of Lu, but to a subsequent Duke of Chou. Cf. however, *Hsün Tzu*, P'ien, 8, fol. 5, where the wealth of Tan is referred to.
⁶ i.e. Jan Ch'iu. The form in which the name is given suggests that these words were spoken by Confucius or a disciple and are not a statement of the compiler's.

is no follower of mine. My little ones, you may beat the drum and set upon him. I give you leave.[1]

17. [The Master said], Ch'ai[2] is stupid, Shên[3] is dull-witted, Shih[4] is too formal; Yu, too free and easy.[5]

18. The Master said, Hui comes very near to it.[6] He is often empty.[7] Ssu (Tzu-kung) was discontented with his lot and has taken steps to enrich himself.[8] In his calculations he often hits the mark.

19. Tzu-chang asked about the Way of the good people.[9] The Master said, He who does not tread in the tracks[10] cannot expect to find his way into the Inner Room.

20. The Master said (of someone), That his conversation is sound one may grant. But whether he is indeed a true gentleman or merely one who adopts outward airs of solemnity, it is not so easy to say.

21. Tzu-lu asked, When one hears a maxim, should

---

[1] This is, of course, meant metaphorically. The same anecdote occurs in *Mencius*, IV, I, XIV.

[2] Kao Ch'ai, associated with Tzu-lu in the Wei accession troubles.

[3] Master Tsêng.

[4] Tzu-chang. The meaning of the epithet *p'i* is very uncertain. See textual notes. Chu Hsi's 'it means that he was expert in ritual attitudes and deportment, but lacked sincerity' is not a philological gloss on *p'i*, but an application to this passage of what is said about Tzu-chang in XIX, 16.

[5] Tradition represents Tzu-lu as a converted swashbuckler. See also textual notes.

[6] To Goodness. The rest of the paragraph runs very awkwardly and is probably corrupt.   [7] Hard up?

[8] 'Traded without official permission' is a possible interpretation.

[9] Possibly a rival Way to that of Confucius, see Introduction, p. 30.

[10] Of the Ancients.

one at once seek occasion to put it into practice? The Master said, Your father and elder brother are alive. How can you whenever you hear a maxim at once put it into practice? Jan Ch'iu asked, When one hears a maxim, should one at once seek occasion to put it into practice? The Master said, When one hears it, one should at once put it into practice.

Kung-hsi Hua said, When Yu asked, 'When one hears a maxim, should one at once put it into practice?' you said, You have a father and elder brother alive. But when Ch'iu asked, 'When one hears a maxim, should one at once put it into practice,' you said, 'When you hear it, put it into practice.' I am perplexed, and would venture to ask how this was. The Master said, Ch'iu is backward; so I urged him on. Yu is fanatical about Goodness;[1] so I held him back.

22.   When the Master was trapped in K'uang,[2] Yen Hui fell behind. The Master said, I thought you were dead. Hui said, While you are alive how should I dare to die?

23.   Chi Tzu-jan[3] asked whether Tzu-lu and Jan Ch'iu could be called great ministers. The Master said, I thought you were going to ask some really interesting question; and it is after all only a question about Yu and Ch'iu! What I call a great minister is one who will only serve his prince while he can do so without infringement of the Way, and as soon as this is impossible, resigns. But in the present case, so far as concerns Yu and Ch'iu, I should merely call them stop-gap ministers. Tzu-jan said, So you think they would merely do what they were told? The Master

---

[1] See textual notes.
[2] See above, IX, 5. The story is also found in *Lü Shih Ch'un Ch'iu*, 17.
[3] Brother of the head of the Chi Family.

said, If called upon to slay their father or their prince,
even *they* would refuse.

24.   Tzu-lu got Kao Ch'ai made Warden of Pi.[1]
The Master said, You are doing an ill turn to another
man's son. Tzu-lu said, What he will take charge of
at Pi will be the peasants and the Holy Ground and
Millet.[2] Surely 'learning consists in other things besides
reading books.'[3] The Master said, It is remarks of that
kind that make me hate glib people.[4]

25.   Once when Tzu-lu, Tsêng Hsi, Jan Ch'iu and
Kung-hsi Hua were seated in attendance upon the
Master, he said, you consider me as a somewhat older
man than yourselves. Forget for a moment that I am
so.[5] At present you are out of office and feel that your
merits are not recognized. Now supposing someone
were to recognize your merits, what employment would
you choose? Tzu-lu promptly and confidently replied,
Give me a country of a thousand war-chariots, hemmed
in by powerful enemies, or even invaded by hostile
armies, with drought and famine to boot; in the space
of three years I could endow the people with courage
and teach them in what direction[6] right conduct lies.
    Our Master smiled at him. What about you, Ch'iu?
he said. Ch'iu replied saying, Give me a domain of
sixty to seventy or say fifty to sixty (leagues), and in
the space of three years I could bring it about that the
common people should lack for nothing. But as to

---

[1] See VI, 7.   [2] See additional notes.
[3] In which the 'stupid' (see XI, 17) Ch'ai was not proficient.
[4] The pertness of Tzu-lu's remark consists of the fact that he throws
in the Master's teeth a favourite Confucian maxim. Cf. I, 14 and
Tzu-hsia's saying, I, 7.   [5] See textual notes.
[6] For *fang*, 'direction,' cf. VI, 28. Courage, it will be remembered,
is the lowest of the three virtues. Next comes wisdom; next Goodness.

rites and music,¹ I should have to leave them to a real gentleman.

What about you, Ch'ih?

(Kung-hsi Hua) answered saying, I do not say I could do this; but I should like at any rate to be trained for it. In ceremonies at the Ancestral Temple or at a conference or general gathering² of the feudal princes I should like, clad in the Straight Gown and Emblematic Cap, to play the part of junior assistant.

Tien,³ what about you?

The notes of the zithern he was softly fingering died away; he put it down, rose and replied saying, I fear my words will not be so well chosen as those of the other three.⁴ The Master said, What harm is there in that? All that matters is that each should name his desire.

Tsêng Hsi said, At the end of spring, when the making of the Spring Clothes⁵ has been completed, to go with five times six newly-capped youths and six times seven uncapped boys, perform the lustration in the river I, take the air⁶ at the Rain Dance altars, and then go home singing. The Master heaved a deep sigh and said, I am with Tien.

When the three others went away, Tsêng Hsi remained behind and said, What about the sayings of

---

¹ Which are the perquisites of the upper classes as opposed to the common people.

² Scrupulously defined as 'Audiences' by the later ritualists, because in theory they were presided over by the Son of Heaven (the king of Chou).

³ i.e. Tsêng Hsi; he was the father of Master Tsêng.

⁴ Or 'I fear my choice will seem inferior to that of . . .'

⁵ A technical name for the clothes worn at the ceremony?

⁶ Cf. *Mencius*, II, 2, II, 1, where *fêng* means 'expose oneself to the wind.' Freak interpretations such as 'scatter,' 'sing,' 'sacrifice to the wind' are merely instances of wasted ingenuity.

those three people? The Master said, After all, it was agreed that each should tell his wish; and that is just what they did.

Tsêng said, Why did you smile at Yu?

The Master said, 'Because it is upon observance of ritual that the governance of a State depends; and his words were lacking in the virtue of cession.[1] That is why I smiled at him.'

'I suppose you were contrasting him with Ch'iu, who (by domain) certainly did not mean kingdom?'

'Where have you ever seen "a domain of sixty to seventy or fifty to sixty leagues" that was not a kingdom?'

'I suppose, then, you were contrasting him with Ch'ih, who was certainly not asking for a kingdom.'

'The business of the Ancestral Temple and such things as conferences and general gatherings can only be undertaken by feudal princes. But if Ch'ih were taking a minor part, what prince is there who is capable of playing a major one?'[2]

---

[1] *Jang*, 'giving up,' 'ceding to others.'

[2] i.e. it is impossible to conceive of Kung-hsi Hua functioning on such an occasion except as the ruler of a Kingdom; so that, in effect, all three were asking for kingdoms.

BOOK XII

1.   Yen Hui asked about Goodness. The Master said, 'He who can himself submit to ritual is Good.'[1] If (a ruler) could for one day 'himself submit to ritual,' everyone under Heaven would respond to his Goodness. For Goodness is something that must have its source in the ruler himself; it cannot be got from others.

Yen Hui said, I beg to ask for the more detailed items of this (submission to ritual). The Master said, To look at nothing in defiance of ritual, to listen to nothing in defiance of ritual, to speak of nothing in defiance of ritual, never to stir hand or foot in defiance of ritual. Yen Hui said, I know that I am not clever; but this is a saying that, with your permission, I shall try to put into practice.[2]

2.   Jan Jung asked about Goodness.[3] The Master said, Behave when away from home[4] as though you were in the presence of an important guest. Deal with the common people as though you were officiating at an important sacrifice. Do not do to others what you would not like yourself. Then there will be no feelings of opposition to you, whether it is the affairs of a State that you are handling or the affairs of a Family.[5]

Jan Yung said, I know that I am not clever; but

---

[1] In the *Tso Chuan* (Chao Kung, 12th year) Confucius is made to quote this as a saying from 'an old record.' The commentators, not understanding the archaic use of *k'o* ('able to') turned *k'o chi* into 'self-conquest,' an error fruitful in edification; see above, p. 74.

[2] A formula of thanks for instruction; cf. *Mencius*, I, i, VII, 19.

[3] i.e. ruling by Goodness, not by force.

[4] i.e. in handling public affairs.

[5] A ruling clan, such as that of the Chi in Lu.

this is a saying that, with your permission, I shall try to put into practice.

3. Ssu-ma Niu[1] asked about Goodness. The Master said, The Good (*jên*) man is chary (*jên*) of speech. Ssu-ma Niu said, So that is what is meant by Goodness —to be chary of speech? The Master said, Seeing that the doing of it is so difficult, how can one be otherwise than chary of talking about it?[2]

4. Ssu-ma Niu asked about the meaning of the term Gentleman. The Master said, The Gentleman neither grieves nor fears. Ssu-ma Niu said, So that is what is meant by being a gentleman—neither to grieve nor to fear? The Master said, On looking within himself he finds no taint; so why should he either grieve or fear?

5. Ssu-ma Niu grieved, saying, Everyone else has brothers; I alone have none.[3] Tzu-hsia said, I have heard this saying, 'Death and life are the decree of Heaven; wealth and rank depend upon the will of Heaven. If a gentleman attends to business and does not idle[4] away his time, if he behaves with courtesy to others and observes the rules of ritual, then all within

---

[1] A native of Sung; brother of Huan T'ui, VII, 22.

[2] Here again Confucius is evasive about the meaning of Goodness. He first puns on *jên*, 'chary,' and *jên*, 'goodness'; and then in his second reply answers as though his first reply had meant 'Goodness is a thing one ought to be chary of talking about.' The implication is that the questioner had not yet reached a stage at which the mysteries of *jên* could be revealed to him.

[3] This may merely mean that his brother Huan T'ui, being an enemy of Confucius, could no longer be regarded by Niu as a brother. When Niu died in 481 B.C. he left behind him at least three brothers.

[4] See textual notes.

the Four Seas¹ are his brothers.' How can any true gentleman grieve that he is without brothers?

6.   Tzu-chang asked the meaning of the term 'illumined.' The Master said, He who is influenced neither by the soaking in of slander nor by the assault of denunciation may indeed be called illumined.² He who is influenced neither by the soaking in of slander nor by the assault of denunciation may indeed be called 'aloof.'

7.   Tzu-kung asked about government. The Master said, Sufficient food, sufficient weapons, and the confidence of the common people. Tzu-kung said, Suppose you had no choice but to dispense with one of these three, which would you forgo? The Master said, Weapons. Tzu-kung said, Suppose you were forced to dispense with one of the two that were left, which would you forgo? The Master said, Food. For from of old death has been the lot of all men; but a people that no longer trusts its rulers is lost indeed.

8.   Chi Tzu-ch'êng³ said, A gentleman is a gentleman in virtue of the stuff he is made of. Culture cannot make gentlemen. Tzu-kung said, I am sorry, Sir, that you should have said that. For the saying goes that 'when a gentleman has spoken, a team of four horses cannot overtake his words.'⁴

Culture is just as important as inborn qualities; and

---

¹ That bound the universe.

² Cf. the section on posthumous titles in the *I Chou Shu*: 'He whom neither slander nor denunciation can influence is called clear-sighted,' i.e. in his choice of subordinates.

³ A statesman of Wei.

⁴ Common people can say what they like, and no harm is done. But a person in your position will at once be quoted as an authority. I read a full stop after *shuo*.

inborn qualities, no less important than culture. Remove the hairs from the skin of a tiger or panther, and what is left looks just like the hairless hide of a dog or sheep.[1]

9.　Duke Ai enquired of Master Yu, saying, It is a year of dearth, and the State has not enough for its needs. What am I to do? Master Yu replied, saying, Have you not got your tithes? The Duke said, Even with two-tenths instead of one, I still should not have enough. What is the use of talking to me about tithes? Master Yu said, When the Hundred Families[2] enjoy plenty, the prince necessarily shares in that plenty.[3] But when the Hundred Families have not enough for their needs, the prince cannot expect to have enough for his needs.

10.　Tzu-chang asked what was meant by 'piling up moral force'[4] and 'deciding when in two minds.'[5] The Master said, 'by piling up moral force' is meant taking loyalty and good faith as one's guiding principles, and migrating to places where right prevails.[6] Again, to love a thing means wanting it to live, to hate a thing means wanting it to perish. But suppose I want

---

[1] The man of good birth is potentially capable of 'patterning his coat' with culture, and thus distinguishing himself from the common herd. But good birth alone, though essential as a basis for culture, is not enough to make a gentleman in the Confucian sense.

[2] All the people.　　　　[3] See textual notes.

[4] No wonder Tzu-chang asked this question; for *ch'ung tê* (a very common expression in old texts) sometimes (e.g. *Hsi Tz'u* I, 7; *Tso Chuan*, Hsi Kung, 7th year) means 'to pile up *tê*, sometimes (e.g. *Tso Chuan*, Wên Kung, 2nd year), 'to do honour to, exalt possessors of *tê*.'

[5] The two phrases in inverted commas rhyme, and no doubt Tzu-chang is asking for an explanation of a particular passage in an ancient rhymed text.

[6] 'If right prevails in a country, then serve it; if right does not prevail, then seek service elsewhere.'

something to live and at the same time want it to perish; that is 'being in two minds.'

> Not for her wealth, oh no!
> But merely for a change.[1]

11.　Duke Ching of Ch'i[2] asked Master K'ung about government. Master K'ung replied saying, Let the prince be a prince, the minister a minister, the father a father and the son a son. The Duke said, How true! For indeed when the prince is not a prince, the minister not a minister, the father not a father, the son not a son, one may have a dish of millet in front of one and yet not know if one will live to eat it.[3]

12.　The Master said, Talk about 'deciding a lawsuit with half a word'—Yu is the man for that.

[1] Couplet from *Song* 105, 3, in which a lady says: I came all this long way to marry you, and you do not give me enough to eat. I shall go back to my country and home. Your thoughts are occupied with a new mate. If it is true that it is not because of her riches, then it is simply for the sake of a change. The last phrase ('only for a change') is susceptible of other interpretations. But it is clearly thus that Confucius understands it, and he uses this story of a man who got a wife from a far country, and then promptly neglected her in favour of someone taken up 'simply for a change,' as an example of 'being in two minds,' 'not knowing one's own mind.'

[2] Died 490 B.C. The last of a long line of powerful and successful dukes. The closing years of his reign were clouded by the intrigues of the Ch'ên Family, which menaced the security of the dynasty (the prince was no longer a prince; ministers, i.e. the leaders of the Ch'ên faction, were no longer content to be ministers); and by succession-squabbles among his sons (the father no longer had the authority of a father; the sons were not content to be sons).

[3] Figure of speech denoting utter insecurity. Legend makes Duke Ching haunted by the fear of death. Cf. *Lieh Tzu* VI, end. Advice very like that which Confucius gives here was given to Duke Ching's ancestor Duke Huan by Kuan Chung. See *Kuo Yü*, Ch. VI, last fol., and *Han Shih Wai Chuan*, X, 9.

Tzu-lu never slept over a promise.[1]

13. The Master said, I could try a civil suit as well as anyone. But better still to bring it about that there were no civil suits![2]

14. Tzu-chang asked about public business. The Master said, Ponder over it untiringly at home; carry it out loyally when the time comes. (Literally, 'Home it untiringly, carry it out loyally.')

15. Repetition of VI, 25.

16. The Master said, The gentleman calls attention to the good points in others; he does not call attention to their defects. The small man does just the reverse of this.

17. Chi K'ang-tzu asked Master K'ung about the art of ruling. Master K'ung said, Ruling (*chêng*) is straightening (*chêng*). If you lead along a straight way, who will dare go by a crooked one?

18. Chi K'ang-tzu was troubled by burglars. He asked Master K'ung what he should do. Master K'ung replied saying, If only you were free from desire, they would not steal even if you paid them to.[4]

---

[1] 'He never agreed to do anything that could not be done till next day; for during the night circumstances might alter and prevent him from carrying out his word.' Such is the interpretation of the early commentators. Chu Hsi takes it in the sense of 'never putting off till the morrow.' Cf. *Shang Tzu's Su Chih*, 'dilatory government.'

[2] Cf. *Ta Hsüeh* ('Great Learning'), Commentary, Para. 4.

[3] See textual notes.

[4] This is a rhetorical way of saying that if K'ang-tzu did not accumulate valuables, he would not be robbed. But coupled with this meaning is the suggestion that the ruler's moral force operates directly on the people, as a magic, not merely as an example.

19.   Chi K'ang-tzu asked Master K'ung about
government, saying, Suppose I were to slay those
who have not the Way in order to help on those who
have the Way, what would you think of it? Master
K'ung replied saying, You are there to rule, not to
slay. If you desire what is good, the people will at
once be good. The essence of the gentleman is that
of wind; the essence of small people is that of grass.
And when a wind passes over the grass, it cannot
choose but bend.[1]

20.   Tzu-chang asked what a knight must be like
if he is to be called 'influential.'[2] The Master said,
That depends on what you mean by 'influential.' Tzu-
chang replied saying, If employed by the State, certain
to win fame, if employed by a Ruling Family, certain
to win fame. The Master said, That describes being
famous; it does not describe being influential. In order
to be influential a man must be by nature straightforward and a lover of right. He must examine men's
words and observe their expressions, and bear in mind
the necessity of deferring to others.[3] Such a one, whether
employed by the State or by a Ruling Family, will
certainly be 'influential'; whereas the man who wins
fame may merely have obtained, by his outward airs,
a reputation for Goodness which his conduct quite
belies. Anyone who makes his claims with sufficient
self-assurance is certain to win fame in a State, certain
to win fame in a Family.

21.   Once when Fan Ch'ih was taking a walk with
the Master under the trees at the Rain Dance altars,
he said, May I venture to ask about 'piling up moral

---

[1] Cf. *Mencius*, III, 1, II, 4.
[2] *Ta*, able to turn his *tê* to account. See VI, 6.
[3] See additional notes.

force,' 'repairing shortcomings' and 'deciding when in two minds'?[1] The Master said, An excellent question. 'The work first; the reward afterwards'; is not that piling up moral force? 'Attack the evil that is within yourself;[2] do not attack the evil that is in others.' Is not this 'repairing shortcomings'?

> 'Because of a morning's blind rage
> To forget one's own safety
> And even endanger one's kith and kin'[3]

is that not a case of 'divided mind'?

22.   Fan Ch'ih asked about the Good (ruler). The Master said, He loves men. He asked about the wise (ruler). The Master said, He knows men. Fan Ch'ih did not quite understand.[4] The Master said, By raising the straight and putting them on top of the crooked, he can make the crooked straight.[5] Fan Ch'ih withdrew, and meeting Tzu-hsia said to him, Just now I was with the Master and asked him about the wise (ruler). He said, By raising the straight and putting them on top of the crooked he can make the crooked straight. What did he mean?

Tzu-hsia said, Oh, what a wealth of instruction is in those words! When Shun had all that is under Heaven, choosing from among the multitude he raised up Kao Yao,[6] and straightway Wickedness disappeared. When T'ang had all that is under Heaven, choosing

---

[1] See above, para. 10. Here all three phrases rhyme; the phrases supplied by Confucius also rhyme, and are presumably quotations from a didactic poem.   [2] See textual notes.

[3] A rhyming triplet. Not knowing the full context either of the poem which the disciple quotes or of the one which Confucius utilizes in his reply, we cannot hope to understand the exact force of this passage.

[4] This applies only to the second answer.

[5] See above, II, 19.   [6] See *The Book of Songs*, p. 268.

from among the multitude he raised up I Yin;[1] and straightway Wickedness disappeared.

23.   Tzu-kung asked about friends. The Master said, inform them loyally and guide them discreetly. If that fails, then desist. Do not court humiliation.

24.   Master Tsêng said, The gentleman by his culture collects friends about him, and through these friends promotes Goodness.

[1] See *The Book of Songs*, p. 278.

BOOK XIII

1. Tzu-lu asked about government. The Master said, Lead them; encourage them! Tzu-lu asked for a further maxim. The Master said, Untiringly.

2. Jan Yung, having become steward of the Chi Family, asked about government. The Master said, Get as much as possible done first by your subordinates.[1] Pardon small offences. Promote men of superior capacity. Jan Yung said, How does one know a man of superior capacity, in order to promote him? The Master said, Promote those you know, and those whom you do not know other people will certainly not neglect.[2]

3. Tzu-lu said, If the prince of Wei were waiting for you to come and administer his country for him, what would be your first measure? The Master said, It would certainly be to correct language. Tzu-lu said, Can I have heard you aright? Surely what you say has nothing to do with the matter. Why should language be corrected? The Master said, Yu! How boorish you are! A gentleman, when things he does not understand are mentioned, should[3] maintain an attitude of reserve. If language is incorrect, then what is said does not concord with what was meant; and if what is said does not concord with what was meant, what is to be done cannot be effected. If what is to be done cannot be effected,[4] then rites and music will not flourish. If rites and music do not flourish, then mutila-

---

[1] So that your time may not be taken up with petty preliminaries.
[2] i.e. will certainly bring to your notice.   [3] See textual notes.
[4] The 'chain argument' clanks rather heavily in English; but it is essential to preserve the form of the original.

tions and lesser punishments will go astray. And if mutilations and lesser punishments go astray, then the people have nowhere to put hand or foot.

Therefore the gentleman uses only such language as is proper for speech, and only speaks of what it would be proper to carry into effect. The gentleman, in what he says, leaves nothing to mere chance.[1]

4.   Fan Ch'ih asked the Master to teach him about farming. The Master said, You had much better consult some old farmer. He asked to be taught about gardening. The Master said, You had much better go to some old vegetable-gardener. When Fan Ch'ih had gone out, the Master said, Fan is no gentleman! If those above them love ritual, then among the common people none will dare to be disrespectful. If those above them love right, then among the common people none will dare to be disobedient. If those above them love good faith, then among the common people none will dare depart from the facts.[2] If a gentleman is like that, the common people will flock to him from all sides with their babies strapped to their backs. What need has he to practise farming?[3]

5.   The Master said, A man may be able to recite the three hundred *Songs;* but, if when given a post in the government, he cannot turn his merits to account, or when sent on a mission to far parts he cannot answer

---

[1] The whole of this highly elaborate, literary paragraph bears the stamp of comparatively late date. See Introduction, p. 22. The links in chain-arguments of this kind are always rhetorical rather than logical; and it would be a waste of time to seek for a causal sequence. Later Confucian literature supplies many examples of such rhetorical 'chains.' For *kou*, 'chance,' see additional notes.

[2] Bear false witness in lawsuits.   [3] See additional notes.

particular questions,¹ however extensive his knowledge may be, of what use is it to him?

6.   The Master said, If the ruler himself is upright, all will go well even though he does not give orders. But if he himself is not upright, even though he gives orders, they will not be obeyed.

7.   The Master said, In their politics Lu and Wei are still brothers.²

8.   The Master said of the Wei grandee Ching,³ He dwelt as a man should dwell in his house. When things began to prosper with him, he said, 'Now they⁴ will begin to be a little more suitable.' When he was better off still, he said, 'Now they will be fairly complete.' When he was really rich, he said, 'Now I shall be able to make them quite beautiful.'

9.   When the Master was going to Wei, Jan Ch'iu drove him. The Master said, What a dense population! Jan Ch'iu said, When the people have multiplied, what next should be done for them? The Master said, Enrich them. Jan Ch'iu said, When one has enriched them, what next should be done for them? The Master said, Instruct them.

10.   The Master said, If only someone were to make

---

¹ Besides delivering his message, he must be able to give an answer of his own to particular enquiries relative to this message.

² On the rise of the Chou dynasty to power, Lu was given to the fourth and Wei to the seventh son of King Wên. The saying expresses, one may suppose, the disillusionment of Confucius on finding that things in Wei were no better than in Lu. In early times, however, it was understood as a commendation of Wei.

³ Flourished about 558 B.C.

⁴ My household rites. For *kou*, see textual notes.

use of me, even for a single year, I could do a great deal; and in three years I could finish off the whole work.

11. The Master said, 'Only if the right sort of people had charge of a country for a hundred years would it become really possible to stop cruelty and do away with slaughter.' How true the saying is!

12. The Master said, If a Kingly Man[1] were to arise, within a single generation Goodness would prevail.

13. The Master said, Once a man has contrived to put himself aright, he will find no difficulty at all in filling any government post. But if he cannot put himself aright, how can he hope to succeed in putting others right?[2]

14. Once when Master Jan came back from Court,[3] the Master said, Why are you so late? He replied, saying, There were affairs of State. The Master said, You must mean private business. If there had been affairs of State, although I am not used,[4] I too should have been bound to hear of them.

15. Duke Ting[5] asked if there were any one phrase that sufficed to save a country. Master K'ung replied saying, No phrase could ever be like that.[6] But here is one that comes near to it. There is a saying among

---

[1] See Introduction, p. 49.

[2] The play on *chêng* 'to straighten, put right' and *chêng* 'to govern' makes this passage impossible to translate satisfactorily.

[3] From the Court of the Chi Family, who had usurped the Duke's powers.   [4] i.e. have no official post.

[5] See above, III, 19.   [6] The stop should come after *jo shih*.

men: 'It is hard to be a prince and not easy to be a minister.' A ruler who really understood that it was 'hard to be a prince' would have come fairly near to saving his country by a single phrase.

Duke Ting said, Is there any one phrase that could ruin a country? Master K'ung said, No phrase could ever be like that. But here is one that comes near to it. There is a saying among men: 'What pleasure is there in being a prince, unless one can say whatever one chooses, and no one dares to disagree?'[1] So long as what he says is good, it is of course good also that he should not be opposed. But if what he says is bad, will it not come very near to his ruining his country by a single phrase?

16.   The 'Duke' of Shê[2] asked about government.[3] The Master said, When the near approve and the distant approach.

17.   When Tzu-hsia was Warden of Chü-fu,[4] he asked for advice about government. The Master said, Do not try to hurry things. Ignore minor considerations. If you hurry things, your personality will not come into play.[5] If you let yourself be distracted by minor considerations, nothing important will ever get finished.

18.   The 'Duke' of Shê addressed Master K'ung saying, In my country there was a man called Upright Kung.[6] His father appropriated a sheep, and Kung

---

[1] This saying also occurs in *Han Fei Tzu*, P'ien, 36.
[2] See above VII, 18. Cf. *Han Fei Tzu*, P'ien, 38 and *Mo Tzu*, P'ien, 46 (*Kêng Chu*).   [3] i.e. about the tokens of good government.
[4] A town in Lu.   [5] For *ta*, see VI, 6.
[6] A legendary paragon of honesty; see *Huai-nan Tzu*, ch. XIII, fol. 6, where he is coupled with Wei-sheng Kao, *Han Fei Tzu*, P'ien, 49, and *Lü Shih Ch'un Ch'iu*, P'ien, 54. See also textual notes.

bore witness against him. Master K'ung said, In my
country the upright men are of quite another sort. A
father will screen his son, and a son his father—which
incidentally[1] does involve a sort of uprightness.

19.   Fan Ch'ih asked about Goodness. The Master
said, In private life, courteous, in public life, diligent,
in relationships, loyal. This is a maxim that no matter
where you may be, even amid the barbarians of the
east or north, may never be set aside.

20.   Tzu-kung asked, 'What must a man be like in
order that he may be called a true knight (of the Way)?
The Master said, he who

> In the furtherance of his own interests
> Is held back by scruples,
> Who as an envoy to far lands
> Does not disgrace his prince's commission

may be called a true knight.
    Tzu-kung said, May I venture to ask who would
rank next? The Master said, He whom his relatives
commend for filial piety, his fellow-villagers, for deference to his elders. Tzu-kung said, May I venture to
ask who would rank next? The Master said, He who
always stands by his word, who undertakes nothing
that he does not bring to achievement. Such a one may
be in the humblest[2] possible circumstances, but all the
same we must give him the next place.
    Tzu-kung said, What would you say of those who
are now conducting the government? The Master
said, Ugh! A set of peck-measures,[3] not worth taking
into account.

[1] For the idiom see II, 18 and VII, 15.
[2] For *k'êng k'êng*, see textual notes and XIV, 42.
[3] 'Mere thimblefuls,' as we should say.

21. The Master said, If I cannot get men who steer a middle course to associate with, I would far rather have the impetuous and hasty.[1] For the impetuous at any rate assert themselves; and the hasty have this at least to be said for them, that there are things they leave undone.[2]

22. The Master said, The men of the south have a saying, 'Without stability[3] a man will not even make a good *shaman* or witch-doctor.'[4] Well said! Of the maxim: if you do not stabilize an act of *tê*, you will get evil by it (instead of good), the Master said, They (i.e. soothsayers) do not simply read the omens.[5]

23. The Master said, The true gentleman is conciliatory but not accommodating. Common people are accommodating but not conciliatory.[6]

24. Tzu-kung asked, saying, What would you feel about a man who was loved by all his fellow-villagers? The Master said, That is not enough.

What would you feel about a man who was hated

---

[1] than the timid and conscientious. See textual notes.

[2] Cf. *Mencius*, VII, 2, XXXVII.

[3] Play on *hêng* (1) a rite for stabilizing, perpetuating the power of good omens and auspicious actions (see additional notes); (2) steadfast, in the moral sense.

[4] For '*shaman* or witch-doctor' the *Li Chi* (33, fol. 3) has 'diviner by the yarrow stalks.'

[5] To 'read the omens' is the first step in any undertaking. Cf. our own word 'inaugurate.' In its moral application Confucius's remark means that it is not enough to embark on the Way; the real test is whether one can continue in it. For 'evil' see textual notes.

[6] 'Accommodating' (*t'ung*) means ready to sacrifice principles to agreement. Cf. the common phrase *kou t'ung*, 'to agree somehow or other,' i.e. at all costs.

The Analects of Confucius   M

by all his fellow-villagers? The Master said, That is
not enough. Best of all would be that the good people
in his village loved him and the bad hated him.

25.   The Master said, The true gentleman is easy
to serve, yet difficult to please.[1] For if you try to please
him in any manner inconsistent with the Way, he
refuses to be pleased; but in using the services of
others he only expects of them what they are capable
of performing. Common people are difficult to serve,
but easy to please. Even though you try to please
them in a manner inconsistent with the Way, they will
still be pleased; but in using the services of others
they expect them (irrespective of their capacities) to
do any work that comes along.

26.   The Master said, The gentleman is dignified,
but never haughty; common people are haughty, but
never dignified.

27.   The Master said, Imperturbable, resolute, tree-
like,[2] slow to speak—such a one is near to Goodness.

28.   Tzu-lu asked, What must a man be like, that
he may be called a true knight of the Way? The
Master said, he must be critical and exacting,[3] but at
the same time indulgent. Then he may be called a
true knight. Critical and exacting with regard to the
conduct of his friends; indulgent towards his brothers.

29, 30.   The Master said, Only when men of the
right sort[4] have instructed a people for seven years

---

[1] Cf. *Hsün Tzu*, P'ien, 27, end.
[2] Or 'wooden,' i.e. simple. But see textual notes.
[3] See textual notes.
[4] i.e. followers of the Way. The 'instruction' is, of course, in virtue,
not in the use of arms.

ought there to be any talk of engaging them in warfare. The Master said, To lead into battle a people
that has not first been instructed is to betray them.[1]

[1] Cf. *Mencius*, VI, 2, VIII, 2, and *Ku-liang Chuan*, Duke Hsi,
23rd year.

BOOK XIV

1.   Yüan Ssu asked about compunction.[1] The Master said, When a country is ruled according to the Way, (the gentleman) accepts rewards. But when a country is not ruled according to the Way, he shows compunction in regard to rewards.

2.   Of the saying 'He upon whom neither love of mastery, vanity, resentment nor covetousness have any hold may be called Good,' the Master said, Such a one has done what is difficult;[2] but whether he should be called Good I do not know.

3.   The Master said, The knight of the Way who thinks only of sitting quietly at home is not worthy to be called a knight.[3]

4.   The Master said, When the Way prevails in the land, be bold in speech and bold in action. When the Way does not prevail, be bold in action but conciliatory in speech.

5.   The Master said, One who has accumulated moral power (*tê*) will certainly also possess eloquence; but he who has eloquence does not necessarily possess moral power. A Good Man will certainly also possess courage; but a brave man is not necessarily Good.

6.   Nan-kung Kuo[4] asked Master K'ung, saying,

[1] With regard to accepting rewards. It will be remembered that it was Yüan Ssu (see above, VI, 3) who was rebuked for refusing a salary. The omission of his surname has led to the supposition that he was the compiler of this chapter.   [2] Cf. VI, 20.
[3] See Introduction, p. 33.   [4] Son of Mêng I Tzu; see II, 5.

Yi[1] was a mighty archer and Ao shook the boat;[2] yet both of them came to a bad end.[3] Whereas Yü and Chi, who devoted themselves to agriculture, came into possession of all that is under Heaven.[4]

At the time our Master made no reply, but when Nan-kung had withdrawn he said, He is a true gentleman indeed, is that man! He has a right apprisal of 'virtue's power' (*tê*),[5] has that man!

7. The Master said, It is possible to be a true gentleman and yet lack Goodness. But there has never yet existed a Good man who was not a gentleman.

8. The Master said, How can he be said truly to love,[6] who exacts no effort from the objects of his love? How can he be said to be truly loyal, who refrains from admonishing the object of his loyalty?

9. The Master said, When a ducal mandate was being prepared[7] P'i Ch'ên[8] first made a rough draft, Shih Shu[9] checked and revised it, Tzu-yü[10] the

[1] A legendary hero. His name is cognate to the word for rainbow.

[2] Shook his enemies out of it, at the great battle in which he destroyed the Shên-hsün clan. See also textual notes.

[3] Yi was slain by his minister Shu (or Cho) of Han. Shu's son Ao was in turn slain by Shao K'ang. For the legend, see *Tso Chuan*, Hsiang Kung, 4th year, and the *T'ien Wên*, verse 90 (Conrady-Erkes edition, p. 246).

[4] For Great Yü drained the land and so made it suitable for agriculture. Hou Chi, from whom the Chou people were descended, was (as his name implies; *chi* = millet) the patron deity of agriculture.

[5] As opposed to physical strength such as that displayed by Yi and Ao.

[6] As a father loves a son or a prince his people.

[7] In the State of Chêng.

[8] Flourished in the middle of the sixth century B.C.

[9] Grandson of Duke Mou of Chêng; died in 506 B.C.

[10] Perhaps Yü Chieh, great-grandson of Duke Mou. He is the 'Receiver of Envoys Tzu-yü of Chêng' mentioned in *Tso Chuan*, Hsiang kung, 29th year.

Receiver of Envoys amended and embellished it;
Tzu-ch'an[1] of Tung-li gave it amplitude and colour.

10, 11.   Someone asked about Tzu-ch'an. The
Master said, A kindly[2] man! Asked about Tzu-hsi[3]
he said, That man! That man! Asked about Kuan
Chung[4] he said, This is the sort of man he was: he
could seize the fief of Pien with its three hundred
villages[5] from its owner, the head of the Po Family;
yet Po, though he 'lived on coarse food'[6] to the end
of his days, never uttered a single word of resentment.[7]
The Master said, To be poor and not resent it[8] is far
harder than to be rich, yet not presumptuous.[9]

12.   The Master said, Mêng Kung Ch'o would
have done well enough as Comptroller of the Chao or

---

[1] See page 110.

[2] The word (see above, p. 104) is often used in a bad sense. Kindli-
ness is often a feeble amends for neglect of duty. Thus Tzu-ch'an took
people across the rivers in his own carriage; but he ought to have
mended the bridges. *Mencius*, IV, 2, I, 2.

[3] A famous minister of the Ch'u State; assassinated in 479 B.C.
According to the accounts of him in the *Tso Chuan* he did and said
much of which Confucius would certainly have approved. The exclamation with which his name is here received is, however, certainly one
of disapprobation. The story that he prejudiced his prince against
Confucius was probably merely invented to explain this passage.

[4] See III, 22.   [5] Cf. *Hsün Tzu*, P'ien, 7, fol. 1.

[6] A stock expression, merely meaning 'in humble circumstances.'

[7] So great was Kuan Chung's prestige. This is the tenor of many
stories about Kuan Chung. He struck with an arrow the man who was
afterwards to become Duke Huan of Ch'i; yet the Duke forgave him
and made him Prime Minister. He broke all the sumptuary laws; yet
it never occurred to the people of Ch'i to regard him as 'presumptuous.'

[8] As the head of the Po Family managed to do.

[9] In which respect, according to Confucius's view (see III, 22), Kuan
Chung signally failed.

Wei families; but he was not fit to be a State minister even in T'êng or Hsüeh.[1]

13. Tzu-lu asked what was meant by 'the perfect man.' The Master said, If anyone had the wisdom of Tsang Wu Chung,[2] the uncovetousness of Mêng Kung Ch'o, the valour of Chuang Tzu of P'ien[3] and the dexterity of Jan Ch'iu,[4] and had graced these virtues by the cultivation of ritual and music, then indeed I think we might call him 'a perfect man.'

He said, But perhaps to-day we need not ask all this of the perfect man. One who, when he sees a chance of gain, stops to think whether to pursue it would be right; when he sees that (his prince) is in danger, is ready to lay down his life; when the fulfilment of an old promise is exacted, stands by what he said long ago—him indeed I think we might call 'a perfect man.'

14. The Master asked Kung-ming Chia[5] about Kung-shu Wên-tzu,[6] saying, Is it a fact that your master neither 'spoke nor laughed nor took?' Kung-

---

[1] Let alone in a great State like Lu. Mêng Kung Ch'o was a Lu politician who flourished about 548 B.C. The Chao and Wei were noble families in Chin.

[2] Middle of the sixth century; grandson of Tsang Wên Chung, V, 17.

[3] The paragon of legendary prowess. See *Hsin Hsü*, VIII.

[4] It is very odd to find the disciple Jan Ch'iu ranged alongside of worthies who belonged to a past generation and contrasted with the men of 'to-day.' I suspect that some earlier member of the Jan family is intended, perhaps Jan Shu, whose marksmanship at a battle between Ch'i and Lu (516 B.C.) is mentioned in the *Tso Chuan*. The familiar name of Jan Ch'iu might then easily have been substituted by a scribe.

[5] Presumably a retainer of Kung-shu Wên-tzu.

[6] Spoken of as 'very aged' in 504 B.C., and apparently dead in 497 B.C., the year (according to the traditional chronology) of Confucius's first visit to Wei, Wen-tzu's native place. See *Tso Chuan*, Ting Kung, 6th year and 13th year.

ming Chia replied saying, The people who told you
this were exaggerating. My master never spoke till
the time came to do so; with the result that people
never felt that they had had too much of his talk. He
never laughed unless he was delighted; so people
never felt they had had too much of his laughter. He
never took[1] unless it was right to do so, so that people
never felt he had done too much taking. The Master
said, Was that so? Can that really have been so?

15.   The Master said, Tsang Wu Chung occupied
the fief of Fang and then demanded from (the Duke
of) Lu that (his brother) Wei should be allowed to
take the fief over from him. It is said that he applied
no pressure upon his prince; but I do not believe it.[2]

16.   The Master said, Duke Wên of Chin could
rise to an emergency, but failed to carry out the plain
dictates of ritual. Duke Huan of Ch'i carried out the
dictates of ritual, but failed when it came to an
emergency.[3]

17.   Tzu-lu said, When Duke Huan put to death
(his brother) Prince Chiu, Shao Hu gave his life in an
attempt to save the prince; but Kuan Chung did not.[4]

[1] Took rewards.
[2] In 550 Tsang Wu Chung, accused of plotting a revolt, was obliged
to go into exile. On his way he seized the fief of Fang, and then sent
word to the Duke offering to proceed into exile and relinquish Fang,
on condition that he should be allowed to hand the fief over to his
brother Tsang Wei. The request was granted. (*Tso Chuan*, Duke
Hsiang, 23rd year.) The later commentators fail to realize that 'Wei'
is a proper name and unsuccessfully attempt to turn it into *wei*, 'to do.'
Translators have followed suit.   [3] See additional and textual notes.
[4] Both Kuan Chung and Shao Hu were supporting Prince Chiu's
claim to the dukedom. Prince Hsiao Po (afterwards to become Duke
Huan) murdered his brother Prince Chiu and seized the ducal throne;
whereupon Kuan Chung, the great opportunist, transferred his allegiance .
to the murderer.

Must one not say that he fell short of Goodness? The Master said, That Duke Huan was able to convene the rulers of all the States without resorting to the use of his war-chariots was due to Kuan Chung. But as to his[1] Goodness, as to his Goodness!

18. Tzu-kung said, I fear Kuan Chung was not Good. When Duke Huan put to death his brother Prince Chiu, Kuan Chung so far from dying on Chiu's behalf became Duke Huan's Prime Minister. The Master said, Through having Kuan Chung as his Minister Duke Huan became leader of the feudal princes, uniting and reducing to good order all that is under Heaven; so that even to-day the people are benefiting by what he then did for them. Were it not for Kuan Chung we might now be wearing our hair loose and folding our clothes to the left![2] We must not expect from him what ordinary men and women regard as 'true constancy'—to go off and strangle oneself in some ditch or drain, and no one the wiser.

19. Kung-shu Wên-tzu, when summoned to office by the Duke (of Wei), brought with him and presented to the Duke his retainer Chuan,[3] the same Chuan who became a State officer. The Master hearing of it[4] said, With good reason was he accorded the title Wên.[5]

---

[1] i.e. Kuan Chung's.

[2] As the barbarians do. Duke Huan stemmed the great invasion of the Ti tribes.

[3] Or Hsien. It is necessary slightly to paraphrase this sentence in order to bring out the meaning with clarity.

[4] As a historical event; not at the time when it happened.

[5] Cf. *I Chou Shu*, 54, fol. 1, 'He who helps commoners to rank and position is called Wên.' So various were Kung-shu Wên-tzu's merits that the business of choosing his posthumous title was unusually difficult. See *Li Chi*, IV, fol. 5.

20.   The Master referred to Duke Ling of Wei as being no follower of the true Way. K'ang-tzu[1] said, How is it then that he does not come to grief? Master K'ung said, He has Chung-shu Yü[2] to deal with foreign envoys and guests, the priest T'o[3] to regulate the ceremonies in his ancestral temple and Wang-sun Chia[4] to command his armies. Why then should he come to grief?

21.   The Master said, Do not be too ready to speak of it,[5] lest the doing of it should prove to be beyond your powers.

22.   When Ch'ên Hêng assassinated Duke Chien of Ch'i, Master K'ung washed his head and limbs,[6] went to Court and informed Duke Ai of Lu, saying, Ch'ên Hêng has slain his prince. I petition that steps should be taken to punish him. The Duke said, You had better inform the Three.[7] Master K'ung said, As I rank next to the Great Officers,[8] I could not do otherwise than lay this information before you. And now your Highness says 'Inform the Three?' He then went to the Three and informed them. They refused his petition. Master K'ung said, As I rank next to the Great Officers, I could not do otherwise than lay this petition before you.

23.   Tzu-lu asked him how to serve a prince. The Master said, Never oppose him by subterfuges.[9]

---

[1] The head of the Chi Family.
[2] Known posthumously as K'ung Wên Tzu. See V, 14.
[3] See VI, 14.   [4] See III, 13.   [5] Goodness. Cf. XII, 3.
[6] As became a suppliant. The assassination took place in 481 B.C.
[7] The heads of the three great families Chi, Shu and Mêng.
[8] Cf. XI, 7. This anecdote, in a very similar form, occurs in the *Tso Chuan*, Ai, 14th year.
[9] But if you have to oppose him, do so openly.

24. The Master said, The gentleman can influence those who are above him; the small man can only influence those who are below him.

25. The Master said, In old days men studied for the sake of self-improvement; nowadays men study in order to impress other people.[1]

26. Ch'ü Po Yü[2] sent a messenger to Master K'ung. Master K'ung bade the man be seated and asked of him saying, What is your master doing? He replied, saying, My master is trying to diminish the number of his failings;[3] but he has not hitherto been successful. When the messenger had gone away, the Master said, What a messenger, what a messenger![4]

27, 28. When the Master said, He who holds no rank in a State does not discuss its policies,[5] Master Tsêng said, 'A true gentleman, even in his thoughts, never departs from what is suitable to his rank.'[6]

29. The Master said, A gentleman is ashamed to let his words outrun his deeds.[7]

---

[1] Cf. *Hsün Tzu*, P'ien, 1.

[2] A famous Wei minister. See below, XV, 6.

[3] Or 'is trying to lessen his offence.' Chü Po Yü may have promised to get Confucius a post in Wei and failed to do so. The message may mean that he is still trying, but has not yet succeeded arranging anything.

[4] This is usually taken as an exclamation of approval. I very much doubt if that is so. [5] See above, VIII, 14.

[6] Tsêng illustrates Confucius's saying by quoting an old maxim, which also figures, in practically identical form, in the first appendix (*Hsiang*) of the *Book of Changes*, section 52. In my paper on the *Book of Changes* (Bulletin of the Museum of Far Eastern Antiquities, No. 5), I quote this saying as though it occurred in the text of the *Book* itself, an error which I take this opportunity of correcting.

[7] See textual notes.

30.   The Master said, the Ways of the true gentleman are three. I myself have met with success in none of them. For he that is really Good is never unhappy, he that is really wise is never perplexed, he that is really brave is never afraid. Tzu-kung said, That, Master, is your own Way![1]

31.   Tzu-kung was always criticizing other people. The Master said, It is fortunate for Ssu that he is so perfect himself as to have time to spare for this. I myself have none.

32.   The Master said, (A gentleman) does not grieve that people do not recognize his merits; he grieves at his own incapacities.

33.   The Master said, Is it the man who 'does not count beforehand upon the falsity of others nor reckon upon promises not being kept,' or he who is conscious beforehand of deceit, that is the true sage?[2]

34.   Wei-shêng Mou said to Master K'ung, 'Ch'iu,[3] what is your object in going round perching now here, now there? Is it not simply to show off the fact that you are a clever talker?' Master K'ung said, I have no desire to be thought a clever talker; but I do not approve of obstinacy.[4]

[1] Is precisely how you yourself behave. Usually taken as referring to Confucius's disclaimer ('I myself have met with success in none,' etc.) and meaning, 'So you yourself say; (but we know that is only due to your modesty, and do not take your words literally).'

[2] See additional and textual notes.

[3] Familiar name of Confucius, the form of address is discourteous. It is surmised that Wei-shêng Mou was a recluse.

[4] It is no use going on and on trying to convert a prince. After a time one must give it up, and try elsewhere.

35. The Master said, The horse Chi[1] was not famed for its strength but for its inner qualities (*tê*).

36. Someone said, What about the saying 'Meet resentment with inner power (*tê*)'?[2] The Master said, In that case, how is one to meet inner power? Rather, meet resentment with upright dealing and meet inner power with inner power.

37. The Master said, The truth is, no one knows me![3] Tzu-kung said, What is the reason that you are not known? The Master said, I do not 'accuse Heaven, nor do I lay the blame on men.'[4]

But the studies[5] of men here below are felt on high, and perhaps after all I am known; not here, but in Heaven!

38. Kung-po Liao spoke against Tzu-lu to the Chi Family. Tzu-fu Ching-po[6] informed the Master saying, I fear my master's[7] mind has been greatly unsettled by this. But in the case of Kung-po Liao, I believe my influence is still great enough to have his carcase exposed in the market-place. The Master said, If it is the will of Heaven that the Way shall prevail, then the Way will prevail. But if it is the will of Heaven

---

[1] A famous horse of ancient times. A rhymed couplet.

[2] The same saying is utilized in the *Tao Tê Ching*, Ch. 63. It originally meant 'Let the ruler meet discontent among his subjects with *tê* and not with violence.' Confucius here uses it in a much more general sense.   [3] No ruler recognizes my merits and employs me.

[4] 'A gentleman neither accuses Heaven nor blames men.' *Mencius*, II, 2, XIII, 1.

[5] The self-training consisting in the study of antiquity.

[6] A retainer of the Chi Family.

[7] Chi K'ang-tzu's.

that the Way should perish, then it must needs perish. What can Kung-po Liao do against Heaven's will?

39.   The Master said, Best of all, to withdraw from one's generation; next to withdraw to another land; next to leave because of a look; next best to leave because of a word.[1]

40.   The Master said, The makers[2] were seven. . . .

41.   Tzu-lu was spending the night at the Stone Gates.[3] The gate-keeper said, Where are you from? Tzu-lu said, From Master K'ung's. The man said, He's the one who 'knows it's no use, but keeps on doing it,' is that not so?

42.   The Master was playing the stone-chimes, during the time when he was in Wei. A man carrying a basket passed the house where he and his disciples had established themselves. He said, How passionately he beats his chimes! When the tune was over, he said, How petty and small-minded![4] A man whose talents

---

[1] This continues the theme of the last paragraph. If *Tao* (the Way) does not prevail, it is better to flee altogether from the men of one's generation, rather than to go round 'perching first here, then there' as Confucius himself had unsuccessfully done, or to wait till the expression of the ruler's face betrays that he is meditating some enormity; or worst of all, to wait till his words actually reveal his intention.

[2] i.e. inventors, 'culture-heroes,' originators of fire, agriculture, metallurgy, boats, carriages, the potter's wheel, the loom. Their names are variously given. It is natural to suppose that the compilers could not agree as to which names Confucius had enumerated, and therefore left the paragraph unfinished.

[3] On the frontiers of Lu and Ch'i? Both this and the next paragraph belong to popular legend rather than to the traditions of the school. Cf. Book XVIII.

[4] Cf. XIII, 20. He sees in Confucius's passionate playing an expression of discontent at his failure to get office.

no one recognizes has but one course open to him—to mind his own[1] business! 'If the water is deep, use the stepping-stones; if it is shallow, then hold up your skirts.'[2] The Master said, That is indeed[3] an easy way out!

43. Tzu-chang said, The Books[4] say, 'When Kao Tsung was in the Shed of Constancy,[5] he did not speak for three years.' What does this mean? The Master said, Not Kao Tsung in particular. All the men of old did this. Whenever a prince died, the ministers (of the last prince) all continued in their offices, taking their orders from the Prime Minister;[6] and this lasted for three years.

44. The Master said, So long as the ruler loves ritual,[7] the people will be easy to handle.

45. Tzu-lu asked about the qualities of a true gentleman. The Master said, He cultivates in himself the capacity to be diligent in his tasks. Tzu-lu said, Can he not go further than that? The Master said, He cultivates in himself the capacity to ease the lot of other people.[8] Tzu-lu said, Can he not go further than that? The Master said, He cultivates in himself the capacity to ease the lot of the whole populace. If he

---

[1] See textual notes.

[2] In *Song* 54. The meaning here is, 'Take the world as you find it.'

[3] *Kuo* here means '*en effet*,' not 'effective,' 'resolute.' Cf. *Mencius*, IV, 2, XXXII.

[4] See *Shu Ching*, Wu Yi. Cf. *Kuo Yü*, 20, fol. 2.

[5] i.e. in mourning for his father. The *liang-an* was a penthouse set up for the habitation of a mourner against the wall of a tomb. Kao Tsung's traditional date is 1324–1266 B.C.

[6] Cf. *Mencius*, III, 1, II, 4.

[7] i.e. carries on immemorial usages and customs.

[8] Other gentlemen.

can do that, could even Yao or Shun find cause to criticize him?[1]

46.   Yüan Jang sat waiting for the Master in a sprawling position.[2] The Master said, Those who when young show no respect to their elders achieve nothing worth mentioning when they grow up. And merely to live on, getting older and older, is to be a useless pest.[3]
And he struck him across the shins with his stick.

47.   A boy from the village of Ch'uëh used to come with messages. Someone asked about him, saying, Is he improving himself?[4] The Master said, Judging by the way he sits in grown-up people's places and walks alongside of people older than himself, I should say he was bent upon getting on quickly rather than upon improving himself.

[1] Cf. VI, 28.
[2] Whereas he ought to have been standing when his teacher arrived and only to have sat down when told to do so.
[3] This paragraph is usually translated in a way which makes it appear that Yüan Jang was an old man, whom Confucius brutally reproaches with 'being old and not dying.' It is, on the contrary, clear that he was a young man, like the boy of the next paragraph.
[4] i.e. taking advantage of his visits to the house of Confucius.

BOOK XV

1. Duke Ling of Wei asked Master K'ung about the marshalling of troops. Master K'ung replied saying, About the ordering of ritual vessels I have some knowledge; but warfare is a thing I have never studied. Next day he resumed his travels.[1] In Ch'ên supplies fell short and his followers became so weak that they could not drag themselves on to their feet. Tzu-lu came to the Master and said indignantly, Is it right that even gentlemen should be reduced to such straits? The Master said, A gentleman can withstand hardships; it is only the small man who, when submitted to them, is swept off his feet.[2]

2. The Master said, Ssu,[3] I believe you look upon me as one whose aim is simply to learn and retain in mind as many things as possible. He replied, That is what I thought. Is it not so? The Master said, No; I have one (thread) upon which I string them all.[4]

3. The Master said, Yu,[5] Those who understand moral force (*tê*) are few.

4. The Master said, Among those that 'ruled by inactivity'[6] surely Shun may be counted. For what action did he take? He merely placed himself gravely and reverently with his face due south;[7] that was all.

---

[1] There is a similar story in the *Tso Chuan*, Ai Kung, 11th year.
[2] As though by a flood.   [3] Familiar name of Tzu-kung.
[4] Cf. IV, 15.   [5] Familiar name of Tzu-lu.
[6] *Wu-wei*, the phrase applied by the Taoists to the immobility of self-hypnosis.
[7] The position of the ruler. Shun was a Divine Sage (*shêng*) whose *tê* was so great that it sufficed to guide and transform the people.

5.   Tzu-chang asked about getting on with people.
The Master said, Be loyal and true to your every word,
serious and careful in all you do; and you will get on
well enough, even though you find yourself among
barbarians. But if you are disloyal and untrustworthy
in your speech, frivolous and careless in your acts, even
though you are among your own neighbours, how can
you hope to get on well? When standing,[1] see these
principles ranged before you; in your carriage, see
them resting on the yoke. Then you may be sure that
you will get on. Tzu-chang accordingly inscribed the
maxim upon his sash.

6.   The Master said, Straight and upright indeed
was the recorder Yü![2] When the Way prevailed in the
land he was (straight) as an arrow; when the Way
ceased to prevail, he was (straight) as an arrow. A
gentleman indeed is Ch'ü Po Yü.[3] When the Way
prevailed in his land, he served the State; but when
the Way ceased to prevail, he knew how to 'wrap it[4] up
and hide it in the folds of his dress.'

7.   The Master said, Not to talk to[5] one who could
be talked to, is to waste a man. To talk to those who
cannot be talked to, is to waste one's words. 'He who

[1] In your place at Court. For 'ranged,' see textual notes.
[2] Having failed to persuade Duke Ling of Wei to use the services
of Ch'ü Po Yü, the recorder Yü gave directions that when he (the
recorder) died his body should not receive the honours due to a minister,
as a posthumous protest against the Duke Ling's offences. The story is
told in *Han Shih Wai Chuan*, 7, and many other places.
[3] Ch'ü Po Yü left Wei owing to the tyrannical conduct of Duke
Hsien in 559 B.C. No tense is expressed in the first clause. I say 'is'
because in XIV, 26, Ch'ü Po Yü appears to be still alive. It is, however,
not very probable that he was, as legend asserts, still alive when
Confucius visited Wei in 495 B.C.
[4] His jewel; i.e. his talents.   [5] About the Way. Cf. VII, 28.

is truly wise never wastes a man';[1] but on the other hand, he never wastes his words.

8. The Master said, Neither the knight who has truly the heart of a knight nor the man of good stock who has the qualities that belong to good stock[2] will ever seek life at the expense of Goodness; and it may be that he has to give his life in order to achieve Goodness.

9. Tzu-kung asked how to become Good. The Master said, A craftsman, if he means to do good work, must first sharpen his tools. In whatever State you dwell

> Take service with such of its officers as are worthy,
> Make friends with such of its knights as are Good.

10. Yen Hui asked about the making of a State. The Master said, One would go by the seasons of Hsia;[3] as State-coach for the ruler one would use that of Yin,[4] and as head-gear of ceremony wear the Chou hat.[5] For music one would take as model the Succession Dance,[6] and would do away altogether with the tunes

---

[1] I suspect that this is a proverbial saying.

[2] The written forms of *chih* and *jên* are here half-punningly insisted upon.

[3] It was believed that in the Hsia dynasty the year began in the spring.

[4] Which were less ornate than those of Chou, say the commentators. But this is a mere guess. *Han Fei Tzu*, P'ien, 10, says that the Yin invented state coaches.

[5] Which had some resemblance to our scholastic mortar-board.

[6] See above. III, 25 and VII, 13.

of Chêng;[1] one would also keep clever talkers at a distance. For the tunes of Chêng are licentious and clever talkers are dangerous.

11.　　The Master said, He who will not worry about what is far off will soon find something worse[2] than worry close at hand.

12.　　The Master said, In vain have I looked for one whose desire to build up his moral power was as strong as sexual desire.[3]

13.　　The Master said, Surely one would not be wrong in calling Tsang Wên Chung[4] a stealer of other men's ranks? He knew that Liu-hsia Hui was the best man for the post, yet would not have him as his colleague.[5]

14.　　The Master said, To demand much from one-self and little from others is the way (for a ruler) to banish discontent.

15.　　The Master said, If a man does not continually ask himself 'What am I to do about this, what am I to do about this?' there is no possibility of my doing anything about him.

16.　　The master said, Those who are capable of spending a whole day together without ever once discussing questions of right or wrong, but who content

[1] The words to these tunes are in the seventh book of the *Songs*. But it was probably to the character of the music not to that of the words that Confucius objected. See additional notes.

[2] *Yu* is a much stronger word than *lü*.　[3] Cf. IX, 17.　[4] See V, 17.

[5] 'Degraded him,' says the *Tso Chuan*, Wên Kung, 2nd year. For Liu-hsia Hui, see below, XVIII, 2.

themselves¹ with performing petty acts of clemency,²
are indeed difficult.³

17. The Master said, The gentleman who takes the
right as his material to work upon and ritual as the
guide in putting what is right into practice, who is
modest in setting out his projects and faithful in
carrying them to their conclusion, he indeed is a true
gentleman.

18. The Master said, A gentleman is distressed by
his own lack of capacity; he is never distressed at the
failure of others to recognize his merits.

19. The Master said, A gentleman has reason to
be distressed if he ends his days without making a
reputation for himself.⁴

20. The Master said, 'The demands that a gentleman makes are upon himself; those that a small man
makes are upon others.'⁵

21. The Master said, A gentleman is proud, but
not quarrelsome, allies himself with individuals, but
not with parties.

22. The Master said, A gentleman does not

> Accept men because of what they say,
> Nor reject sayings, because the speaker is
> what he is.

---

¹ 'Satisfy their consciences,' as we should say.
² See textual notes.   ³ To lead into the Way.
⁴ Which contradicts the saying before. As both sayings completely
lack context, it would be a waste of time to try to reconcile the
contradiction.
⁵ This is a proverbial saying, capable of many interpretations. To
the Taoists it meant 'Seek Tao in yourself (through the practice of
quietism) and not in the outside world.'

23.   Tzu-kung asked saying, Is there any single saying that one can act upon all day and every day?[1] The Master said, Perhaps the saying about considera-tion:[2] 'Never do to others what you would not like them to do to you.'[3]

24.   The Master said, In speaking of the men of the day I have always refrained from praise and blame alike. But if there is indeed anyone whom I have praised, there is a means by which he may be tested. For the common people here round us are just such stuff as the three dynasties[4] worked upon in the days when they followed the Straight Way.

25.   The Master said, I can still remember the days when a scribe left blank spaces,[5] and when someone using a horse (for the first time)[6] hired a man to drive it.[7] But that is all over now!

26.   The Master said, Clever talk can confound the workings of moral force, just as small impatiences can confound great projects.

27.   The Master said, When everyone dislikes a man, enquiry is necessary; when everyone likes a man, enquiry is necessary.

---

[1] For *chung shên*. Cf. IX, 26   [2] Ch. IV, 15.
[3] Cf. V, 11.   [4] Hsia, Yin and Chou.
[5] When in doubt; instead of trusting to his imagination.
[6] Some such words must have slipped out. Pao Hsien's (first century A.D.) commentary suggests that they were still there in his text.
[7] Another instance of diffidence, parallel to 'leaving blanks.' See additional notes.

28.   The Master said, A man can enlarge his Way; but there is no Way that can enlarge a man.[1]

29.   The Master said, To have faults and to be making no effort to amend them is to have faults indeed![2]

30.   The Master said, I once spent a whole day without food and a whole night without sleep, in order to meditate.[3] It was no use. It is better to learn.[4]

31.   The Master said, A gentleman, in his plans, thinks of the Way; he does not think how he is going to make a living. Even farming sometimes entails[5] times of shortage; and even learning may incidentally lead to high pay. But a gentleman's anxieties concern the progress of the Way; he has no anxiety concerning poverty.

32.   The Master said, He whose wisdom brings him into power, needs Goodness to secure that power. Else, though he get it, he will certainly lose it. He whose wisdom brings him into power and who has Goodness whereby to secure that power, if he has not dignity wherewith to approach the common people, they will not respect him. He whose wisdom has

---

[1] Without effort on his part. Play on 'Way' and 'road.' 'A man can widen a road . . . ,' etc.

[2] Whereas one should never condemn one who is amending his faults. The *Ku-liang Chuan* (Hsi, 22) adds two words, which give a very different turn to the saying. See textual notes.   [3] See II, 15.

[4] This paragraph reads at first sight as though it were the record of a personal experience. In reality it is meant in a much more general way. *Hsün Tzu* (P'ien, i, fol. 2) quotes the proverb 'I spent a whole day meditating; I should have done better to learn. I stood on tip-toe in order to get a good view; I should have done better to climb a hill.'

[5] For the idiom, see II, 18; VII, 15; XIII, 18 and XIX, 6.

brought him into power, who has Goodness whereby
to secure that power and dignity wherewith to approach
the common people, if he handle them contrary to the
prescriptions of ritual, is still a bad ruler.[1]

33.   The Master said, It is wrong for a gentleman
to have knowledge of menial matters[2] and proper that
he should be entrusted with great responsibilities. It
is wrong for a small man to be entrusted with great
responsibilities, but proper that he should have a
knowledge of menial matters.

34.   The Master said, Goodness is more to the
people than water and fire. I have seen men lose their
lives when 'treading upon' water and fire; but I have
never seen anyone lose his life through 'treading upon'
Goodness.[3]

35.   The Master said, When it comes to Goodness
one need not avoid competing with one's teacher.

36.   The Master said, From a gentleman consistency
is expected, but not blind fidelity.

[1] This paragraph with its highly literary, somewhat empty elabora-
tion, and its placing of ritual on a pinnacle far above Goodness, is
certainly one of the later additions to the book. For the chain-like
rhetorical development, cf. XIII, 3.

[2] The usual interpretation is 'It is impossible for us to recognize a
gentleman when he is merely employed in small matters.' But I do not
see how such a sense can be forced out of the text as it stands. For the
undesirability of a gentleman's having miscellaneous accomplishments,
cf. IX, 6.

[3] A symbolic 'treading upon fire' is still used in China as a rite of
purification. According to the *Lun-hêng* (P'ien, 45) a processional
wading along the river was part of the rain-making ceremony. Confucius
says ʌnat Goodness (on the part of the ruler) is a greater and safer
purifier than even water or fire.

37. The Master said, In serving one's prince one should be

> Intent upon the task,
> Not bent upon the pay.

38. The Master said, There is a difference[1] in instruction but none in kind.

39. The Master said, With those who follow a different Way it is useless to take counsel.

40. The Master said, In official speeches[2] all that matters is to get one's meaning through.

41. The Music-master Mien came to see him. When he reached the steps, the Master said, Here are the steps.[3] When he reached the mat, the Master said, Here is the mat. When everyone was seated the Master informed him saying, So-and-so is here, So-and-so is there. When the Music-master Mien had gone, Tzu-chang asked saying, 'Is that the recognized way to talk to a Music-master?' The Master said, Yes, certainly it is the recognized way to help a Music-master.

[1] Between us and the Sages. Any of us could turn into a Yao or Shun, if we trained ourselves as they did. Cf. XVII, 2, and *Mencius*, II, 1, II, 28.

[2] *Tz'u* means pleas, messages, excuses for being unable to attend to one's duties, etc.   [3] Music-masters were blind.

BOOK XVI

1. 1 The Head of the Chi Family decided to attack Chuan-yü.[1] 2 Jan Ch'iu and Tzu-lu[2] came to see Master K'ung and said to him, The Head of the Chi Family has decided to take steps with regard to Chuan-yü. 3 Master K'ung said, Ch'iu, I fear you must be held responsible for this crime. 4 Chuan-yü was long ago appointed by the Former Kings[3] to preside over the sacrifices to Mount Tung-mêng. Moreover, it lies within the boundaries of our State, and its ruler is a servant of our own Holy Ground and Millet. How can such an attack be justified?

5 Jan Ch'iu said, It is our employer who desires it. Neither of us two ministers desires it. 6 Master K'ung said, Ch'iu, among the sayings of Chou Jên[4] there is one which runs: 'He who can bring his powers into play steps into the ranks;[5] he who cannot, stays behind.' Of what use to anyone are such counsellors as you, who see your master tottering, but do not give him a hand, see him falling, but do not prop him up? 7 More-over, your plea is a false one. For if a tiger or wild buffalo escapes from its cage or a precious ornament of tortoise-shell or jade gets broken in its box, whose fault is it?[6]

8 Jan Ch'iu said, The present situation is this: Chuan-yü is strongly fortified and is close to Pi.[7] If

---

[1] A small independent State within the borders of Lu.
[2] Who were in the service of the Chi Family.
[3] The Chou Emperors.
[4] An ancient sage. Further sayings by him are quoted in *Tso Chuan*, Yin Kung, 6th year, and Chao Kung, 5th year. I fancy he is the same person as the Ch'ih Jên of the *Shu Ching* (P'an Kêng, Part I).
[5] Military metaphor, here applied to politics.
[6] i.e. it is the fault of the person in charge of these things.
[7] The chief castle of the Chi Family.

he does not take it now, in days to come it will certainly give trouble to his sons or grandsons. 9 Master K'ung said, Ch'iu, a true gentleman, having once denied that he is in favour of a course, thinks it wrong to make any attempt to condone that course. 10 Concerning the head of a State or Family I have heard the saying:

> He is not concerned lest his people should
>   be poor,
> But only lest what they have should be ill-
>   apportioned.
> He is not concerned lest they should be few,
> But only lest they should be divided against
>   one another.[1]

And indeed, if all is well-apportioned, there will be no poverty; if they are not divided against one another, there will be no lack of men.[2] 11 If such a state of affairs exists, yet the people of far-off lands still do not submit, then the ruler must attract them by enhancing the prestige (*tê*) of his culture; and when they have been duly attracted,[3] he contents them. And where there is contentment there will be no upheavals.

12 To-day with you two, Yu and Ch'iu, acting as counsellors to your master, the people of far lands do not submit to him, and he is not able to attract them. The State itself is divided and tottering, disrupted and cleft, but he can do nothing to save it and is now planning to wield buckler and axe within the borders of his own land. I am afraid that the troubles of the

---

[1] The text of this little poem is slightly corrupt. See textual notes.

[2] The words *an wu ch'ing* have become displaced. They belong after *an chih*, 21 characters further on; see textual notes.

[3] For the ideas underlying this passage, see Introduction, p. 39.

Chi Family are due not to what is happening in Chuan-yü, but to what is going on behind the screen-wall of his own gate.[1]

2.   Master K'ung said, When the Way prevails under Heaven all orders concerning ritual, music and punitive expeditions are issued by the Son of Heaven himself. When the Way does not prevail, such orders are issued by the feudal princes; and when this happens, it is to be observed that ten generations rarely pass before the dynasty falls. If such orders are issued by State Ministers, five generations rarely pass before they lose their power. When the retainers[2] of great Houses seize a country's commission,[3] three generations rarely pass before they lose their power. When the Way prevails under Heaven, policy is not decided by Ministers; when the Way prevails under Heaven, commoners[4] do not discuss public affairs.

3.   Master K'ung said, Power over the exchequer was lost by the Ducal House[5] five generations ago, and government has been in the hands of Ministers[6]

---

[1] His own lack of *tê* and the fact that he has bad advisers.

[2] Such as Yang Huo, who seized power in Lu in 505 B.C.

[3] The *ming* of a State is the charge whereby the Emperor appoints its feudal lord.

[4] People not belonging to the Imperial family.

[5] Surrendered by the Duke to the Three Families.

[6] The heads of the Chi Family. The first three paragraphs of this book seem to form a connected unity. It was under Chi K'ang-tzu (succeeded in 492 B.C.) that Tzu-lu and Jan Ch'iu were colleagues. If we take paragraph 3 as having been spoken subsequent to 492 B.C., the five powerless Dukes must be Ch'êng, Hsiang, Chao, Ting and Ai; and the four Ministers, Chi Wu-tzu, Chi P'ing-tzu, Chi Huan-tzu and Chi K'ang-tzu. But it would be a mistake to try to fit into too strict a chronology sayings that may be purely legendary. For the late date of Book XVI, see Introduction, p. 25.

for four generations. Small wonder that the descendants of the Three Huan¹ are fast losing their power!

4.　Master K'ung said, There are three sorts of friend that are profitable, and three sorts that are harmful. Friendship with the upright, with the true-to-death and with those who have heard much is profitable. Friendship with the obsequious,² friendship with those who are good at accommodating their principles, friendship with those who are clever at talk² is harmful.

5.　Master K'ung said, There are three sorts of pleasure that are profitable, and three sorts of pleasure that are harmful. The pleasure got from the due ordering of ritual and music, the pleasure got from discussing the good points in the conduct of others, the pleasure of having many wise friends is profitable. But pleasure got from profligate enjoyments, pleasure got from idle gadding about, pleasure got from comfort and ease is harmful.

6.　Master K'ung said, There are three mistakes that are liable to be made when waiting upon a gentleman. To speak before being called upon to do so; this is called forwardness.² Not to speak when called upon to do so; this is called secretiveness. To speak without without first noting the expression of his face; this is called 'blindness.'³

7.　Master K'ung said, There are three things against which a gentleman is on his guard. In his

---

¹ The Three Families, Chi, Mêng and Shu.
² See textual notes.　　　　³ Cf. *Hsün Tzu*, P'ien, 1, end.

youth, before his blood and vital humours[1] have settled
down, he is on his guard against lust. Having reached
his prime, when the blood and vital humours have
finally hardened, he is on his guard against strife.
Having reached old age, when the blood and vital
humours are already decaying, he is on his guard
against avarice.

8.   Master K'ung said, There are three things that
a gentleman fears: he fears the will of Heaven, he
fears great men,[2] he fears the words of the Divine
Sages. The small man does not know the will of Heaven
and so does not fear it. He treats great men with con-
tempt, and scoffs at the words of the Divine Sages.

9.   Master K'ung said, Highest are those who are
born wise. Next are those who become wise by learning.
After them come those who have to toil painfully in
order to acquire learning. Finally, to the lowest class
of the common people belong those who toil painfully
without ever managing to learn.

10.   Master K'ung said, The gentleman has nine
cares. In seeing he is careful to see clearly, in hearing
he is careful to hear distinctly, in his looks he is careful
to be kindly; in his manner to be respectful, in his
words to be loyal, in his work to be diligent. When
in doubt he is careful to ask for information; when
angry he has a care for the consequences, and when

---

[1] The physiological theories which underlie this paragraph are, I
suspect, considerably posterior to Confucius.

[2] *Ta-jen* means (1) giants; (2) ministers, persons in authority;
(3) morally great, as in *Mencius*, IV, 2, VI: IV, 2, XI and XII, etc.
Probably the meaning here is 'morally great'; that is to say, people
like Confucius himself.

he sees a chance of gain, he thinks carefully whether
the pursuit of it would be consonant with the Right.

11, 12.   Master K'ung said, 'When they see what
is good, they grasp at it as though they feared it would
elude them. When they see what is not good, they test
it cautiously, as though putting a finger into hot water.'
I have heard this saying; I have even seen such men.[1]
'It is by dwelling in seclusion that they seek the fulfilment of their aims; it is by deeds of righteousness that
they extend the influence of their Way.' I have heard
this saying; but I have never seen such men. 'Duke
Ching of Ch'i had a thousand teams of horses; but on
the day of his death the people could think of no good
deed for which to praise him.[2] Po I and Shu Ch'i[3]
starved at[4] the foot of Mount Shou-yang; yet the
people sing their praises down to this very day.' Does
not this saying illustrate the other?[5]

13.   Tzu-ch'in[6] questioned Po Yü[7] saying, As his
son[8] you must after all surely have heard something
different from what the rest of us hear. Po Yü replied
saying, No. Once when he was standing alone and I
was hurrying[9] past him across the court-yard, he said,

---

[1] These two clauses are accidentally inverted in the original.

[2] This is clearly the same formula as VIII, 1 (end), where, however,
it is used in praise and not, as here, in condemnation.   [3] See V, 22.

[4] This form of the preposition, which occurs twice here but nowhere
else in the *Analects*, marks the passage as a quotation from some other
text. Moreover, the passage is closed by a formula (*ch'i ssu chih wei*)
which regularly follows quotations.

[5] i.e. are not Po I and Shu Ch'i examples of people who dwelt in
seclusion to fulfil their aims, by deeds of righteousness extended the
influence of the Way?

[6] See I, 10.   [7] Confucius's son; see XI, 7.

[8] *Tzu* here means 'son' and not 'you, my master.'

[9] As a sign of respect.

Have you studied the *Songs*? I replied saying, No. (He said) If you do not study the *Songs*, you will find yourself at a loss in conversation. So I retired and studied the *Songs*. Another day he was again standing alone, and as I hurried across the courtyard, he said, Have you studied the rituals? I replied saying, No. (He said) If you do not study the rituals, you will find yourself at a loss how to take your stand.[1] So I retired and studied the rituals. These two things I heard from him.

Tzu-ch'in came aw?v delighted, saying, I asked about one point, but got information about three. I learnt about the *Songs*, about the rituals, and also learnt that a gentleman keeps his son at a distance.[2]

14.   The wife of the ruler of a State is referred to by the ruler as 'That person.' She refers to herself as Little Boy. The people of the country call her 'That person of the Prince's.' When speaking of her to people of another State the ruler calls her 'This lonely one's little prince.' But people of another State likewise call her 'That person of the Prince's.'[3]

----

[1] On public occasions.

[2] The reasons why a gentleman must not teach his own son are discussed in *Mencius*, IV, 1, XVIII. There is a definite ritual severance between father and son. A father may not carry his son in his arms. A son may not, when sacrifice is being made to his deceased father, act as the 'medium' into whom the spirit of the deceased passes. See *Li Chi*, I, fol. 5.

[3] This paragraph is a passage on etiquette from some old handbook of ritual, and was probably inserted here merely because it was found along with the manuscript of this *p'ien* ('chapter'). See additional notes, and cf. *Li Chi*, II, fol. 3.

BOOK XVII

1. Yang Huo[1] wanted to see Master K'ung; but Master K'ung would not see him. He sent Master K'ung a sucking pig. Master K'ung, choosing a time when he knew Yang Huo would not be at home, went to tender acknowledgment; but met him in the road. He spoke to Master K'ung, saying, 'Come here, I have something to say to you.' What he said was, 'Can one who hides his jewel[2] in his bosom and lets his country continue to go astray be called Good? Certainly not. Can one who longs to take part in affairs, yet time after time misses the opportunity to do so— can such a one be called wise? Certainly not.[3] The days and months go by, the years do not wait upon our bidding.' Master K'ung said, All right;[4] I am going to serve.

2. The Master said, By nature, near together; by practice far apart.[5]

3. The Master said, It is only the very wisest and the very stupidest who cannot change.

4. When the Master went to the walled town of

---

[1] See XVI, 2, note. For the anecdote, cf. *Mencius;* III, 2, VII, 3. For 'sent' see textual notes.

[2] i.e. his talents. Cf. XV, 6.

[3] Yang Huo answers his own rhetorical questions, a common formula in Chinese.

[4] The form of assent Confucius uses implies reluctance. This story, like those in Books XVIII and XIII, certainly originated in non-Confucian circles and comes from the same sort of source as the Confucius Anecdotes in the Taoist works *Chuang Tzu* and *Lieh Tzu.*

[5] This proverbial saying has wide possibilities of application. It here presumably means that goodness is a matter of training and application and not an inborn quality.

Wu,[1] he heard the sound of stringed instruments and singing. Our Master said with a gentle[2] smile, 'To kill a chicken one does not use an ox-cleaver.'[3] Tzu-yu replied saying, I remember once hearing you say, 'A gentleman who has studied the Way will be all the tenderer towards his fellow-men; a commoner who has studied the Way will be all the easier to employ.' The Master said, My disciples, what he says is quite true. What I said just now was only meant as a joke.

5. Kung-shan Fu-jao,[4] when he was holding the castle of Pi in revolt (against the Chi Family), sent for the Master, who would have liked to go; but Tzu-lu did not approve of this and said to the Master, After having refused in so many cases, why go to Kung-shan of all people? The Master said, It cannot be for nothing[5] that he has sent for me. If anyone were to use me, I believe I could make a 'Chou in the east.'[6]

6. Tzu-chang asked Master K'ung about Goodness. Master K'ung said, He who could put the Five into practice everywhere under Heaven would be Good. Tzu-chang begged to hear what these were. The Master said, Courtesy, breadth, good faith, diligence

[1] Where Tzu-yu was in command. See VI, 12. [2] See textual notes.
[3] A saying of proverbial type meaning, in effect, that in teaching music to the inhabitants of this small town Tzu-yu is 'casting pearls before swine.' The proverb may well have had a second, balancing clause, here alluded to, but not expressed; such as, 'To teach commoners one does not use a zithern.'
[4] Warden of Pi, the chief stronghold of the Chi Family. He revolted in 502, but in 498 he fled to Ch'i and later to Wu where he is said to have plotted, in a spirit of petty revenge, against his native State of Lu.
[5] Confucius believes that Kung-shan intends to restore the Duke to his rightful powers.
[6] Create a second Golden Age, comparable to the early days of the Chou dynasty.

and clemency. 'He who is courteous is not scorned,
he who is broad wins the multitude, he who is of good
faith is trusted by the people, he who is diligent
succeeds in all he undertakes, he who is clement can
get service from the people.'[1]

7.   Pi Hsi[2] summoned the Master, and he would
have liked to go. But Tzu-lu said, I remember your
once saying, 'Into the house of one who is in his own
person doing what is evil, the gentleman will not enter.'
Pi Hsi is holding Chung-mou[3] in revolt. How can
you think of going to him? The Master said, It is
true that there is such a saying. But is it not also said
that there are things 'So hard that no grinding will
ever wear them down,' that there are things 'So white
that no steeping will ever make them black'? Am I
indeed to be forever like the bitter gourd that is only
fit to hang up,[4] but not to eat?[5]

8.   The Master said, Yu, have you ever been told
of the Six Sayings about the Six Degenerations?[6] Tzu-lu
replied, No, never. (The Master said) Come, then; I
will tell you. Love of Goodness without love of learning[7]
degenerates into silliness. Love of wisdom without love
of learning degenerates into utter lack of principle.
Love of keeping promises without love of learning
degenerates into villainy.[8] Love of uprightness without
love of learning[9] degenerates into harshness. Love of

---

[1] This is almost certainly a quotation from some text of the *Shu
Ching.* Cf. XX, 1, where most of it reappears.   [2] A Chin officer.
[3] A town in Wei, captured by the Chin (in 490?).
[4] Till it is dry and can be used as a vessel.
[5] Play on two senses of *shih* (1) to eat; (2) to get a salary, an official
post.   [6] See textual notes.   [7] i.e. learning the Way of the ancients.
[8] i.e. keeping regrettable pacts and promises to the detriment of *i*
('what is right under the circumstances').
[9] Like that of Upright Kung, XIII, 18.

courage without love of learning degenerates into turbulence.[1] Love of courage without love of learning degenerates into mere recklessness.

9.   The Master said, Little ones, Why is it that none of you study the *Songs*? For the *Songs* will help you to incite people's emotions, to observe their feelings, to keep company, to express your grievances. They may be used at home in the service of one's father; abroad, in the service of one's prince.[2] Moreover, they will widen your acquaintance with the names[3] of birds, beasts, plants and trees.

10.   The Master addressed Po Yü[4] saying, Have you done the *Chou Nan* and the *Shao Nan*[5] yet? He who has not even done the *Chou Nan* and the *Shao Nan* is as though he stood with his face pressed against a wall!

11.   The Master said, Ritual, ritual! Does it mean no more than presents of jade and silk?[6] Music, music! Does it mean no more than bells and drums?[7]

12.   The Master said, To assume an outward air of fierceness when inwardly trembling is (to take a com-

---

[1] The tendency to fling oneself into any revolutions or upheavals that are going on in the world around one.

[2] For the uses of the *Songs* here inculcated, see *The Book of Songs*, p. 335.

[3] i.e. the 'correct names,' the names in the ancient Court dialect used in ritual, as opposed to the local names.

[4] Son of Confucius. See XVI, 13.

[5] The first two books of the *Songs*.

[6] Cf. *Hsün Tzu*, P'ien, 27, fol. 1.

[7] For tne particle *yün*, see my paper in *Bulletin of the School of Oriental Studies*, Vol. VII, pt. III, 1934.

parison from low walks of life) as dishonest as to sneak
into places where one has no right to be, by boring a
hole or climbing[1] through a gap.

13. The Master said, The 'honest villager' spoils[2]
true virtue (*tê*).

14. The Master said, To tell in the lane what you
have heard on the highroad is to throw merit (*tê*) away.

15. The Master said, How could one ever possibly
serve one's prince alongside of such low-down creatures?
Before they have got office, they think about nothing
but how to get it; and when they have got it, all they
care about is to avoid losing it. And so soon as they
see themselves in the slightest danger of losing it, there
is no length to which they will not go.

16. In old days the common people had three faults,
part[3] of which they have now lost. In old days the
impetuous were merely impatient of small restraints;
now they are utterly insubordinate. In old days the
proud were stiff and formal; now they are touchy and
quarrelsome. In old days simpletons were at any
rate straightforward; but now 'simple-mindedness'
exists only as a device of the impostor.

17. The Master said, Clever talk and a pretentious
manner are seldom found in the Good.[4]

---

[1] See textual notes.

[2] As we should say 'Spoils the market for . . . .' For a long discussion
of this saying, see *Mencius*, VII, 2, XXXVII.

[3] What follows is a paradox, for we expect to hear that the people
have improved; whereas it turns out that the 'lost parts' were redeeming
features.   [4] Identical with I, 3.

18.   The Master said, I hate to see roan killing red,
I hate to see the tunes of Chêng¹ corrupting Court
music, I hate to see sharp mouths overturning kingdoms
and clans.

19.   The Master said, I would much rather not have
to talk. Tzu-kung said, If our Master did not talk,
what should we little ones have to hand down about
him? The Master said, Heaven does not speak; yet
the four seasons run their course thereby,² the hundred
creatures, each after its kind, are born thereby. Heaven
does no speaking!

20.   Ju Pei³ wanted to see Master K'ung. Master
K'ung excused himself on the ground of ill-health. But
when the man who had brought the message was going
out through the door he took up his zithern and sang,
taking good care that the messenger should hear.

21.   Tsai Yü⁴ asked about the three years' mourning,⁵
and said he thought a year would be quite long enough:
'If gentlemen suspend their practice of the rites⁶ for
three years, the rites will certainly decay; if for three
years they make no music, music will certainly be
destroyed.'⁷ (In a year) the old crops have already
vanished, the new crops have come up, the whirling

---

¹ See XV, 10. Cf. also *Mencius*, VII, 2, XXXVII.

² By command of Heaven.

³ Of whom practically nothing is known. He had evidently disgraced
himself.   ⁴ See V, 9.

⁵ For parents. Three years is often interpreted as meaning 'into the
third year,' i.e. 25 months.

⁶ The mourning for parents entailed complete suspension of all
ordinary activities.

⁷ A traditional saying. Cf. *Shih Chi*, Ch. 28, beginning.

drills have made new fire.¹ Surely a year would be
enough?

The Master said, Would you then (after a year)
feel at ease in eating good rice and wearing silk
brocades? Tsai Yü said, Quite at ease. (The Master
said) If you would really feel at ease, then do so.
But when a true gentleman is in mourning, if he eats
dainties, he does not relish them, if he hears music,
it does not please him, if he sits in his ordinary seat,
he is not comfortable. That is why he abstains from
these things. But if you would really feel at ease, there
is no need for you to abstain.

When Tsai Yü had gone out, the Master said, How
inhuman² Yü is! Only when a child is three years old
does it leave its parents' arms. The three years'
mourning is the universal mourning everywhere under
Heaven.³ And Yü—was he not the darling of his
father and mother for three years?

22. The Master said, Those who do nothing all
day but cram themselves with food and never use their
minds are difficult.⁴ Are there not games such as

---

¹ The ritualists describe four 'fire-changing' rites, one for each
season, the new fire being in each case kindled on the wood of a tree
appropriate to the season. But perhaps the only actual 'fire-changing,'
when all fires were put out and after three days rekindled from a new
ritually-obtained flame, was in the spring. See *Hou Han Shu*, LXI,
fol. 6, recto and *Chou Li*, Ch. 57 (commentary).

² *Jên* is here used in its later sense, 'possessing human feelings,'
'kind.' This chapter, it will be remembered (see Introduction, p. 21),
shows many signs of late date.

³ The whole object of this paragraph is to claim Confucius as a
supporter of the three years' mourning. This custom was certainly far
from being 'universal,' and was probably not ancient. Cf. *Mencius*,
III, 1, III, where the people of Têng protest that even in Lu 'the former
princes none of them practised it.'   ⁴ Cf. XV, 16.

draughts?[1] To play them would surely be better than doing nothing at all.

23.   Tzu-lu said, Is courage to be prized by a gentleman? The Master said, A gentleman gives the first place to Right. If a gentleman has courage but neglects Right, he becomes turbulent. If a small man has courage but neglects Right, he becomes a thief.

24.   Tzu-kung said, Surely even the gentleman must have his hatreds? The Master said, He has his hatreds. He hates those who point out what is hateful in others.[2] He hates those who dwelling in low estate[3] revile all who are above them. He hates those who love deeds of daring but neglect ritual. He hates those who are active and venturesome, but are violent in temper.[4] I suppose you also have your hatreds? Tzu-kung said,[5] I hate those who mistake cunning[6] for wisdom. I hate those who mistake insubordination for courage. I hate those who mistake tale-bearing for honesty.

25.   The Master said, Women and people of low birth are very hard to deal with. If you are friendly

---

[1] For draughts, see *Tso Chuan*, Duke Hsiang, 25th year, end. It no doubt resembled the current game of *wei-ch'i*. I think *po* (cognate with *po* 'to strike,' cf. Japanese *utsu*, 'to strike,' i.e. make a move in board-games) is to be taken with *i* and is not the name of a separate game.
[2] Cf. *Kuan Tzu*, P'ien, 66, end.
[3] *liu* has been wrongly inserted here on the analogy of XIX, 20.
[4] See textual notes.
[5] This 'said' has accidentally been transferred to the clause above.
[6] See textual notes.

with them, they get out of hand, and if you keep your distance, they resent it.[1]

26.   The Master said, One who has reached the age of forty and is still disliked will be so till the end.

[1] Like Liu Pao-nan, I take *nü-tzu* in its ordinary sense of 'women' as opposed to 'men,' and *hsiao jên* in its ordinary sense of 'cads' as opposed to gentlemen. The standard interpreters soften the saying by making it apply to 'maids and valets.'

BOOK XVIII

1.   'The lord of Wei fled from him,[1] the lord of Chi suffered slavery at his hands, Pi Kan rebuked him and was slain.' Master K'ung said, In them the Yin had three Good men.

2.   When Liu-hsia Hui[2] was Leader of the Knights,[3] he was three times dismissed. People said to him, Surely you would do well to seek service elsewhere? He said, If I continue to serve men in honest ways, where can I go and not be three times dismissed? If, on the other hand, I am willing to serve men by crooked ways, what need is there for me to leave the land of my father and mother?

3.   Duke Ching of Ch'i received Master K'ung; he said, To treat him on an equality with the head of the Chi Family is impossible. I will receive him as though he ranked between the head of the Chi and the head of the Mêng. (At the interview) he said, I am old and have no use for you. Whereupon Master K'ung left (the land of Ch'i).[4]

4.   The people of Ch'i sent[5] to Lu a present of female

---

[1] i.e. from the tyrant Chou, last sovereign of the Yin dynasty. The lord of Wei was his step-brother. The lord of Chi and Pi Kan were his uncles. For his enormities, see *The Way and Its Power*, p. 126.

[2] See XV, 13.

[3] A comparatively humble post. Its occupant was chiefly concerned with criminal cases.

[4] As pointed out in the Introduction, Book XVIII is wholly legendary in content. The Confucius who ranked above the head of the Mêng family is already well on the way towards apotheosis.

[5] See textual notes.

musicians,[1] and Chi Huan-tzu[2] accepted them. For
three days no Court was held, whereupon Master
K'ung left Lu.

5.   Chieh Yü,[3] the madman of Ch'u, came past
Master K'ung, singing as he went:

> Oh phoenix, phoenix
> How dwindled is your power!
> As to the past, reproof is idle,
> But the future may yet be remedied.
> Desist, desist![4]
> Great in these days is the peril of those who
>   fill office.

Master K'ung got down,[5] desiring to speak with him;
but the madman hastened his step and got away, so
that Master K'ung did not succeed in speaking to him.

6.   Ch'ang-chü and Chieh-ni[6] were working as
plough-mates together. Master K'ung, happening to
pass that way, told Tzu-lu to go and ask them where
the river could be forded. Ch'ang-chü said, Who is
it for whom you are driving? Tzu-lu said, For K'ung
Ch'iu. He said, What, K'ung Ch'iu of Lu? Tzu-lu
said, Yes, he. Ch'ang-chü said, In that case he already

---

[1] In order to weaken the power of the government. A common
folk-lore theme.
[2] The father of Chi K'ang-tzu; died 492. This is the only passage
in the *Analects* where he is directly mentioned.
[3] See *Chuang Tzu*, IV, 8, where this typically Taoist, anti-Confucian
story is told in a slightly longer form. For the 'madman,' see also *Chuang
Tzu*, I, 4 and VII, 2, *Hsin Hsü*, III. *Han Fei Tzu*, P'ien, 20. *Chan Kuo
T'sê*, Ch'in stories, Pt. II.   [4] See textual notes.   [5] From his carriage.
[6] The names recall in their formation those of the fictitious personages
in *Chuang Tzu* and *Lieh Tzu*.

knows where the ford is.¹ Tzu-lu then asked Chieh-ni.
Chieh-ni said, Who are you? He said, I am Tzu-lu.
Chieh-ni said, You are a follower of K'ung Ch'iu of
Lu, are you not? He said, That is so. Chieh-ni said,
Under Heaven there is none that is not swept along
by the same flood.² Such is the world and who can
change it? As for you, instead of following one who
flees from this man and that, you would do better to
follow one who shuns this whole generation of men.
And with that he went on covering the seed.

Tzu-lu went and told his master, who said ruefully,
One cannot herd with birds and beasts. If I am not to
be a man among other men, then what am I to be?³
If the Way prevailed under Heaven, I should not be
trying to alter things.

7.   Once when Tzu-lu was following (the Master)
he fell behind and met an old man carrying a basket⁴
slung over his staff. Tzu-lu asked him, saying, Sir,
have you seen my master? The old man said, You who

> With your four limbs do not toil,
> Who do not sift the five grains,⁵

who is your master? And with that he planted his staff
in the ground and began weeding, while Tzu-lu stood
by with his hands pressed together.⁶

He kept Tzu-lu for the night, killed a fowl, prepared
a dish of millet for his supper and introduced him to
his two sons. Tzu-lu said, It is not right to refuse to
serve one's country. The laws of age and youth may

---

¹ Or should do; for he claims to be a Sage.   ² See textual notes.
³ I think the second *yü*, like the first, is interrogative.
⁴ Cf. XIV, 20.
⁵ Who would not know how to choose the right seed for sowing.
The five kinds of grain are rice, two kinds of millet, wheat and pulse.
⁶ The palms pressed together in an attitude of respect.

not be set aside. And how can it be right for a man to set aside the duty that binds minister to prince, or in his desire to maintain his own integrity, to subvert the Great Relationship?[1] A gentleman's service to his country consists in doing such right as he can. That the Way does not prevail, he knows well enough beforehand.

Next day[2] Tzu-lu went on his way and reported what had happened. The Master said, He is a recluse, and told Tzu-lu to go back and visit him again. But on arriving at the place he found that the old man had gone away.[3]

8. Subjects whose services were lost to the State: Po I, Shu Ch'i,[4] Yü Chung,[5] I I, Chu Chang,[6] Liu-hsia Hui, Shao Lien.[7] The Master said, Those of them who 'would neither abate their high resolve nor bring humiliation upon themselves' were, I suppose, Po I and Shu Ch'i. It means that[8] Liu-hsia Hui and Shao-lien did abate their high resolve and bring humiliation

---

[1] This is the only book in the *Analects* in which the term *lun*, 'relationship,' which figures so prominently in later Confucianism, makes its appearance.

[2] In the original this clause down to 'gone away' follows the words 'his two sons.' This makes the whole story run very awkwardly; see T.T. 2036. The clauses have certainly become accidentally inverted.

[3] Fearing that Confucius might recommend him for public service? Compare the very similar story, *Chuang Tzu*, XXV, 5.

[4] For Po I and Shu Ch'i, see V, 22.

[5] Brother of T'ai Po, VIII, 1.

[6] I I and Chu Chang are unknown. I suspect that Chu Chang at any rate is not a proper name at all, but a corruption of part of the sentence. This was clearly suspected by Lu Tê-ming (*c*. 600 A.D.).

[7] For Liu-hsia Hui, see XV, 13. Shao-lien is said to have been an 'eastern barbarian.'

[8] Confucius seems here to be commenting on some text which is unknown to us.

upon themselves. 'Their words were consonant with
the Relationships, their deeds were consonant with
prudence; this and no more,' means that Yü Chung
and I I, on the contrary, lived in seclusion and refrained
from comment. They secured personal integrity; and
when set aside maintained due balance.[1] As for me,
I am different from any of these. I have no 'thou shalt'
or 'thou shalt not.'

9.   The Chief Musician Chih[2] betook himself to
Ch'i; Kan, the leader of the band at the second meal,[3]
betook himself to Ch'u, Liao (leader of the band at
the third meal) went to Ts'ai, and Ch'üeh (leader of
the band at the fourth meal) went to Ch'in. The big
drummer Fang Shu went within[4] the River, the kettle-
drummer Wu went within the River Han, the Minor
Musician Yang and Hsiang, the player of the stone-
chimes, went within the sea.[5]

10.   The Duke of Chou addressed the Duke of Lu,[6]
saying: A gentleman never discards[7] his kinsmen; nor
does he ever give occasion to his chief retainers to
chafe at not being used. None who have been long in

---

[1] For variants, see textual notes. This whole paragraph is certainly
corrupt. Liu-hsia Hui hung on to office despite every rebuff, and
cannot be counted as a 'lost subject.' After the name of I I some
phrase must have followed meaning 'Those who concealed their
discontent,' or the like. See texual notes.

[2] Cf. VIII, 15. It is natural to suppose that this migration took
place when Duke Chao of Lu fled to Ch'i in 517 B.C.

[3] Or 'at the second course.'   [4] i.e. to the north of.

[5] to an island. This paragraph and the two which follow it are stray
fragments arbitrarily inserted at the end of the Book. Cf. the terminations
of Books X and XVI.   [6] His son.

[7] The original sense of the maxim may have been 'never reserves
all his largesses for his own kinsmen.'

his service does he ever dismiss without grave cause.
He does not expect one man to be capable of everything.[1]

11.   Chou had its Eight Knights:

Elder-brother Ta	(d'ât)
Elder-brother Kua	(g'uât)
Middle-brother T'u	(t'ut)
Middle-brother Hu	(hut)
Younger-brother Yeh	(zia)
Younger-brother Hsia	(g'a)
Youngest-brother Sui	(d'uâ)
Youngest-brother Kua	(Kuâ)[2]

---

[1] Cf. XIII, 25.

[2] A sign that a country had reached the maximum of plenty and
fertility was that one woman should bear four pairs of twins. Cf. the
similar set of twins mentioned in Tsang Wên Chung's great discourse,
Tso Chuan, Duke Wên, 18th year. The present set is unknown elsewhere, and commentators cannot decide in what reign the happy
phenomenon took place. I give the names in their approximate ancient
pronunciation, to show that they form a sort of jingle. 'The names go
in pairs, as becomes those of twins,' says Huang K'an. For the
pronunciation of the last name I follow Lu Tê-ming.

BOOK XIX

1. Tzu-chang said, A knight who confronted with danger is ready to lay down his life, who confronted with the chance of gain thinks first of right, who judges sacrifice by the degree of reverence shown and mourning by the degree of grief[1]—such a one is all that can be desired.

2. Tzu-chang said, He who sides with moral force (*tê*) but only to a limited extent,[2] who believes in the Way, but without conviction—how can one count him as with us, how can one count him as not with us?

3. The disciples of Tzu-hsia asked Tzu-chang about intercourse with others. Tzu-chang said, What does Tzu-hsia tell you? He replied saying, Tzu-hsia says:

> Go with those with whom it is proper to go;
> Keep at a distance those whom it is proper to
>   keep at a distance.

Tzu-chang said, That is different from what I have been told:

> A gentleman reverences those that excel, but
>   'finds room'[3] for all;
> He commends the good and pities the
>   incapable.

Do I myself greatly excel others? In that case I shall certainly find room for everyone. Am I myself inferior to others? In that case, it would be others who would

---

[1] And not by the elaborateness of the ceremonies. For the first part of the saying, Cf. XIV, 13.

[2] Saying for example that *tê* has its uses, but that the ultimate appeal must always be to physical compulsion.   [3] i.e. tolerates.

keep me at a distance. So that the question of keeping others at a distance does not arise.¹

4.   Tzu-hsia said, Even the minor walks² (of knowledge) have an importance of their own. But if pursued too far they tend to prove a hindrance; for which reason a gentleman does not cultivate them.

5.   Tzu-hsia said, He who from day to day is conscious of what he still lacks, and from month to month never forgets what he has already learnt, may indeed be called a true lover of learning.

6.   Tzu-hsia said,

> One who studies widely and with set purpose,
> Who questions earnestly, then thinks for himself about what he has heard

—such a one will incidentally³ achieve Goodness.

7.   Tzu-hsia said, Just as the hundred⁴ apprentices must live in workshops to perfect themselves in their craft, so the gentleman studies, that he may improve himself in the Way.

8.   Tzu-hsia said, When the small man goes wrong, it is always on the side of over-elaboration.⁵

---

¹ Literally, what becomes of that (*ch'i* in such usages corresponds to the Latin *iste*) 'keeping others at a distance' of yours?

² Such as agriculture, medicine, etc. The idea that specialized knowledge is incompatible with true gentility prevailed in England till well towards the close of the nineteenth century.

3 Cf. II, 18, VII, 15, XIII, 18 and XV, 31.

4 i.e. all the different sorts of . . .

5 Lu Tê-ming does not gloss this character, and therefore presumably read *wên* in its ordinary pronunciation. I see no reason to read it in the 'departing tone,' with the meaning 'gloss over,' 'make excuses.' The sole authority for the usual interpretation is the pseudo K'ung An-kuo.

9. Tzu-hsia said, A gentleman has three varying aspects: seen from afar, he looks severe, when approached he is found to be mild, when heard speaking he turns out to be incisive.

10. Tzu-hsia said, A gentleman obtains the confidence of those under him, before putting burdens upon them. If he does so before he has obtained their confidence, they feel that they are being exploited.[1] It is also true that he obtains the confidence (of those above him) before criticizing them. If he does so before he has obtained their confidence, they feel that they are being slandered.

11. Tzu-hsia said, So long as in undertakings of great moral import a man does not 'cross the barrier', in undertakings of little moral import he may 'come out and go in.'[2]

12. Tzu-yu said, Tzu-hsia's disciples and scholars, so long as it is only a matter of sprinkling and sweeping floors, answering summonses and replying to questions, coming forward and retiring, are all right. But these are minor matters. Set them to anything important, and they would be quite at a loss.

Tzu-hsia, hearing of this, said, Alas, Yen Yu is wholly mistaken. Of the Way of the True Gentleman it is said:

> If it be transmitted to him before he is ripe[3]
> By the time he is ripe, he will weary of it.

---

[1] See textual notes.

[2] In matters such as loyalty, keeping promises, obedience to parents, the laws which govern his conduct are absolute. In lesser matters he is allowed a certain latitude. Several early writers attribute the saying to Confucius himself.   [3] See textual notes.

Disciples may indeed be compared to plants and trees. They have to be separately treated according to their kinds.

In the Way of the Gentleman there can be no bluff. It is only the Divine Sage who embraces in himself both the first step and the last.

13.   Tzu-hsia said, The energy that a man has left[1] over after doing his duty to the State, he should devote to study; the energy that he has left after studying, he should devote to service of the State.

14.   Tzu-yu said, The ceremonies of mourning should be carried to the extreme that grief dictates, and no further.

15   Tzu-yu said, My friend Chang does 'the things that it is hard to be able to do';[2] but he is not yet Good.

16.   Master Tsêng said, Chang is so self-important. It is hard to become Good when working side by side with such a man.

17.   Master Tsêng said, I once heard the Master say, Though a man may never before have shown all that is in him, he is certain to do so when mourning for a father or mother.

18.   Master Tsêng said, I once heard the Master say, Filial piety such as that of Mêng Chuang Tzu[3] might in other respects be possible to imitate; but the way in which he changed neither his father's[4] servants

---

[1] Cf. I, 6.   [2] Cf. XIV, 2.
[3] Died in 550 B.C.   [4] Mêng Hsien Tzu, died in 554 B.C

nor his father's domestic policy, that would indeed be hard to emulate.

19.   When the Chief of the Mêng Family[1] appointed Yang Fu as Leader of the Knights,[2] Yang Fu[3] came for advice to Master Tsêng. Master Tsêng said, It is long since those above lost the Way of the Ruler and the common people lost their cohesion. If you find evidence of this, then be sad and show pity rather than be pleased at discovering such evidence.

20.   Tzu-kung said, The tyrant Chou[4] cannot really have been as wicked as all this! That is why a gentleman hates to 'dwell on low ground.' He knows that all filth under Heaven tends to accumulate there.

21.   Tzu-kung said, The faults of a gentleman are like eclipses of the sun or moon. If he does wrong, everyone sees it. When he corrects his fault, every gaze is turned up towards him.

22.   Kung-sun Ch'ao of Wei[5] asked Tzu-kung, From whom did Chung-ni[6] derive his learning? Tzu-kung said, The Way of the kings Wên and Wu has never yet utterly fallen to the ground. Among men,[7] those of great understanding have recorded the major principles

---

[1] Mêng Wu Po, who succeeded to the headship of the clan in 481 B.C. Usually explained as meaning Mêng I Tzu, predecessor of Mêng Wu Po. But in his time (if we are to follow the traditional chronology) Master Tsêng would have been too young to be consulted. It must be remembered, however, that the Confucian legend was not built up by people who had chronological tables open in front of them.

[2] A post involving the judging of criminal cases. See above, p. 15.

[3] Unknown.   [4] See above, p. 218.

[5] So called to distinguish him from a number of Kung-sun Chaos in other countries.   [6] i.e. Confucius.

[7] The usual interpretation: 'It is still here among men', implies a very abrupt construction.

of this Way and those of less understanding have recorded the minor principles. So that there is no one who has not access to the Way of Wên and Wu. From whom indeed did our Master *not* learn? But at the same time, what need had he of any fixed and regular teacher?

23.   Shu-sun Wu-shu[1] talking to some high officers at Court said, Tzu-kung is a better man than Chung-ni. Tzu-fu Ching-po[2] repeated this to Tzu-kung. Tzu-kung said, Let us take as our comparison the wall round a building. My wall only reaches to the level of a man's shoulder, and it is easy enough to peep over it and see the good points of the house on the other side. But our Master's wall rises many times a man's height, and no one who is not let in by the gate can know the beauty and wealth of the palace that, with its ancestral temple, its hundred ministrants, lies hidden within. But it must be admitted that those who are let in by the gate are few; so that it is small wonder His Excellency should have spoken as he did.

24.   Shu-sun Wu-shu having spoken disparagingly of Chung-ni, Tzu-kung said, It is no use; Chung-ni cannot be disparaged. There may be other good men; but they are merely like hillocks or mounds that can easily be climbed. Chung-ni is the sun and moon that cannot be climbed over. If a man should try to cut himself off from them, what harm would it do to the sun and moon? It would only show that he did not know his own measure.

25.   Tzu-ch'in[3] said to Tzu-kung, This is an affectation of modesty. Chung-ni is in no way your superior.

---

[1] Flourished *c.* 500 B.C.

[2] Cf. XIV, 38.   [3] See I, 10. and XVI, 13

Tzu-kung said, You should be more careful about what you say. A gentleman, though for a single word he may be set down as wise, for a single word is set down as a fool. It would be as hard to equal our Master as to climb up on a ladder to the sky. Had our Master ever been put in control of a State or of a great Family, it would have been as is described in the words: 'He raised them, and they stood, he led them and they went. He steadied them as with a rope, and they came. He stirred them, and they moved harmoniously. His life was glorious, his death bewailed.'[1] How can such a one ever be equalled?

[1] Probably a quotation from a *lei* (funeral eulogy).

BOOK XX

1. Yao said, Oh you, Shun!

Upon you in your own person now rests the
    heavenly succession;[1]
Faithfully grasp it by the centre.
The Four Seas may run dry;[2]
But this heavenly gift lasts forever.

Shun too, when giving his charge to Yü . . . (hiatus).
(T'ang)[3] said, I, your little son Li, venture to
sacrifice a black ox and tell you, oh most august
sovereign God, that those who are guilty[4] I dare not
spare; but God's servants I will not slay. The decision
is in your heart, O God.

If I in my own person do any wrong, let it never
be visited upon the many lands. But if anywhere in
the many lands wrong be done, let it be visited upon
my person.[5]

When Chou gave its great largesses,
It was the good who were enriched:
'Although I have my Chou kinsmen,
They are less to me than the Good Men.[6]

---

[1] See additional notes.

[2] i.e. 'sooner shall the sea run dry, than this gift. . . .' For *yung-chung*, cf. *Shu Ching*, Metal Casket, 10.

[3] Founder of the Yin dynasty, when informing the Supreme Ancestor of his (T'ang's) accession. Li was his personal name.

[4] The Hsia, whom T'ang had defeated.

[5] This 'scape-goat' formula is constantly referred to in early Chinese literature. Mo Tzu (Universal Love, Pt. III), after quoting this same passage, says that T'ang 'did not scruple to make of himself a sacrificial victim.' The passage has been reinterpreted in a very drastic fashion.

[6] i.e. those who distinguished themselves in the campaign against Yin. The speaker is presumably King Wu.

> If among the many families
> There be one that does wrong,
> Let the wrong be visited on me alone.'

(King Wu)[1] paid strict attention to weights and measures, reviewed the statutes and laws, restored disused offices, and gave a polity to all the four quarters of the world. He raised up States that had been destroyed, re-established lines of succession that had been broken, summoned lost subjects back to prominence, and all the common people under Heaven gave their hearts to him. What he cared for most was that the people should have food, and that the rites of mourning and sacrifice should be fulfilled.

He who is broad[2] wins the multitude, he who keeps his word is trusted by the people, he who is diligent succeeds in all he undertakes, he who is just is the joy (of the people).

2.　　Tzu-chang asked Master K'ung, saying, What must a man do, that he may thereby be fitted to govern the land? The Master said, He must pay attention to the Five Lovely Things[3] and put away from him the Four Ugly Things. Tzu-chang said, What are they, that you call the Five Lovely Things? The Master said, A gentleman 'can be bounteous without extravagance, can get work out of people without arousing resentment, has longings but is never covetous, is proud but never insolent, inspires awe but is never ferocious.'

Tzu-chang said, What is meant by being bounteous without extravagance? The Master said, If he gives to the people only such advantages as are really advan-

---

[1] Or the Duke of Chou?
[2] 'He who is broad' down to 'undertakes' occurs also in XVII, 6.
[3] For these enumerations, cf. XVI, 4–8.

tageous[1] to them, is he not being bounteous without extravagance? If he imposes upon them only such tasks as they are capable of performing, is he not getting work out of them without arousing resentment? If what he longs for and what he gets is Goodness, who can say that he is covetous? A gentleman, irrespective of whether he is dealing with many persons or with few, with the small or with the great, never presumes to slight them. Is not this indeed being 'proud without insolence'? A gentleman sees to it that his clothes and hat are put on straight, and imparts such dignity to his gaze that he imposes on others. No sooner do they see him from afar than they are in awe. Is not this indeed inspiring awe without ferocity?

Tzu-chang said, What are they, that you call the Four Ugly Things? The Master said, Putting men to death, without having taught them (the Right); that is called savagery. Expecting the completion of tasks, without giving due warning; that is called oppression. To be dilatory about giving orders, but to expect absolute punctuality, that is called being a tormentor. And similarly, though meaning to let a man have something, to be grudging about bringing it out from within, that is called behaving like a petty functionary.

3. The Master said, He who does not understand the will of Heaven cannot be regarded as a gentleman. He who does not know the rites cannot take his stand.[2] He who does not understand words,[3] cannot understand people.

---

[1] For example, if he promotes agriculture instead of distributing doles and largesses.   [2] Cf. XVI, 13.

[3] i.e. cannot get beneath the surface-meaning and understand the state of mind that the words really imply. Cf. *Mencius*, II, 1, II, 17. Para. 3 was lacking in the Lu version.

ADDITIONAL NOTES

II, 18. *tsai ch'i chung* is an idiom (cf. VII, 15, XIII, 18, XV, 31, XIX, 6) which can never be translated literally. It is used of results that occur incidentally without being the main object of a certain course of action.

III, 1.   Eight teams of dancers.

The exact number of performers is in every ritual a matter of extreme importance. The Chi family's crime consisted in usurping rites which were proper only to the Ducal House; or, possibly, proper only to the Emperor. They were 'making the twigs heavy and the trunk light'—the surest way to ruin.

III, 8.   An alternative interpretation of Confucius's reply is 'In painting, the plain colour (i.e. the white) is put on last,' because otherwise it would get soiled. This explanation lands us in all kinds of difficulties, and is based, I think, on a misunderstanding of a passage in the *Chou Li*, LXXIX (page 17; Biot's translation, II, 516), which in reality means: 'When birds, beasts and snakes are combined with the symbols of the four seasons and with the five colours in their proper arrangements, and are thus duly displayed, this is called "skilled work." In the business of painting (i.e. of decorating the personal possessions of officials with designs appropriate to their rank) plain work comes after (i.e. is not considered so highly).'

'Plain work' is painted in the appropriate colours, but lacks the birds, beasts and snakes that decorate the appurtenances of the mighty. Confucius uses the same maxim as the *Chou Li*, but reinterprets it as meaning not 'In painting plain work is not so highly esteemed,' but 'The painting comes after the plain groundwork.'

The *Chou Li* commentary tries to force upon 'plain work' the impossible sense of 'application of white pigment,' thus making the last sentence totally disconnected from the context.

III, 15. The poem *T'ien Wên* is supposed to embody the questions asked by the poet Ch'ü Yüan when he visited the shrines of former kings and ministers, and to concern legends depicted on the walls of these shrines.

III, 16. According to the *Chou Li* (XXI, 52) the local archery meeting was made the occasion for a general review of conduct, 'points' in the competition being given for (1) not quarrelling; (2) correct deportment; (3) *chu-p'i*, explained as meaning 'skill in archery'; (4) singing; (5) dancing.

It is clear, then, that the *Chou Li* does not give to *chu* the meaning 'give chief place to'; it is, however, equally clear that in the *Lun Yü* passage *chu* can only bear this meaning. Moreover, the mention in *Lun Yü* of 'strength' suggests that 'piercing the hide' and not merely hitting the mark is what is meant.

III, 21. *Shê* ('holy ground') was an earth-mound at the borders of a town or village, interpreted as symbolizing the whole soil of the territory in which it stood. It was often associated with a sacred tree or grove, and with a block or pillar of wood[1] which served as a 'stance' (resting-place) for spirits. This wooden

---

[1] In other parts of the world objects analogous to the *chu* vary within comparatively small areas between being made of stone and being made of wood. The typical Chinese *chu* has always been a wooden object; but *chu* of other materials including stone probably also existed.

object was called *chu*; see textual notes. In parallel passages the question at issue is what sort of wood was used in making the *chu*. This passage is generally taken as referring to the trees of the Holy Ground and not to the material of the *chu*.

The *fêng*, a terminal earth-mound where a road reached the borders of a State, is analogous to the *shê*, and the same official was responsible for the maintenance of both.

IV, 11.   The Chu Hsi interpretation is 'The gentleman thinks of *tê*, the small man of material comfort; the gentleman, of punishments (i.e. justice); the small man of favours.' In his conversations (section on *Lun Yü* in *Chu Tzu Ch'üan Shu*) he records that Yin Shun (1071–1142) construed the sentence as I have done; and Huang K'an (sixth century) notes this rendering as an alternative one. The absence of any 'then,' 'in that case' in the second and fourth clauses makes the sentence obscure, and I fancy that *tsê* ('then') has been suppressed in order to admit of an interpretation such as Chu Hsi's, by people who unlike Confucius, believed in government by penalties. Chu Hsi's interpretation of *huai-t'u* is hopelessly forced.

IV, 26.   The character that I have translated 're-peated scolding' means literally 'to enumerate.' Hence to 'enumerate people's faults,' to 'tick off.' Cf. *Shih Chi*, ch. 86, fol. 4.

It is taken in this sense here by Yü Yüeh[1] (died 1906). The *Chi Chieh* gives it the meaning 'quick,' 'hasty.' Cf. *Lieh Tzu*, II, 8: 'Anyone who is good at swimming can quickly learn . . . ,' and *Chuang Tzu*, XIX, 4. But Chêng Hsüan, the great Han dynasty commentator, explains it as meaning 'enumerating

[1] H.P. 1391, 10.

one's own services.' Finally, the current explanation
gives it the meaning 'numerously,' 'repeatedly.' Comparison with XII, 23 seems to show that this last
explanation is right.

V, 2.   For this saying, set in the context of a longer
anecdote, see *K'ung Tzu Chia Yü*, XIX (Tzu-lu
Ch'u Chien) and *Shuo Yüan*, VII. A work called
Fu Tzu (i.e. sayings of Master Fu) was current until
the first century A.D., and the stories about Fu's ideal
governorship which are found in works of the third
century B.C. and onwards may be extracts from *Fu
Tzu*. See G. Haloun, *Asia Major*, VIII, fasc. 3, pp.
437 *seq*. But there is no reason to suppose that any
of these stories supplies us with the original context
of this saying in the *Analects*.

V, 21.   This saying exists in two forms. The version
of the *Analects* reoccurs *verbatim* in the *Ju-lin Chuan*
(ch. 121 of the *Shih Chi*) and, apart from the insertion
of one superfluous character,[1] also in the Life of
Confucius[2] (ch. 47 of the *Shih Chi*). But in another
passage[3] of the Life and in *Mencius*[4] Confucius is made
to say 'Let us return . . . the little ones . . . push
themselves forward and grab' (the opposite of the
essential principle *jang*, 'yield,' 'give place to others').
'They cannot forget their beginnings' (i.e. they are
always lapsing back into the old ways of greed and
push that are inconsistent with my Way of Goodness).

V, 24.   When later Confucians were attempting to
make Confucius in some way responsible (either as
author or editor) for the whole of early Chinese litera-

---

[1] *Wu* ('I') is inserted before 'do not know how to'; which does not
make sense.   [2] Chavannes' translation, V, p. 359.
[3] Chavannes, V, 343.   [4] VII, 2, XXXVII.

ture, they turned Tso Ch'iu Ming into a disciple of Confucius and credited him with the authorship (under the Master's direction) of the *Tso Chuan* chronicle. Nothing further is known about him.

VI, 6.   *Ta* means 'to put through,' 'penetrate.' So (1) To 'put oneself through,' to turn one's *tê* to account, to get on in the world, to progress; to get one's meaning or one's doctrines through, i.e. to 'put them across.' (2) To get through, penetrate, i.e. understand.

VI, 11.   From the Han dynasty onwards the word *ju*, which is of very uncertain origin, was applied to those who devoted themselves to the study of the *Songs*, the *Books*, the ritual treatises, etc., and hence to followers of Confucius in general. It seems, however, to have originally been a contemptuous nickname given by the warlike people of Ch'i to their more pacific neighbours in Lu. Cf. *Tso Chuan*, Ai kung, 21st year. But since the word occurs only this once in the *Analects*, without adequate context, it is impossible to know for certain what meaning the compilers attached to it.

VI, 21.   This saying, in the form in which it now occurs, is completely Taoistic, save that the word Good (Goodness) has been substituted for 'Tao.' Taoism, it is true, drew its vocabulary and ideas partly from a stock common to all early Chinese thought. But nowhere else in the *Analects* is it suggested that anyone save the *Shêng* (Divine Sage) can achieve his ends by inactivity, and as this passage stands it is impossible not to give it a more general application. But comparison with other sayings in the *Analects* and elsewhere suggests that this saying originally had a very different form. In XV, 32, it is *shou* 'keeping what one has gained'[1] (and not *shou* 'longevity') which is the consequence of Goodness, but cannot result from wisdom alone. Moreover, in the *Ku-liang Chuan*[2] we twice get the saying 'The wise man schemes (*lü*) . . . the Good man keeps' ('secures,' *shou*) what the scheming has achieved. Both passages are concerned with politics, not with the moral life of the individual, and mean that State successes gained by cleverness will not be permanent; only the State that is based on Goodness can have any permanence.

As it stands, the saying runs very awkwardly. It is first said that the Good man delights (*lo*) in mountains and then that it is the wise man who 'delights'; whereas the Good man is long-lived (*shou*) as opposed to 'delighting' (*lo*). I cannot help believing that the original sense of the last two phrases was: 'The wise ruler schemes; but the Good ruler alone can give permanent effect to schemes,' as in the *Ku-liang Chuan*.

The Good 'stay still,' because their effects are achieved by *tê* ('moral force') not by *li* ('physical force'). The dictum easily passes into the vocabulary of full-blown, systematic quietism.

Pao Hsien, in the first century, takes the whole saying as referring to the ruler. But it is usually taken to refer to the individual in general, and is interpreted in a completely Taoist sense: all exercise of the emotions destroys the soul and leads to early death.

VI, 26.   'Made a solemn declaration,' literally 'arrowed it.' Here metaphorical; but probably the character 'arrow' has its ideogrammatic sense and is not a phonetic substitute. For the use of a bundle of arrows in oath-taking, see H. Maspero (Mélanges chinois et bouddhiques, III, p. 270). *Le Serment dans la procédure judiciaire. . . .* The bundle of arrows is a

---

[1] See textual notes.   [2] Yin 2 and Huan 18.

symbol of the unbreakable, in contrast with a single arrow, that can easily be snapped. Cf. the memorial inscription of the Mongol leader Mêng-ku (13th century) by Yao Sui[1] (A.D. 1238–1314): He broke an arrow and swore saying: 'May every act in which I am not utterly faithful to the Khan be snapped like this!' We see here that it is against his acts and not against himself that the speaker invokes destruction. Confucius's *yeh chih* is generally translated 'crush (reject, forsake) me.' But the text says 'it' not 'me,' following a formula similar to that of the Mongol oath. There is no evidence that *yeh* can mean 'reject.' Nor is there any suggestion in the text that improper conduct had taken place between Nan-tzu and Confucius, but only that his seeing her at all, as a means of obtaining influence at the Wei Court, was improper.

VI, 27.   It is upon this passage that the whole Confucian philosophy of compromise, of 'too much is as bad as too little,' is built. What *chung-yung* meant to start with is very doubtful. To the compilers of the *Analects*, I do not think it meant anything different from *chung tao*, the Middle Way. But the interpretation 'middle and usual,' i.e. 'traditional,' is a quite possible one.

A Confucian treatise of very mixed content, strongly tinged with Taoism, deals in several passages with the power of *chung-yung*, and bears these two words as its title. (It is known in Europe as the *Doctrine of the Mean*.) The material that this treatise contains is partly, at any rate, as old as the first half of the third century; but the unification of China is referred to, and the actual compilation of the work must be as late as the end of the third century B.C.

Is there not, however, some connection between

[1] Collected Works, XIV, 1 verso.

this passage and *Song* 142, which recounts the virtues of Chung Shan Fu? The 6th verse says: 'Moral force (*tê*) is light as a hair; but among the people there are few that can lift it' (i.e. that can use it).

I suspect that in its original form the saying was parallel to that about T'ai Po in VIII, 1, and ran: 'How transcendent was the *tê* of Chung Shan Fu (Minister of King Hsüan of Chou). That among the people there are few (who know how to use *tê*) is an old story!' in allusion to *Song* 142, verse 6. The two characters *shan* and *fu*, written too close one above the other, were later misread as a single character *yung*. This however is merely a tentative suggestion.

VII, 7.   As in modern Chinese school-fees are called 'the bundle of dried flesh,' it would not occur to the average reader that *shu-hsiu* in this passage could possibly mean anything but 'a bundle of dried flesh,' brought as a humble present to the teacher. This, however, was not the view of many outstanding commentators. Chêng Hsüan (died A.D. 200) says it means 'fourteen years old': the Master accepted any pupil who had attained to years of discretion. The alternatives arise in this way: *Shu* = to tie, tie one's belt. *Hsiu* = 'to put right,' 'to cure'; hence to 'cure' meat, so that 'tied cured' means 'a bundle of dried flesh' or one who has 'tied his belt and put himself to rights,' i.e. has donned the garb of manhood. There is, however, no trace of this idiom till Han times; whereas 'dried flesh,' as a humble form of offering, occurs in texts which have every chance of being pre-Han. I therefore think that Huang K'an (sixth century) was right in championing the 'dried flesh' theory against the view of Chêng Hsüan.

VII, 17.   There is not much doubt that *ya* ('refined,'

'standard,' 'correct' as applied to speech) is etymologically the same word as the ethnic term Hsia, the common name of the Chinese, as opposed to the barbarians. Mo Tzu calls the third part of the *Book of Songs* 'Ta Hsia' instead of the usual *Ta Ya*.[1]

To avoid the implication that Confucius sometimes spoke in his native dialect, Ch'êng Hao in the eleventh century interpreted *ya* as meaning not 'standard,' but 'standardly,' i.e. frequently. Hence Legge's 'His frequent themes were. . . .' But Chêng Hsüan interprets the passage exactly as I have done.

VII, 18.   It is the 'Duke' of Shê who is the subject of the following anecdote. There was once a man who said he had a passion for dragons. He was always talking about them, and had them painted all over the walls of his house. After all, he said, there is nothing pleasanter to look at than a dragon. One day a huge, shiny, slimy paw flopped on to his window-sill; soon a green and golden scaly face reared itself up at the window and grinned a dank greeting. The lover of dragons was beside himself with terror. He fled shrieking to the hall, where he tripped over the oozing, slithery tail which the monster had thrust in friendly salutation through the doorway of the house.

The story is told as a warning against insincere enthusiasms. (See Waley, *Introduction to the Study of Chinese Painting*, p. 37.)

VIII, 3.   The passage quoted from the *Li Chih* [1] refers, it must be admitted, to the death of an emperor, not a private person.

Trussing up of various kinds and the placing of heavy weights on the body occur in many parts of the

[1] The variant has been smoothed away from Mo Tzu's text by modern editors.

world, in some cases before death, in some cases after it. Where such practices take place after death, they are explained by anthropologists as being due to fear of the dead returning to life.[1] Where they occur before death this explanation obviously does not hold good. The question is complicated by the fact that in China (and probably elsewhere?) many practices originally belonging to the period preceding death were in less primitive days delayed until death had actually taken place; see De Groot, *The Religious Systems of China*, I, p. 9.

VIII, 15.   The interpretation of *shih* ('began') as 'when he first entered on his duties' seems to date from Sung times.

VIII, 20.   King Wu's statement that he had 'ten ministers' is found in several passages of old literature; e.g. *Tso Chuan*, Duke Hsiang, 28th year.[2]

IX, 2.   The commentators take the villager's 'vastly learned,' etc. not as irony but as praise; for to achieve a reputation in any one line is unworthy of a *chün-tzu*. This seems to make Confucius's comment unintelligible. I take the villager to be a boorish, ignorant man who does not know that a true gentleman ought not to be known as a specialist in any one line.

IX, 5.   The people of K'uang are supposed to have mistaken Confucius for the adventurer Yang Huo (see XVII, 1) who had formerly created a disturbance in

---

[1] Cf. Frazer, *The Fear of the Dead in Primitive Religion*, 2 vols., 1933 and 1934.
[2] The omission of the word 'ministers' in some early versions (e.g. the T'ang Scriptures on Stone) was a doctrinal not a philological emendation. It is unfilial to speak of a mother as being 'minister' (literally 'servant') to her son.

K'uang. The mistake was made more natural by the fact that Confucius's carriage was being driven by a man who had previously been associated with Yang Huo.

X, 10.   For the No (expulsion rite) see *Chou Li*, ch. 48 and 54. The exorcist accompanied by four 'Madmen' (see *The Book of Songs*, p. 222) 'wearing over their heads a bear's skin with four eyes of yellow metal (copper or gold?), clad in a black coat and red skirt, grasping halberd and raising shield, leads all the house-servants and performs the No of the season, searching the house and driving out noxious influences.'

In many parts of Europe the whole household still visits every corner of the house and outbuildings on New Year's Eve, banging forks on dish-covers and so on, in order to drive out the Old Year.

The *Chi Chieh* says that Confucius stood on the eastern steps of the ancestral shrine during this ceremony 'in order to reassure the ancestral spirits' of the house, who might otherwise have taken flight along with the 'noxious influences.' In T'ang times the No was stylized as a Court dance.

XI, 4.   Min Tzu-ch'ien's mother died when he was a child and his father married again. One day when he was driving his father's carriage he let the reins slip. His father found that he was wearing such thin gloves that his hands were numbed with cold. On going home he looked at the gloves worn by the two children born to him by his second wife and found that they were thick and warm. He said to his wife, 'I married you solely in order to have someone to look after my motherless children. Now I can see that you have been imposing upon me. Leave my home at once!' Tzu-ch'ien said, 'If my step-mother remains, one child will be imperfectly clad; but if she goes, several children will be cold.' His father said no more about it. (Fragment of lost portions of *Shuo Yüan*, quoted under heading 'filial piety' in *I Wên Lei Chü.*)

XI, 7.   *Kuo* (the word translated 'enclosure') meant, as may be seen most clearly from the paragraph on 'Inspecting the *kuo* and grave-figures' in *I Li*, XII, a protection for the coffin made by laying beams longways and crossways, like the framework at the top of a well. Excavation has confirmed this; Cf. S. Umehara, *Selected Relics from the Chin-ts'un Tombs, Lo-yang.* Kyōto, 1937, Figure 3.

In later times *kuo* meant an 'outer coffin,' a 'shell.' In Japan the term 'stone *kuo*' has been applied to the *allées couvertes* of Japanese megalithic structures.

XI, 13.   Duke Chao, who fled from Lu in 517, had used this building as a basis for operations against his enemies, the Chi Family. It is probable, therefore, that the remark of Min Tzu-ch'ien was applauded by Confucius for its loyalist, pro-dynastic tendency.

XI, 24.   For the Holy Ground, see additional note to III, 21. The Millet is in early texts always closely associated with the Holy Ground and not treated as the object of a separate cult.[1] It was interpreted as symbolizing the fruits of the soil in general. It was no doubt a sheaf of millet (if grain had been meant another word would have been used) and may have been the Last Sheaf, kept over from the previous harvest. 'Last Sheaf' ceremonies are common in India, Indo-China and Indonesia.

XI, 25, 7.   The ritualists describe four rain-cere-

[1] 'The *Chi*, "Millet," is a detail of the *shê*,' as Chêng Hsüan puts it, in commenting on *Chou Li*, XXII.

monies, one for each season. But there is reason to believe[1] that the ceremony carried out at the end of spring or beginning of summer and traceable throughout Chinese history down to the present day is the only one that has, as a regular institution, had any real existence. During times of drought an emergency ceremony might indeed be performed; but the four ceremonies, each corresponding to a season, a colour, etc., are a pure fantasy of the ritualists.

A constant feature of these ceremonies is, as Professor Shiratori has shown, the participation of boys and young men.

$5 \times 6 + 6 \times 7$ makes 72, a number used in other dances.[2] The performance of lustrations preceded every sacrifice, and there is not the slightest reason to emend the character *yü* 'bathe,' on the ground that the season was too cold for bathing (cf. *Lun Hêng*, P'ien 45, fol. 11).

The commentator quoted by the *Lun Hêng* (first century A.D.) is trying to explain this passage in the light of the popular rain-ceremonies held in his own day, and I do not think we can accept his interpretation in all its details.[3] The whole of this very literary passage bears the stamp of belonging to a milieu different from that of the brief colloquial sayings. It is noteworthy that *an* (usual sense 'peaceful') is used as an interrogative particle.[4] This usage does not seem

[1] See K. Shiratori, *Tōyō Gakuhō*, XXI, 2, pp. 104 seq.

[2] e.g. the dance to Hou Chi, the god of agriculture, which was performed by 'capped youths five times six which is thirty, and boys six times seven which is forty-two.' See *Han Ch'iu I*, quoted among the fragments collected in *P'ing Ching Kuan Ts'ung Shu*, Supplement, ch. 2, fol. 6.

[3] Cf. M. Granet, *Fêtes et Chansons Anciennes de la Chine*, 1929, p. 158.

[4] But the text used by Lu Tê-ming seems to have had the usual particle *yen*.

to belong either to the older language (only one very doubtful example occurs in the *Songs*) or to the language of Lu (no other example in the *Lun Yü*; none in *Mencius*). On the other hand, it is extremely common in the (more northerly?) dialect of the *Tso Chuan*, and in third century B.C. writings generally.

XII, 20.   *lü i hsia jên.* Cf. *Tso Chuan*, Hsüan Kung 12th year, 'A people whose prince knows how to defer to others (*nêng i hsia jên*) may be treated as reliable.' *lü* sometimes means 'in general,' 'on the whole.' (See Wang Nien-sun, *Tu Shu Tsa Chih* VIII, 4 and Yü Yüeh, H.P. 1392, fol. 7.) I doubt if that is the sense here.

XIII, 3.   For *kou* ('chance') see *Han Shih Wai Chuan*, III, fol. 1 and IV, fol. 1 verso. Also *Tso Chuan*, Chao Kung, 18th year. It is used when things are done 'somehow or other,' in a 'hit or miss' offhand fashion, when everything is 'left to chance.' In hypothetical clauses it means 'If by any chance,' 'If somehow or other.' It applies wherever a result is achieved by mere accident and not as the result of *tê* ('virtue,' moral power). Cf. XIII, 8 and Introduction, p. 66.

XIII, 4.   Confucius took the traditional view that it is for common people to work with their hands, for gentlemen to work with their *tê*. Fan Ch'ih had evidently been influenced by views similar to those of Hsü Hsing (*Mencius*, III, 1, IV) who held that it was unfair to live by the labour of others and maintained that 'the wise man should plough side by side with the common people.' There is a parallel passage in *Mo Tzu* (Lu Wên, *P'ien*, 49), where 'a low fellow, from the south of Lu, called Wu Lü,' reproaches Mo Tzu with preaching justice, while all the time living on the labour of others. Mo Tzu's reply amounts practically to saying that he is promoting justice more by teaching it to others than he would be by practising it himself.

XIII, 15.   Wang Su (died A.D. 256), Huang K'an (died A.D. 545) and Hsing P'ing (died A.D. 1010) all accept that *chi* (current interpretation 'expect,' 'count upon') means 'near.' Chu Hsi bases his 'expect' on an isolated and very uncertain usage in *Song* 199.

XIII, 22.   It seems clear that *hêng* was the name of a ritual. Cf. *Chou Li*, ch. 50: 'If a great calamity befalls the land, then send for *wu* (shamans) and perform the *wu-hêng* (shamanistic *hêng* ceremony).' The explanations given by Chêng Hsüan and other *Chou Li* commentators are forced and unconvincing. *Mo Tzu* (XXXII. Forke's translation, p. 371) quotes from a 'book of the former kings': 'to perform the *hêng* dance in the palace is called yielding to the influence of shamans.' To dance *hêng* 'continually' (which is the usual interpretation) makes poor sense. I would also suggest that the words 'ill, *hêng*, not die' in the *Book of Changes*, section 16, mean 'If anyone is ill, perform the *hêng* rite and he will not die.' The saying of the 'men of the south' (i.e. of Ch'u?) is also quoted in Section 32 of the *Changes*.

XIV, 16.   The usual interpretation, 'Wên was crafty and not upright, Huan was upright and not crafty' is, as Wang Nien-sun long ago observed (*Ching I Shu Wên*, on this passage), nonsensical. The story of Wên (Double Ears,[1] as he was called) is known to us chiefly through a heroic legend embodied in *Kuo Yü*, IX and X. The commentators try to discover a lack of

[1] Like many heroes, he was noted for strange physical peculiarities; his ribs were all in one piece.

ritual correctness in the story of his being visited by the Divine King (T'ien-wang, i.e. the ruler of Chou). But this requires some ingenuity. We only know a legend that praises him; we must suppose Confucius to have known one which denigrated him.

Of Duke Huan's failure in emergencies no convincing example is cited. For this sense of *chüeh*, see Liu Pao-nan's *Lun Yü Chêng I*.

XIV, 33.   Usually taken as meaning 'who does not anticipate deceit . . . and, yet immediately perceives it when it occurs.' There are two objections to this rendering: (1) The *i* of *pu hsin, i* . . . usually means 'or,' not 'but'; (2) *hsien chüeh* normally means to perceive beforehand, not 'to perceive immediately,' and the text says nothing about 'when it has occurred,' or the like. Confucius is criticizing a current maxim about the *chün-tzu*. Cf. the *Ta Tai Li Chi* passage quoted below in the textual notes.

XV, 10.   The tunes of Chêng and Wei are often referred to as 'new music' or the 'common music of the world.' Towards classical music, the 'music of the former Kings' (*Mencius*, I, 2, I) ordinary as opposed to serious-minded people had the same feelings as they have towards our own classical music to-day. 'How is it,' the Prince of Wei asked Tzu-hsia, 'that when I sit listening to old music, dressed in my full ceremonial gear, I am all the time in terror of dropping off asleep; whereas when I listen to the tunes of Chêng and Wei, I never feel the least tired?' (*Li Chi*, XIX, fol. 5).

XV, 25.   The current interpretation is 'lent it to others to drive.'[1] This gives a sense totally unconnected

---

[1] 'To ride' is an anachronism; for horses were not ridden in the time of Confucius.

with what goes before. Moreover, *chieh jên* occurs elsewhere[1] in the sense 'to avail oneself of the services of others,' but never is the sense 'to lend to others.' *Chieh* in the sense 'to lend' is very rare in early texts, while in the sense 'to borrow' it is very common.

XVI, 14. It will be noticed that although the words *jên* (person) and *chün* (prince), here applied to a lady, are not exclusively masculine, they are chiefly and prevailingly applied to men rather than to women. For example, in VIII, 20, Confucius says that King Wu had not really 'ten *jên*' to help him; for one of them was a woman. *Hsiao T'ung* ('Little boy') means a pageboy, and is an exclusively masculine term. Thus it may be said that the sovereign's wife may not be referred to (either by himself or anyone else) by any term that is feminine in implication and must in referring to herself use a term that is definitely masculine.

This is in obedience to the general principle that a sovereign must be spoken of as though he were free from ordinary human needs and desires.[2] It will also be noted that the sovereign speaks of himself as the 'lonely one.' This he does under all circumstances, and not only in reference to his wife. Thus his city is 'the lonely one's city,' etc. In China he was 'lonely' in the sense that his father whose throne he had inherited, was necessarily dead. But a king is often technically motherless as well as fatherless. For at his accession he must either, as in some parts of the world, marry his mother, and so lose her as a mother; or else 'never set eyes on his mother.'[3] Or again, his mother has been ritually sacrificed during the funeral ceremony

[1] *Tso Chuan*, Hsiang Kung, 19th year; and *Kuan Tzu*, P'ien 33, *chieh-jên*, 'set other people to do it for you.'

[2] Cf. C. G. Seligman, *Egypt and Negro Africa*, a Study in Divine Kingship, 1934, p. 47. [3] *Op. cit.*, p. 43.

of his father. It is possible that the expression 'the lonely one' goes back in China to times when the king was technically motherless as well as fatherless.

XX, 1.   *T'ien chih li-shu* was no doubt understood in a quasi-abstract sense by the compilers of the *Analects*: 'Heaven's succession,' i.e. the succession accorded by Heaven. It is possible, however, that in its original setting, as a formula used in the accession-rites of kings, it had a much more concrete sense: 'The calendar[1] and counting-sticks of Heaven' (i.e. of the Ancestors).

There is a hiatus after 'his charge to Yü.' In other Chinese works (e.g. in the forged portions of the *Shu Ching*, in *Mo tzu* and in the *Kuo Yü*) many of the sentences strung together in this paragraph will be found utilized for a different purpose and interpreted with a different meaning. A discussion of all these parallels belongs rather to the textual criticism of the *Shu Ching* than to a study of the *Analects*, and I shall not attempt it here.

The Ku version treated XX, 2 and 3 as a separate book.

[1] i.e. 'succession' of agricultural tasks.

TEXTUAL NOTES

*

Introduction, p. 27 : *Jên,* 仁. *Min,* 民.
   p. 33 : *Shih,* 士.

I. 1.   不 亦, cf. VIII. 7. 2. Sometimes written 不 以 (*Mencius,*
   III, 2, IV, 1). In such phrases *i* seems to mean 'indeed',
   sometimes with a slight concessive form, like the French
   tout de même in *cela, c'est tout de même trop fort.* It seldom
   means 'also' in the *Analects.*

I. 1. 2.[1]   有 variant 友 ('friend').

I. 4.   For 傳 the Lu version read 專.

I. 7.   易 for 惕. Cf. III. 4.

I. 12, end.   可 行. The Han stone-engraved text (*apud* Hung
   K'uo, *Li Shih*) omits 可.

I. 15.   Read 樂 道, which is the reading of the Huang K'an
   text (6th century A.D.). On the T'ang stone-engraved text
   tao was added marginally.

II. 3.   格 is for the obsolete character 佫, which had the meaning
   至.

II. 8.   For 饌 Chêng Hsüan reads 餕.

II. 19.   錯 for 措.

II. 24.   諂 does not make sense. Surely a mistake for 謟. The
   same confusion occurs elsewhere ; cf. Chu Ch'i-fêng's
   Tz'u T'ung (Shanghai, 1934), p. 1073. In future cited as T.T.

III. 4.   易 for 惕. Cf. I. 7 above.

III. 8.   Commentators since Han times have taken 起 in the
   sense 發 明, 'make clear'. It is true that 起 can have the
   sense 發 動, 'set in motion', but it is doubtful if it can mean
   'make clear'. Moreover, such an interpretation involves the
   necessity of understanding after 予 an 意 which is not in the
   text. It is simpler to take 起 in the sense 'keep upright',
   'support' ; cf. *Kuo Yü,* Chin Yü, IV. 世 相 起 : 'From
   generation to generation [Chou and Chin] are to support
   one another'.

---

[1] Where two arabic figures are used, the second refers to the number
of the sentence, as marked in the editions of Legge and Soothill.

III. 11. 示, read *chih*. Phonetic borrowing for 寘, 'put'. Cf. *Hsün Tzu*, 27 : 示 諸 檃 栝, 'If you put it (timber) in a vice'.

III. 12. It is quite certain that there is a pun on 在 and 祭. The phonological relationship between these two words was, however, in Chou times a very slender one and I suspect that 祭 has been substituted for the less familiar word 祠 (dzieg), which could well be called 'like' 在 (dz'eg). Cf. the alleged use of 在 as a phonetic substitute for 司 and 嗣 (Chu Chünshêng's phonetic *Shuo Wên*, under 在).

III. 14. 郁 郁. For other ways of writing this binome, see T.T. 2258.

III. 21. For 社 Chêng Hsüan reads 主, which is also the reading of the *Po Hu T'ung*; the *Shuo Wên* character is 宔. The word 主, *chu*, means a stance for spirits. Chinese etymologies should be made with great reserve ; but it is worth noting that 主 may be cognate to 住, 'bide'. The pictogram 主 is interpreted as representing a wick. This may be another use of the same root ; for a wick is the 'stance' of the flame.

III. 22. The 反 of this phrase here and elsewhere is probably a corruption of 危, i.e. 阽. Cf. *Êrh Ya*, 阽 謂 之 垝.

IV. 2. 因 for 姻.

IV. 5. 造 次 for 躁 趡.
顛 沛 for 躓 跰.

IV. 6. 蓋 for 盍 : 'How not ?', i.e. 'they must exist'. Cf. VII. 27 and XIII. 3.

IV. 10. I adopt Chêng Hsüan's 無 敵 無 慕. 之 in the last clause is for 是. Cf. Shu Ching, *Wu I*, 惟 耽 樂 之 從, modernized as 是 從 in Han quotations of the passage : 'It was solely upon abandoned pleasures that they were bent'. The demonstrative 之 is also closely connected with 是 ; cf. 之 子 in the *Songs* and 之 人, 'this man', in *Chuang Tzu*, I. 4. See also XI. 18 and XIII. 22 below.

IV. 12. 放 is for 倣.

IV. 13. 何 有. Cf. VI. 6 ; VII. 2 ; IX. 15 ; XIII. 13 ; also *Mencius*, VI. 2, I. 4 (Legge, p. 299), and many further examples in *Tso Chuan*, etc. The idiom means 'What more is there to be said ?', 'That settles the matter ', 'On that point at any rate we can be satisfied ', and the like.

IV. 18   勞 for 懲.

V. 4.   給 for 嗑? 合 and 盍 are 'etymologically the same word' (Karlgren, *Analytic Dictionary*, p. 56). Cf. *Lieh Tzu*, IV. 12: 佞 給 而 不 中, 'glibly chattering, but never hitting the mark'.

V. 7. 2.   For 賦 the Lu version read 傅.

V. 13.   有 for 又, as constantly in old texts.

V. 17.   節 is a phonetic borrowing for 梲, cognate to 梧 which has the same meaning. 梲; *Erh Ya* writes this word with the character 棳, which exists here as a variant.

V. 18. 2.   For 崔 the Lu version read 高.

V. 21.   裁 for 載. Cf. 裁 使, 'to turn to account', and *Shih Tzu* (尸 子) fragments : 'Heaven and Earth produced the myriad things ; the Sages 裁 之, turned them to account'.

V. 25. 2.   It is better to omit 輕 ; omitted at first in T'ang stone-engraved Classics, and added later.   For further evidence, see Liu Pao-nan's *Lun Yü Chêng I.*

V. 25. 3.   施 for 訑.

VI. 3. 1.   庚 for 臾斗.

VI. 3. 2.   周 for 賙.

VI. 4.   犂 for 驪, 'brown and black'. 騂 is commonly used of cattle as well as horses ; but 牸 also exists.

VI. 21.   (Additional note) *shou*, 守, 'to secure'.

VI. 24.   Read 井 有 仁. The variant 人 is certainly wrong. 逝 is for 折. Cf. 邁 for 萬 in inscriptions.

VI. 26.   厭, abbreviation for 厭, 'exorcize.'

VII. 3.   講 in sense of 構. The rhyme indicates that 講 (like 溝 and other words in the series) had an alternative reading *kog*.

VII. 4.   燕. Chêng Hsüan reads 宴.

VII. 7.   誨 ; the Lu reading was 悔.

VII. 8.   There is no evidence for the existence of 俳 except as an alternative form of 悲. The word here intended is 啡, 'the sound of spittle', applied to one who is bubbling over with things to say.

憤, 'welling up of emotion', is probably cognate to 噴, 'spurt up', 'spit'.

啟 properly means 'to instruct' ; 启, 'to open'.

VII. 10.   馮 for 淜.

VII. 13.   For 爲 樂, some texts read 嬀 樂, 'music of the Kuei'. Kuei was the clan-name (*hsing*) of the T'ien family who usurped the throne of Ch'i in 386 B.C. Those who follow this reading regard the Master's use of the term Kuei, meaning the rulers of Ch'i, as prophetic ; for Confucius had already been dead for 100 years when the T'ien came into power.

VII. 16.   The Lu version reads 亦 not 易 ; Cf. *Lieh Tzu*, II. 16 : 二 者 亦 知, 'These two things are easy to know' ; variant, 易. There is no evidence that the philosophical interpretation of the *Changes* was adopted by the Confucians till the second half of the 3rd century B.C. The Lu reading is adopted by most modern scholars.

VII. 27.   蓋 for 盍. Cf. IV. 6.

VII. 32.   Read 忝 慎. For various ways of writing this binome, see T.T. 1407. There is no evidence that 莫 can mean 'perhaps'.

VII. 33.   正 ; Lu version 誠.

VII. 36.   蕩 ; Lu version 湯. Perhaps for 暢. 長 for 悵 ?

VII. 37.   子, variant 君 子. 厲 ; variant 例 (homophones).

VIII. 12.   至 should be 志. Cf. *Mencius*, VI. 1. xx (Legge, p. 297), where 志 has a variant 至 ; also *Hsün Tzu*, VIII, Par. 4, where 志 堅 has been corrupted into 至 堅, but *Han Shih Wai Chuan* (III, 3 recto) quotes correctly as 志. There are other examples of this confusion which despite the difference in finals (至 with *d*, 志 with *g*) must be a phonetic one. Neither the seal nor cursive forms could give rise to confusion.

Comparison with the *Mencius* passage shows that a pun on 鵠, 'target' (keep your mind on the target), and 穀, 'salary', is perhaps intended.

VIII. 20.   亂 in such contexts is a misunderstanding of 嗣, archaic for 司, 'to administrate'. The idea that 亂 could mean both to rebel and to rule led to a theory that 'the ancients' constantly said just the opposite of what they meant.

VIII. 21.   There is a chance that the whole passage from 非 to 洫 is intended as rhyme : 食 with 服, 神 with 冕, 室 with 洫. The last word now has a guttural ending ; but 血 (dental ending) must surely be phonetic in 洫. Cf. the transition of 卽 from dental ending (as in the *Songs*) to guttural ending (as in T'ang times).

IX. 2. 絞, 'harsh', ought logically to be written 恔; but this was docketed for another meaning.

IX. 3. For 純 Chêng Hsüan read 紂, old form of 緇. It is easy to see how the unfamiliar 紂 got corrupted into the familiar 純, and Chêng's reading is probably right. The same confusion occurs several times in *Chou Li* and *Li Chi*.

IX. 5. What is supposed to have happened to Confucius in K'uang (as is clear from numerous anecdotes) is that he was surrounded 圍 'by a cordon several men deep' (*Chuang Tzu*, XVII. 3) in the hope of starving him out. Cf. *Shuo Yüan*, XVII: 'They surrounded K'ung Tzu's house'.

畏 does not make sense and it is perhaps a mistake (due to resemblance of sound) for 圍.

IX. 7. Some versions of Chêng Hsüan's text read 悾 悾.

IX. 9. 冕. Chêng Hsüan reads 弁. The Lu version had 絻.

IX. 9. 趨. The Pelliot MS. reads 趍, a reading also current in Sung times. Certainly a corruption.

IX. 12. 沾. The variant 霑 is the correct 'spelling'.

IX. 23. 從 (which does not make sense) is for 聳, 'rouse'; Chêng Hsüan glosses it by 悅.[1]

巽 與 = 選 舉. Cf. *Li Chi*, Li Yün chapter, 選 賢 與 能, 'choose out the superior and promote the competent', where *Ta Tai Li Chi* (Chu Yen[2] chapter, fol. 3) has 舉.

IX. 30. 偏 for 翩 ('swift flight'). Cf. *Songs*, 268. 1.

X. 1. 便 for 辯, which is the reading in the Life of Confucius (*Shih Chi*, ch. 47).

X. 2. 侃 is here for 衎 (cf. T.T. 1383). Hence the *Chi Chieh*: 和 樂 之 貌. Cf. *Lieh Tzu*, IV. 5, 與 言 衎 衎 然, 'conversed amiably with him'; and also the 侃 侃 of XI. 12, below, which makes better sense if taken in this way.

X. 2. 踧 踖. The idea is 'stepping warily'; cf. 蹐 and 踈.

---

[1] Pelliot MS.

[2] Some versions call the chapter 'Wang Yen'.

與 constantly interchanges with 豫, and 'relaxed' is the idea here. Cf. *The Book of Songs*, Vol. II, p. 14.

X. 3.   襜 (TIAM) does not involve the idea of 'straight', but merely of hanging down, 'flopping'. Cf. 耽 (TAM), 'pendulous ears'; also 眈, 黕 and 膽 (TIAM) in the same sense.

X. 3.   翼 如 is simply another way of saying 翼 翼, a descriptive compound very common in old texts, with the meaning 'noble', 'majestic'. It has nothing to do with outstretched wings.

X. 4.   鞠 躬 is an alliterative compound. The sense is 跼 弓, 'bent and bowed'.

逞 is for 裎, alternative form of 綎, 'slacken'.

X. 5.   For 蹜, cf. 蹴 and 縮, 'recoil'. For 循 we should, as Chu Chün-shêng has pointed out in his phonetic *Shuo Wên*, write 遁. 有, as often, has the sense of 或. 'As though he were dragging something' (the usual interpretation) would be 如 有 所 曳, or the like.

X. 6, end.   吉 is a mistake for 告. The confusion is a very frequent one.

X. 10.   儺. The proper character is presumably 魑 which the *Yü P'ien* defines as meaning 'to startle and drive away pestilent spirits'. For 儺 (NA) the Lu version read 獻 (HIAN).

The same saying occurs in the Chiao T'ê Shêng (11th) chapter of the *Li Chi*, with 禓 for 儺, and the note 'for 禓 (SHIANG) some texts read 獻, others 儺'. 禓 is understood to mean 'spirits of those who died in battle', and subsequently turned into noxious spirits.

The meaning of 獻 and its relationship to 儺 are very uncertain. It may simply mean 'offering' and have originally signified the alternative method of dealing with evil influences, i.e. by propitiation instead of by violent expulsion.

X. 13.   拖. Also written 拕, 袉 and 扡.

X. 16.   容. Variant 客 ('guest').

X. 17.   The Lu version read 內 顧, omitting the negative. This is probably right.

XI. 13.   For 仍 the Lu version read 仁.

XI. 17.   辟 for 躃.

Chêng Hsüan defines 嗲 as 畔 嗲, a phrase which is also written 阪 嗲 and seems to mean careless deportment.

XI. 18.　之 不 欲.　之 is the copulative ＝ 是 ; cf. IV. 10 above.

XI. 21.　兼 人 for 磏 仁 ? Literally, ' is angular in his Goodness '. In *Han Shih Wai Chuan*, I. 11 磏 仁 is the lowest of the four kinds of Goodness, and the examples given show that ' fanatical ' is the nearest English equivalent of 磏.

Old texts constantly confuse 人 and 仁. Thus the Pelliot MS. from Tun-huang reads 仁 for 人 in both clauses of *Analects*, VIII. 6.　All attempts to make sense of 兼 人 reading it as it stands have been hopelessly forced.　兼 cannot mean ' wants to excel ', nor can 兼 人 mean ' does the work of two men ', on the analogy of such phrases as 兼 任, ' do two jobs at once '.

XI. 25. 1.　For 吾 以 Chêng Hsüan reads 吾 己.

XI. 25. 3.　For 居, 'living as private persons', cf. 居 士, used in same sense as 處 士.

XI. 25. 4.　牽, variant 卒.

XI. 25. 5.　足 民 should surely be 民 足 ?

XI. 25. 7.　鏗. The *Yü P'ien* reads 挶.
　　撰. Cf. 譔, ' eloquent '.
For 歸 the Lu version and Chêng Hsüan read 饋. This is, I think, merely a phonetic borrowing. The two characters constantly interchange.

XII. 5. 4.　失 for 迭.

XII. 9.　孰 與 seems to mean ' how ? ', rhetorical question implying a negative.

XII. 12.　For 折 the Lu version read 制.　(Approximately TIAT and TIAD.)

XII. 16.　成 seems to be for 稱. Cf. *Lieh Tzu*, V. 6, 成 爲 孝 子, ' acclaimed as a filial son '.

XII. 21.　其 for 己. Cf. 彼 其 之 子 (frequent in the *Songs*), also written 彼 己 之 子.

XII. 22.　錯 for 措. Cf. II. 19.

XIII. 3.　蓋 for 盍 ' How not ? ', i.e. ' he must '. Cf. IV. 6.

XIII. 8.　苟 in this sense is sometimes written 姑 ; a cognate but not identical word.

XIII. 11.　勝 for 踆, in *Shih Ching* written 懲.　Cf. 淩 also written 朕 (*Shuo Wên*).　Original TL initial?

XIII. 18.　躬.　Chêng Hsüan read 弓.　Despite the frequency with which this Kung is mentioned in early literature, Chu Hsi failed to recognize it as a proper name.

XIII. 20.　硜 硜 is a descriptive binome written phonetically and has nothing to do with 'pebbles' or 'grit'.　Cf. 輕 in the senses 'cheap', 'unimportant', etc.

XIII. 21.　狷 (*Mencius*, 獧) is the 懁 'hasty' of *Shuo Wên*; cognate to the 儇 'nimble' of *Song* 265.　狂 and 狷 are complementary not contrasted terms.　*Mencius*, in his version of this passage (VII. 2, XXXVII. 2) seems to interpret the word as though it were 涓, 'clean'.

XIII. 22.　之 羞.　之 is for 是.　Cf. above, IV. 10.　羞 for 醜 (both words are of the SIOG type), according to Chu Chün-shêng, phonetic *Shuo Wên*.

XIII. 27.　I suspect that 木 is a textual mistake for 朴.

XIII. 28.　偲, variant 𢚩.　I suspect that it is cognate to 責, which is used to define it.　The relationship according to Karlgren's reconstruction is *si̯əg* and *tṣĕk*.

XIV. 6.　Ao's name is also written 澆 and 傲.

XIV. 16.　譎, talk 'crookedly'.　遹, 'act crookedly', would be more in place.　The usual contrast is between 權 and 正.

XIV. 29.　For 而 read 之 (Huang K'an text).

XIV. 31.　方; Chêng Hsüan read 謗.

XIV. 33.　Cf. *Ta Tai Li Chi*, chapter *Tsêng Tzu Li Shih*: fol. 3; 君子不先人以惡, 不 疑 (ngjieg; for 逆 ngiag) 人以不信.　For 抑, cf. *Mencius*, II. 2, IV. 3.

XIV. 42.　Read 斯 己 not 斯 巳.

XIV. 46.　夷 is for 跠.

XV. 5.　Some texts read 參 然 for 參.

XV. 16.　The Lu reading 惠 makes better sense.　Cf. *Han Fei Tzu*, 9: 行小惠以取百姓.

XV. 29.　*Ku-liang Chuan* (Hsi kung, 22nd year) adds 又之 after 改: 'If one points out a man's mistake and he does not change, to repeat it (i.e. rebuke him again) may, indeed, be called a mistake.'

XVI. 1. 4.　邦, variant 封.

XVI. 1. 10.　寡 and 貧 in lines 1 and 3 of the poem should be

transposed. 安 at the end of line 4 should be 和. See Y. Ojima in *Shinagaku*, Vol. II, No. 10, p. 65. Omit 安無傾, which should come at the end of paragraph 11.

XVI. 4.　便辟, also written 盤辟, 'bending at the knee'. 便佞 for 諞佞; so quoted by *Shuo Wên*.

XVI. 6.　For 躁 the Lu version read 傲 'presumptuous'. The saying occurs in several Han texts, always with the reading 傲.

XVII. 1. 1.　歸 is a Lu version reading. The Ku version read 饋.

XVII. 4.　莞爾; for various ways of writing this descriptive, see T.T. 628.

XVII. 8.　蔽 for 弊.

XVII. 8. 2.　居 appears to be an exclamatory particle, demanding attention. Sometimes written 姬. Cf. *Lieh Tzu*, II. 3.

XVII. 12.　窬 means a gap, and does not mean to climb. Cf. *Mencius*, VII, 2 ; XXXI, 2. 窬 may be merely a phonetic borrowing for 踰, 'climb', 'cross'. See T.T. 357.

XVII. 16.　廉 (LIAM) ; Lu version 貶 (PIAM). Cf. 律 (LIUET) and 筆 (PIET). The reasons that admit these two words into the same phonetic series are clearly the same as those that give rise to LIAM, variant PIAM. What those reasons are is a matter for phonologists to decide.

XVII. 19. 3.　The Lu version read 夫 for 天, apparently in both cases. Possibly the second 天 should be 夫.

XVII. 24.　窒. This is the word that is also written 疐, 懥 and 懫. The Lu version read 室.
　　For 儌 Chêng Hsüan read 絞 ; the meaning intended is clearly 狡.

XVIII. 4.　For 歸 Chêng Hsüan read 饋.

XVIII. 5.　The Lu version read 期斯已矣, and omitted 而 after 殆 : 'The only thing to do is to choose one's time'.

XVIII. 6.　滔滔 is an exception to the general rule that descriptive binomes are written phonetically not ideogrammatically in early texts. It is, therefore, not surprising to find that Chêng Hsüan read 悠悠.

XVIII. 8.　*Shih Chi*, 47, reads 行中清. For 廢 Chêng Hsüan read 發.

XVIII. 10.　施 for 弛.

XIX. 10.　Chêng Hsüan says that 厲 (LIAD) is a phonetic

substitute for (? dialectical for) 賴 (LAD) ; 'throws the burden upon'. This is certainly right ; 'oppresses' is too general.

XIX. 12.　孰 for 熟, as constantly ;　for example, repeatedly in *Li Chi*, *Hsün Tzu*, *Chuang Tzu*. If we take it in the sense of 'which', we have to understand some such words 'as one must take into consideration' before the 'which'. Neither the early commentators nor Chu Hsi make any attempt to construe the sentence.

誣 does not fit the context. There is a variant 憮.

XX. 1.　蔽. 弊 would make better sense ;　but cf. *Mo Tzu*, P'ien, XVI : 有 善 不 敢 蔽, 'The good I dare not keep in obscurity'.

周 親 ; cf. *Shih Tzu* 尸 子 (fragments) : 文 王 曰 苟 有 仁 人, 何 必 周 親, 'Wên Wang said, "If I can find good men, I will not confine my appointments to my own Chou kinsmen"'. It is certain that 'Chou' is here to be taken in this sense.

XX. 2.　戒 for 誡.

視 for 氐, synonymous with 致. Cf. 眂 which is the alternative form (*Shuo Wên*) of 視. 'Look at' does not make sense.

客 rhymes with 人, and the passage runs better if we omit 也.

For 出 納 Huang K'an (6th century) and Lu Tê-ming (7th century) both read 出 內. The reading 納 seems to have begun in Sung times.

ADDENDUM

IX. 23.　The traditional interpretation of 繹 : 'unravel' and so 'carry out,' is rather forced. Perhaps 繹 stands for its homophone 易, 'change.'

Index

Ai, duke of Lu 92, 99, 115, 165, 186
An-yang 19
Ao 181
Āpastamba Dharma Sūtra 59

Chan Kuo Ts'ê 113, 219
Chang Yü 24
Changes, the Book of 48, 126, 187, 249, 256
Chao, duke of Lu 129, 222, 246
Chavannes, E. 76
Ch'ang-chü 219
Ch'ao, prince of Sung 119
Chêng Hsüan 23, 24, 71, 89, 132, 138, 153, 237, 243, 246, 253, 254, 255, 256, 257, 259, 260, 261, 262
Ch'ên Hêng 186
Ch'ên Wên-tzu 28, 112
Ch'êng Hao 73, 76, 112, 243
Ch'êng I 73
Chi Huan-tzu 204, 219
Chi K'ang-tzu 15, 92, 116, 117, 150, 154, 167, 168, 186, 189, 204, 219
Chi Tzu (Marquis of Chi) 29, 218
Chi Tzu-ch'êng 164
Chi Tzu-jan 158
Chi Wên Tzu 112
Chieh-ni 219, 220
Chieh-yü 219
Chien, duke of Ch'i 186
Chih, Chief Musician 135, 222
Ching, duke of Ch'i 166, 207, 218
Ching, grandee of Wei 173
Ching I Shu Wên 76
Chiu, prince of Ch'i 184, 185

Ch'i version 24
Ch'i-tiao K'ai 108
Ch'ih Jên 202
Chou, duke of 17, 47, 123, 134, 156, 222
Chou Jên 202
Chou Li 77, 98, 215, 235, 236, 245, 246, 249
Chou Li Chêng I 77
Chou, the tyrant 218, 228
Chou-shêng Lieh 71
Chu Ch'i-fêng 255
Chu Chün-shêng 254, 258, 260
Chu Hsi 46, 72–74, 148, 157, 167, 237, 249, 262
Chu Tzu Ch'üan Shu 73, 237
Chuang Tzu 79
Chuang Tzu 113, 125, 139, 143, 144, 209, 219, 237, 254, 257, 262
Chuang Tzu of P'ien 183
Chung Ni, see Confucius
Chung Shan Fu 242
Chung-shu Yü 186
Chung-yung, see *Doctrine of the Mean*
Ch'ü Po Yü 187, 194
Confucius 13, and passim
Conrady, August 181
Couvreur, S. 62, 77

De Groot, J. J. 244
Dirges 62, 131, 230
Doctrine of the Mean 23, 67, 96, 122, 144, 242

Êrh Ya 254, 255
Erkes, Eduard 181

Fa Yen 143

Fa Yü 143
Fan Ch'ih 54, 88, 120, 168, 169, 172, 176, 248
Fang Chi 22
fêng ('phoenix') 48
Filial Piety, Canon of (*Hsiao Ching*) 38
Frazer, Sir James 58, 60, 244
Fu Tzu 238
Fu Tzu-chien 107

Genkyo, Fukube 72
Granet, Marcel 78, 247
Great Learning, The 23, 102, 167

Haloun, Gustav 12, 131, 238
Han Ch'iu I 247
Han Fei Tzu 36, 175, 195, 219, 260
Han Shih Wai Chuan 23, 122, 166, 194, 248, 256, 259
Ho Ting-shêng 53
Holy Ground, the (*Shê*) 99, 202, 236, 246
Hou Chi 19, 181, 247
Hou Han Shu 133, 215, 243
Hsi Tz'u 165
Hsia dynasty 18, 95
Hsin-hsü 183, 219
Hsin-lun 24
Hsing P'ing 249
Hsü Hsing 248
Hsüan Chü 143
Hsün Tzu (Confucian philosopher of the 3rd century B.C.) 22, 23
Hsün Tzu 97, 126, 142, 156, 178, 182, 187, 199, 205, 212, 253, 256, 262
Hu Shih 127
Hu Shih Wên Ts'un 127
Huai-nan Tzu 58

Huai-nan-Tzu 113, 175
Huan, duke of Ch'i 50, 166, 182, 184, 185, 249
Huan T'an 24
Huan T'ui 42, 163
Huang Ch'ing Ching Chieh (abbreviation H.C.C.C.) 20, 76
Huang Ch'ing Ching Chieh Hsü Pien (abbreviation H.P.) 76, 237
Huang K'an 71, 156, 223, 249, 253, 260, 262

I Chou Shu 105, 108, 164, 185
I Li 58, 98, 246
I Wên Lei Chü 246
I Yin 170

Jan Ch'iu 15, 20, 28, 54, 95, 108, 115, 117, 118, 125, 153, 155, 156, 158, 159, 160, 161, 173, 174, 183, 202
Jan Kêng 117, 153
Jan Shu 183
Jan Yung 28, 107, 115, 116, 153, 162, 171
Johnston, Sir Reginald 37; 38
Ju Pei 214
Jung (ritual attitude) 55, 56

Kao Ch'ai 157, 159
Kao Tsung 191
Kao Yao 18, 169
Karlgren, B. 87, 254, 260
Knight, see *Shih*
Knights, Leader of, see *Shih-shih*
Ku Chieh-kang 14
Ku Wên version ('Ku version') 24, 126, 252, 261
Ku-liang Chuan 179, 199, 240, 260
Kuan Chung, see Kuan Tzu
Kuan Tzu 28, 99, 100, 166, 182, 184, 185

Kuan Tzu 129, 216, 251
K'ung Wên Tzu 110, 186
K'ung Yeh Ch'ang 107
Kung-hsi Hua 28, 108, 115, 116, 130, 158, 159, 160, 161
Kung-ming Chia 183
Kung-po Liao 189, 190
Kung-shan Fu-jao 210
Kung-shu Wên-tzu 183, 185
Kung-sun Chao 228
Kung-yang Chuan 86
K'ung An-kuo 71, 148, 225
K'ung-tzu Chia Yü 96, 238
Kuo Yü 21, 40, 102, 166, 191, 249, 252, 253

Lao 15, 139
Lao Tzu 46
Legge, James 21, 24, 41, 46, 52, 77, 243
Li Chi 22, 26, 67, 97, 100, 124, 133, 148, 177, 185, 208, 250, 251, 257, 258
Li I Chih, see *Hou Han Shu*
Li Shih 255
Lieh Tzu 166, 209, 219, 237, 254, 256, 257, 259, 261
Lies, polite 44, 214
Lin Fang 94
Ling, duke of Wei 121, 125, 186, 193
Liu Pao-nan 123, 153, 217, 250, 255
Liu T'ai-kung 98
Liu-hsia Hui 18, 196, 218, 221, 222
Lods, A 133
Lu Tê-ming 221, 223, 225, 247, 262
Lu version 24, 126, 233, 255, 256, 258, 259, 260, 261
Lun Hêng 23, 200, 247

Lun Yü 21
Lun Yü Chi Chieh 71, 237, 245, 257
Lun Yü Chi Chu 72
Lun Yü Tsa Chieh 74
Lü Pu-wei 23
Lü Shih Ch'un Ch'iu 39, 144, 151, 152, 158, 175

Ma Jung 71
Magic Square 48, 49
Mārkandeya Purāna 59
Maspero, Henri 16, 79, 241
Mémoires Historiques 76
Mencius 46, 79
Mencius 15, 17, 22, 36, 50, 89, 90, 102, 118, 121, 130, 136, 139, 142, 150, 153, 157, 160, 162, 168, 177, 179, 189, 191, 201, 206, 208, 209, 213, 215, 233, 238, 248, 250, 253, 254, 256, 260, 261
Mêng Chih-fan 118
Mêng Ching Tzu 133
Mêng Chuang Tzu 227
Mêng Hsien Tzu 227
Mêng I Tzu 88, 107
Mêng Kung Ch'o 183
Mêng Wu Po 89, 108, 133
Mien, music-master 201
Min Tzu-ch'ien 117, 153, 155, 156, 245, 246
Ming 41
Ming T'ang, the 49
Mo Tzu 38, 79, 138, 231, 243, 262
Mo Tzu 123, 175, 248, 252

Nan Jung 107, 154
Nan-kung Kuo 107, 180
Nan-tzu 121, 242
Ning Wu Tzu 112
No (expulsion rite) 149, 245

Numbers 19, 48

Ojima, Y. 263
Oracle bones 93

Pao Hsien 71, 89, 198, 241
Pelliot, Paul 12, 71
Pelliot MS. 132, 138
P'êng Tsu 17, 123
Pi Hsi 211
Pi Kan 29, 218
P i Ch'ên 181
P'ing, duke of Chin 68
Po Hu T'ung 256
Po I 28, 113, 126, 207, 221
Po Niu 42
Po Yü (Li), son of Confucius 154, 207, 212

Quietists 28, 30, 46

River Chart, the 48

Seligman, C. G. 7, 251
Shang Ti 42
Shao ('succession dance') 69, 101, 125, 195
Shao Hu 184
Shao K'ang 181
Shao Lien 221
Shê, 'duke' of 127, 175, 239
Shên Ch'êng 109
Shên Chu-liang 127
Shêng 17, 28
Shih (Knight) 15
Shih Chi 26, 108, 237, 238, 257, 262
Shih Ching, see *Songs*
Shih Shu 181
Shih Tzu 255, 262
Shih Wên 24
Shih-shih ('leader of the knights') 15, 154, 218, 228

Shinagaku 263
Shiratori, Professor 247
Shu Ching ('Book of History') 21, 25, 52 seq., 84, 93, 191, 202, 211, 231, 232, 252, 254
Shu Ch'i 29, 113, 126, 207, 221
Shu-sun Wu-shu 229
Shun 18, 122, 136, 169, 192, 193, 201, 231
Shuo Wên 254, 258, 260, 261, 262
Shuo Yüan 121, 238, 246
Songs, the Book of 19, 27, 33, 39, 42, 43, 47, 51, 52, 84, 87, 88, 91, 94, 95, 99, 124, 128, 133, 134, 135, 144, 145, 154, 166, 169, 172, 191, 196, 208, 212, 242, 243, 245, 248, 249, 254, 257, 258, 259, 260
Soothill, E. 46, 54, 77
Ssu-ma Ch'ien, see *Shih Chi*
Ssu-ma Niu 163
Stein, Sir Aurel 71
Succession Dance, see *Shao*
Sun I-jang 77
Sun Yat-sen 77
Sung, State of 19

Ta Tai Li Chi 49, 114, 250, 259, 260
Ta Hsüeh, see *Great Learning*
T'ai, Mount 95
T'ai P'ing Yü Lan 131
T'ai Po 132, 221, 242
Tan, king of Chou 133
T'an-t'ai Mieh-ming 118
T'ang 19, 50, 231
Tao Tê Ching 36, 91, 189
T'ien Wên 181
Ting, duke of Lu 98, 174, 175
T'o, priest 119, 186
Transliteration 77

Tsai Yü 99, 109, 121, 153, 214, 215
Tsang Wên Chung 111, 183, 196
Tsang Wu Chung 183, 184
Tsêng Hsi 159, 160, 161
Tsêng Tzu (Master Tsêng) 20, 21, 67, 84, 85, 89, 105, 132–134, 157, 170, 187, 227, 228
Tso Ch'iu Ming 114, 238
Tso Chuan 20, 21, 39, 40, 97, 108, 127, 139, 155, 162, 165, 181, 182, 183, 184, 186, 193, 196, 202, 216, 223, 239, 244, 248, 251
Tso-wang 116
Ts'ui Tzu 112
Tu Shu Tsa Chih 76
Tun-huang 24
Twins 223
Tzu Ssu Tzu 22
Tzu-chang 20, 91, 93, 111, 156, 157, 164, 165, 167, 168, 191, 194, 210, 224, 232, 233
Tzu-ch'an 110, 182
Tzu-ch'in 85, 207, 208, 229
Tzu-fu Ching-po 189, 229
Tzu-hsi 182
Tzu-hsia 20, 84, 89, 95, 118, 153, 156, 159, 163, 169, 224, 225, 226, 227
Tzu-kung 20, 87, 90, 98, 107, 109, 110, 117, 125, 126, 139, 141, 153, 155, 156, 164, 170, 176, 177, 185, 188, 193, 195, 198, 214, 216, 228, 229, 230
Tzu-lu 15, 20, 22, 28, 32, 62, 62, 91, 108, 110, 114, 116, 121, 124, 130, 131, 140, 144, 152, 153, 155, 156, 157, 158, 159, 161, 166, 167, 171, 179, 183, 186, 189, 190, 191, 193, 202, 210, 211, 216, 219–221

Tzu-sang Po-tzu 115
Tzu-wên 28, 111
Tzu-yu 20, 89, 106, 118, 153, 210, 226, 227
Tzu-yü of Chêng 181
Tz'u T'ung (abbreviation, T. T.) 151, 253, 254, 256, 261

Umehara, S. 246

Wang Nien-sun 76, 248, 249
Wang Su 71, 249
Wang Yin-chih 76
Wang-sun Chia 97, 186
Way and its Power, The 17, 22, 27, 33, 43, 56, 106, 218
Wei Tzu (Marquis of Wei) 29, 218
Wei-shêng Kao 113
Wei-shêng Mou 188
Wên, duke of Chin 50, 184, 249
Wên, king of Chou 47, 139, 173, 228
Wilcox, Ella Wheeler 78
Wilhelm, Richard 48, 77
Wu, king of Chou 47, 136, 228, 231, 232, 244
Wu Mêng Tzu 130
Wu-ma Ch'i 129

Yang Fu 228
Yang Huo 25, 128, 204, 209, 244
Yao 18, 122, 192, 201, 231
Yao Sui 241
Yen Hui 15, 20, 41, 90, 109, 114, 115, 116, 117, 118, 124, 134, 140, 142, 143, 153, 154, 155, 157, 158, 162, 195
Yen Tzu (Ch'i statesman) 25, 111
Yen Yu, see Tzu-yu
Yi, the Archer 181

Yu, Master   20, 86, 165
Yu Tso   74, 75
Yü Chung   221, 222
Yü, the Great   18, 136, 137, 181, 231
Yü P'ien   258, 259

Yü, the Recorder   194
Yü Yüeh   76, 237, 248
Yüan Ssu   116, 180
Yüan Yüan   20, 76

Zen   46, 73

Head Office: 40 Museum Street, London, WC1

Sales, Distribution and Accounts Departments:
Park Lane, Hemel Hempstead, Hertfordshire

Athens: 7 Stadiou Street, Athens 125
Barbados: Rockley New Road, St. Lawrence 4
Bombay: 103/5 Fort Street, Bombay 1
Calcutta: 2850 Bepin Behari Ganguli Street, Calcutta 12
Dacca: Alico Building, 18 Motijheel, Dacca 2
Hornsby, N.S.W.: Cnr. Bridge Road and Jersey Street, 2077
Ibadan: P.O. Box 62
Johannesburg: P.O. Box 23134, Joubert Park
Karachi: Karachi Chambers, McLeod Road, Karachi 2
Lahore: 22 Falettis' Hotel, Egerton Road
Madras: 2/18 Mount Road, Madras 2
Manila: P.O. Box 157, Quezon City, D-502
Mexico: Serapio Rendon 125, Mexico 4, D.F.
Nairobi: P.O. Box 30583
New Delhi: 4/21-22B Asaf Ali Road, New Delhi 1
Ontario: 2330 Midland Avenue, Agincourt
Singapore: 248C-6 Orchard Road, Singapore 9
Tokyo: C.P.O. Box 1728, Tokyo 100-91
Wellington: P.O. Box 1467, Wellington, New Zealand

MADLY SINGING IN THE MOUNTAINS

An Appreciation and Anthology of Arthur Waley

IVAN MORRIS

'Those who already know Arthur Waley's work will treasure this tribute to his memory. As for the rest there could hardly be a better introduction to the works of this many-sided genius.'

New Statesman

'An entertaining miscellany, half tributes, half samples, various enough to be an eye-opener for old readers as well as a starter for new ones.' *The Observer*

'The book can be pressed upon all admirers of this exquisite artist, and will also reveal his genius, I hope, to the young who have not yet read him.'

Raymond Mortimer in *The Sunday Times*

'Gives an admirable all-round picture of a brilliant and unusual figure.' *The Daily Telegraph*

ARTHUR WALEY

BALLADS AND STORIES FROM TUN-HUANG

THE BOOK OF SONGS

CHINESE POEMS

THE LIFE AND TIMES OF PO CHU-I

NINE SONGS: A STUDY OF SHAMANISM IN ANCIENT CHINA

THE NO PLAYS OF JAPAN

THE OPIUM WAR THROUGH CHINESE EYES

THE POETRY AND CAREER OF LI PO

THE REAL TRIPITAKA AND OTHER PIECES

THE SECRET HISTORY OF THE MONGOLS

THREE WAYS OF THOUGHT IN ANCIENT CHINA

THE WAY AND ITS POWER: A STUDY OF THE TAO TE CHING

YUAN MEI: EIGHTEENTH CENTURY CHINESE POET

also

THE TALE OF GENJI by Lady Murasaki
translated by Arthur Waley

THE PILLOW BOOK OF SEI SHONAGON
translated by Arthur Waley

MONKEY by Wu Ch'Eng
translated by Arthur Waley

Eastern philosophy and literature

EASTERN WISDOM AND WESTERN THOUGHT
P. J. Saher

THE ONE-WORLD PHILOSOPHY OF K'ANG YU-WEI
Tat'ung Shu

TAO TE CHING
Tzu Lao

THE WHITE PONY
*An Anthology of Chinese Poetry from Earliest Times
to the Present Day*
Robert Payne

FIFTY SONGS FROM THE YUAN

THE MALICE OF EMPIRE
Yao Hsin-Nung

THE BOOK OF CHANGE
A translation of the ancient treatise *I Ching*
John Blofeld

CHUANG TZU: TAORIST PHILOSOPHER AND MYSTIC
Herbert L. Giles

A NEW ROAD TO ANCIENT TRUTH
Ittoen Tenko-San

THE WAY OF CHUANG TZU
Thomas Merton

Write for our complete list of Eastern philosophy, religion and literature

LONDON: GEORGE ALLEN & UNWIN LTD